GEORGE PEPER | THIRD EDITION

GOLF COURSES OF THE PGA TOUR

HARRY N. ABRAMS, INC., PUBLISHERS

CONTENTS

THE PLANTATION COURSE AT KAPALUA | *Mercedes Championships, Hawaii*

We've all seen them—the gaudy, multicolored junk mail envelopes that scream: "Win an All-Expense-Paid Trip to Paradise!" And we toss them in the trash, knowing those things simply don't happen. Not to ordinary people.

Only to professional golfers. Every year. Dozens of them. Among the perks that come with victory in a PGA Tour event is an invitation to the season-opening Mercedes Championships in Kapalua, Maui. It's the one week in the year where everyone in the field is a winner, and everyone lives like King Kamehameha.

The Mercedes Championships—or "Kapalua" as the players refer to it—is the modern version of the Tournament of Champions, the winners-only event started by a Las Vegas promoter in 1953, when first prize, paid in silver dollars, was a princely $10,000—more money than Ben Hogan would earn that year for winning the Masters, U.S. Open, and British Open combined. These days, even the last-place finisher gets a check for $60,000 or so, along with seven days of fun and frolic in one of the world's premier playgrounds.

But this event, played the week after New Years, is also a treat for millions of snowbound Americans who, because of the time difference, get the rare opportunity to tune into live golf in prime time. It's usually a good show, too, thanks equally to the quality of the field and the quality of the venue.

The Plantation Course at Kapalua , designed in 1991, is the most visually arresting golf course on the PGA Tour—and that includes Pebble Beach. The architects were Ben Crenshaw and Bill Coore, and every inch of turf reflects Crenshaw's reverence for two of the game's most venerable venues—St. Andrews and Augusta National.

As at those courses, the designers had a generous expanse on which to ply their trade—the Plantation Course unfolds on 240 acres of former pineapple fields—and the result is a succession of vast tumbling and climbing fairways leading to gargantuan rolling greens, all routed imaginatively across and around a series of deep, overgrown canyons.

Everything about this golf course is big, and that's as it should be, since the wind in this part of Maui can gust to 50 miles per hour and more, and dead-calm days are encountered about as often as

1ST HOLE

penguins. Bear in mind also that for 51 weeks a year it is not the pros battling those squalls, it is the high-handicap guests of the Kapalua Resort, whose hooks and slices call for a large measure of forgiveness.

Even the pros can be vexed when the prevailing tradewinds turn 180 degrees to become Kona winds from the southwest. On holes such as the first, a downhill 473-yard par four that plays directly toward the Pacific, it can mean hitting as little as a 9-iron approach one day and as much as a 3-wood the next. It was on this hole in 2000 that Tiger Woods rolled in a 40-foot birdie putt in sudden death to defeat Ernie Els and launch the finest season of his career, a year when he would claim nine victories, including the U.S. and British Opens and PGA Championship.

Few courses can claim as intriguing a quartet of par fives, beginning with the fifth hole, which curls 532 yards left-to-right along the edge of a 300-foot-deep gorge running the entire right side of the hole. It's a classic, heroic example of the Cape hole, originated a century ago by C.B. Macdonald, where the player is invited to carry as much of the hazard as he dares—in this case on the tee shot and the approach to the green, perched on a peninsula.

Number nine, another par five and comparatively short by Tour standards at just 521 yards, nonetheless annually plays as one of the toughest holes on the course, requiring three well-struck shots into the teeth of the prevailing wind. The second of those shots must cross an immense valley, or the third shot will be blind to a tightly bunkered plateau green that slopes fiercely. In the final round of the 2002 Mercedes, Sergio Garcia hit a 3-wood within two feet of the hole here to set up an eagle that took him to victory, three days before his 22nd birthday.

Par on the Plantation is 73, which means that it features only three par threes, the last of them coming at hole 11, a downhill, downwind 164-yarder where finesse is paramount and keeping one's head down is a true act of will, as the Pacific in all its glory backdrops the green.

Switchback is the name for number 15, a brilliantly conceived strategic par five that doglegs

5TH HOLE

ABOVE (TOP TO BOTTOM): 11TH, 15TH AND 17TH HOLES **RIGHT:** 18TH HOLE

first right and then left while diving down and up through a deep swale. Another canyon guards the right side of the drive zone and reappears to the left of the elevated green, so shots that can be held tight to these borders will offer rewards. The most frustrating miss on the Plantation Course may be the approach to this green that lands on the front edge, sits for a moment, and then begins to trickle backward, gaining speed until it comes to rest 50 yards or so back down the fairway. When the hole is located up front, birdies here are rare, even for Tour players.

The highest point on the course—and without question one of the two or three most scenic spots in the world of golf—is the tee at number 17, a 486-yard par four that tumbles more than 150 feet from tee to green. Once again, the second shot must negotiate a canyonful of dense vegetation, but even a semi-solidly hit ball, if it clears the greenery, will often bounce and roll all the way to a putting surface the size of a parking lot.

Each year the sponsors offer a brand new Mercedes to the player whose second shot on Sunday stops closest to the pin at the final hole. And why not—that second shot is usually played from a distance of roughly 300 yards. Number 18 at Kapalua is one of the longest holes on the PGA Tour at 663 yards—more than 150 yards longer than the par-five 13th at Augusta National. That said, it does play downhill, downgrain, and on most days, downwind, and the green is an immense 16,000 square feet. In 2000, the playoff between Woods and Els began after both players eagled this hole in regulation, Tiger hitting a 320-yard 3-wood to 15 feet and Els a 286-yard 2-iron to 10 feet.

The winner of this tournament gets $1 million, a new Mercedes SL500 sports car, and a Tiffany crystal trophy—all that plus the expense-paid week in Paradise.

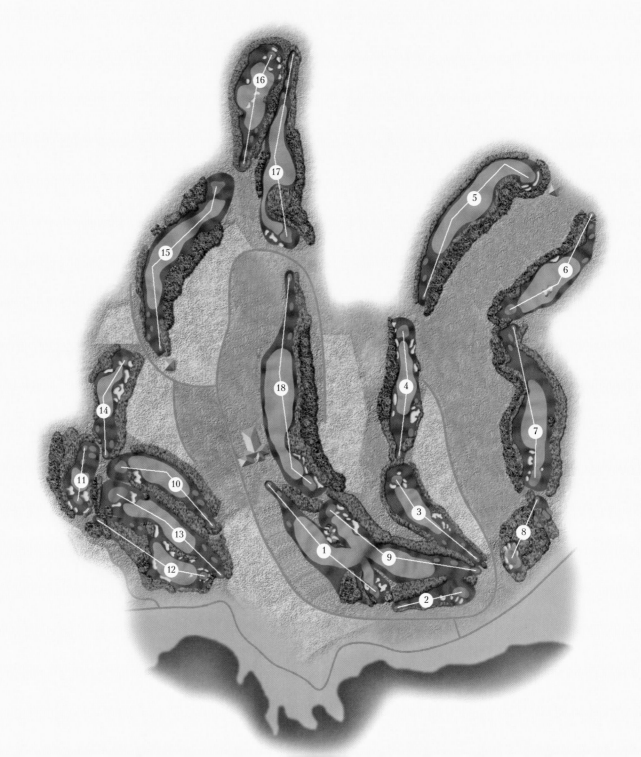

ONLY HERE

Frasier: Don't be surprised to see Kelsey Grammer in the gallery. He owns a huge home a stone's throw from the 18th hole, so close, in fact, that shortly after he moved in—and at the time an innocent non-golfer—he was reprimanded for playing his CDs too loudly. Now he plays the game poorly, his music softly.

Beards: For the players, this isn't so much the beginning of the new season as the end of the off-season. Many arrive early and chill out at the luxurious, laid-back Kapalua Resort, ringing in the New Year there with their families. And some just never get around to using their razors.

Carts: Some of the canyons on the course are so expansive and intrusive that the only way to get from green to tee is by cart—it's one of the only times you'll see PGA Tour players riding.

PLAYING TIP

Start the Season Right
Whether you play your first round of the year in January or June, do yourself a favor and get off on the right foot.

The most important preparation is mental: Manage your expectations. Remember that your muscle memory has been stretched out on the sofa for a while, so you can't count on your rhythm and coordination being very sharp—and you should expect a particularly thick layer of rust on your short game and putting. So on day one, don't even think about shooting a low score—just try to hit some solid shots.

Physically, expect to give your golf muscles a rude awakening, and lessen the jolt by doing some stretching. Ideally, you should do this for a few minutes every day for a week before you play, but minimally on the day of your opening round.

Once on the course, keep the swing slow and smooth. On your tee shots, just try to make good contact and put the ball in the fairway; on your approach shots, take a club more than you think you'll need and swing within yourself. If you can maintain that kind of discipline for 18 holes, you may just surprise yourself with a strong debut.

SCORECARD

HOLE	PAR	YARDS
1	4	473
2	3	218
3	4	380
4	4	382
5	5	532
6	4	398
7	4	484
8	3	203
9	5	521
OUT	36	3591
10	4	354
11	3	164
12	4	373
13	4	407
14	4	305
15	5	555
16	4	365
17	4	486
18	5	663
IN	37	3672
TOTAL	73	7263

TIGER WOODS DEFEATED ERNIE ELS IN A PLAYOFF IN 2000.

ABOVE: WAIALAE OVERVIEW **RIGHT:** 3RD HOLE

Golf in the 21st century may be no easier to master than it was a hundred years ago, but one thing is certain—we're all longer hitters than we used to be. High-performance balls, titanium shafts, and metal drivers with heads the size of toasters have combined with improved course conditioning to add millions of miles to our collective tee shots. As a consequence, numerous older courses have been forced to adapt in order to maintain their challenge and protect the sanctity of par.

The pressure is especially strong on courses that host professional events, since it is the world's best players who have reaped the biggest gains in dis-

tance. Much has been made of the recent lengthening and strengthening of high-profile venues such as Augusta National and the Old Course at St. Andrews, but no course on the pro circuit has seen a more dramatic fortification than the Waialae Country Club in Hawaii.

It was long overdue. Even before the long-ball era, Waialae was one of the two or three most vulnerable courses on the PGA Tour, with an average winning score of nearly 20 under par, despite the appreciable winds that are all but constant.

Designed in 1926 by Seth Raynor and completed a year later by his protégé Charles "Steamshovel"

15TH HOLE

17TH HOLE

18TH HOLE

13TH HOLE

Banks, Waialae was originally intended as a diversion for guests of the exclusive Royal Hawaiian Hotel, a few miles up the road on Honolulu's Waikiki Beach.

The first Hawaiian Open was won here by Wild Bill Mehlhorn in 1928, and the tournament continued here until World War II, when the ocean holes of the course were strung with barbed wire to ward off an enemy invasion. No damage was done to the course, however, until the modern Tour players began their assault after the tournament was revived in 1965.

When Bruce Lietzke won here in 1977, he scored three eagles in one round. In 1981, Hale Irwin won by playing the par fives in 14 under par for the week, and in 1994 Davis Love III blazed through his second round in 60 strokes. The final straw came in 1998, when John Huston set a new PGA Tour record of 28 under par for 72 holes.

The result: Additional bunkers and grass mounds tightened the fairways and greens of several holes, and the back tees were stretched nearly 200 yards while at the same time the par was decreased by two strokes; a pushover par 72 suddenly became a formidable par 70 of 7,060 yards.

One of the most marked changes came at the first hole (although it's technically the tenth, as the nines are reversed for tournament play). Architect Raynor was the sole disciple of C.B. Macdonald, pioneer of American golf-course architects and creator of the first 18-hole course in the United States, the Chicago Golf Club. Macdonald, in turn, was a student of the original courses of the British Isles, having spent a year in St. Andrews at the knee of Old Tom Morris. As a result, many of Raynor's designs owe something to the classic links of Scotland. He crafted Waialae's opener as a dogleg par five with a sternly bunkered green, to mimic the famed Road Hole, number 17 at the Old

Course at St. Andrews. The only problem with that was that the Road Hole is a par four, albeit one of the most daunting fours in golfdom.

The course renovations of 1999 repaired that mistake. By moving the tee forward a few yards, this became a par four of 488 yards, as fierce a first hole as there is on the Tour. Opening birdies at Waialae used to be as common as coconuts, but now they're extremely rare.

The second hole was lengthened a whopping 64 yards, its tee moved back across a creek, with the result that a lake now comes into play on the left side of the drive zone and the bunker-fronted green requires a well-judged, well-struck approach. The toughest hole on the course, however, may be the par-three fourth, 203 yards directly into the prevailing tradewinds to a deep green (55 yards long) with a swale running through the middle of it.

The six par fours on the front nine now average over 450 yards, and the best of them might be number five, a 466-yard bruiser where the tee shot calls for a 225-yard carry over a ditch. Under normal conditions, that 225 yards is nothing for the world's best players, but into a stiff Kona breeze, it can give even John Daly pause, especially since the second shot must clear another ditch. The player who negotiates all that is rewarded with a putt on the course's most fiendishly contoured green.

Hole six, lengthened 25 yards, now beckons a big belt from the tee, but for those who get ahead of themselves on the downswing, out of bounds looms to the right, and the prevailing wind on this par four blows that way as well.

Number 13 is the other hole that was converted from a par five to a four. On most days it plays downwind, but at 478 yards with a tightly bunkered green, it's never an easy par.

Waialae's signature hole is the 17th, a palm-surrounded par three played along the edge of the beach. Most of the pros will hit a middle iron to the green, which has been restored to Raynor's original Redan design with a pronounced pitch from right to left. A large bunker waits on the left and a quartet of small but deep ones lurks to the right, making this a tall assignment when the tournament is on the line.

One hole that saw only a dozen yards of lengthening is the finisher. At 551 yards it remains a very reachable dogleg-left par five, and in a following wind can play more like a four, adding an element of unpredictability to the finish. Just ask Jack Renner, who in 1983 was in the scorer's tent signing what he thought to be the winning scorecard when a thunderous roar arose from the 18th fairway. From 128 yards out, Isao Aoki had holed a wedge shot for eagle to steal the tournament by a stroke, the first Japanese player to win on American soil.

BELOW LEFT: MICHELLE WIE'S PGA TOUR DEBUT WAS AT THE SONY OPEN IN HAWAII.
BELOW RIGHT: ERNIE ELS, 2003 AND 2004 WINNER

SCORECARD

HOLE	PAR	YARDAGE
1	4	488
2	4	426
3	4	423
4	3	203
5	4	466
6	4	459
7	3	167
8	4	459
9	5	510
OUT	35	3601
10	4	353
11	3	196
12	4	446
13	4	478
14	4	433
15	4	396
16	4	417
17	3	189
18	5	551
IN	35	3459
TOTAL	70	7060

ONLY HERE

Hollywood History: Near a bunker on the original first hole, Montgomery Clift filmed a scene as Private Robert E. Lee Prewitt in the 1953 hit *From Here to Eternity*.

Edible Tee Markers: Instead of the usual wooden or metal blocks, the tee markers for the Sony Open are live, succulent versions of the tournament symbol, the pineapple.

Teen Prodigy: Hawaii's own Michelle Wie made her PGA Tour debut here in 2004, shooting rounds of 72 and 68 to miss the cut by only one stroke at the age of 14. She had already been part of the tournament for the previous two years, playing in a special pro-am where she impressed the pros with her play and her distance off the tee. That's when Tom Lehman dubbed the then-12-year-old "The Big Wiesy" because her swing reminded him of Ernie Els, who is known as "The Big Easy."

Foreign Flair: No PGA Tour event is held in closer proximity to the Far East. As a result, the field often includes a number of players from the Asian and Japanese Tours.

PLAYING TIP

The Driver Off the Deck

The constant winds at Waialae, combined with a collection of reachable par fives, mean that both pros and amateurs find themselves gunning for greens from long distances. In such situations, it pays to be able to hit your driver from the fairway.

You might think this shot is hard to hit with the enormous heads on today's metal drivers, but the truth is that those clubs also have a much lower center of gravity than their ancestors, which makes it much easier to get the ball into the air. Just be sure you have a decent lie.

The swing is essentially the same as when hitting from a tee peg, but to give yourself a margin for error, widen your stance a bit. This will lower your swing center and facilitate the shallow, sweeping impact you want. As an added safeguard against a thin or topped shot, put a little extra flex in your knees. Finally, try to keep your swing patient and unrushed—after all, that's a driver in your hands, so there's no need to lunge at the ball.

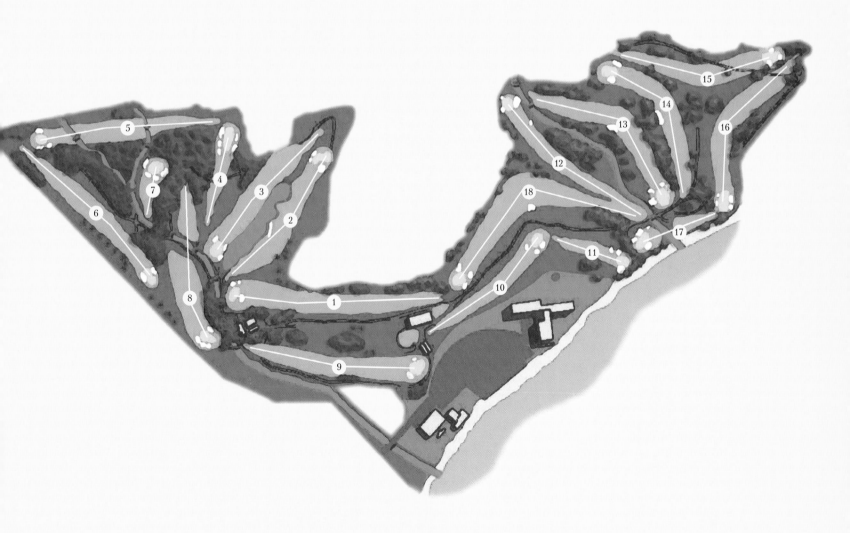

ARNOLD PALMER PRIVATE COURSE AT PGA WEST
BERMUDA DUNES COUNTRY CLUB
LA QUINTA COUNTRY CLUB
TAMARISK COUNTRY CLUB

Bob Hope Chrysler Classic, California

ABOVE: ARNOLD PALMER COURSE, 5TH HOLE **RIGHT:** ARNOLD PALMER COURSE, 15TH HOLE

Ask any self-respecting golf nut the significance of the year 1960, and he'll quickly tell you it's the year Arnold Palmer invented the modern Grand Slam. With the Masters and U.S. Open titles in his pocket, Arnie headed to St. Andrews, Scotland, in hopes of adding the British Open to his laurels, with the ultimate goal of returning to complete the circuit with a win in the PGA Championship. Although he fell short of his dream that summer, he single-handedly revived American interest in the game's oldest championship, and—with the help of an adoring press—created the enduring concept of four major professional championships.

But at least one other important event took shape in 1960—the Palm Springs Golf Classic—known today as the Bob Hope Chrysler Classic. Then as now it was staged over five days and across four different desert courses in California's Coachella Valley. And who won that inaugural event? The same Arnold Palmer—the first of what would be eight victories in that 1960 season, the finest of his career.

In fact, Arnie didn't so much win that Palm Springs Golf Classic as overwhelm it, with a 22-under-par performance that would remain the tournament record for 17 years. He would go on to play in 42 of the next 43 editions of this tournament, winning five times, including playoff victories over Ray Floyd and Deane Beman and, in 1973, a triumph over his arch rival, Jack Nicklaus, for the last of his 60 professional titles. Except for his own Bay Hill Invitational, no event is more closely identified with "The King" than the Bob Hope Chrysler Classic.

It's altogether appropriate, therefore, that one of the venues for this tournament is the Arnold Palmer Private Course at PGA West, designed in 1986 by Palmer and his partner, Ed Seay. By general agreement, this is the most difficult

ABOVE: ARNOLD PALMER COURSE, 16TH HOLE **RIGHT:** ARNOLD PALMER COURSE, 18TH HOLE

of the four courses that currently host the Hope, and the nicknames of a few of its holes—Intimidator, Brutal, Tyrant, and Monster—suggest exactly that. But those rubrics are geared largely to stir the juices of the retiree-members who tackle this course the other 51 weeks a year. To the Tour players, being the most difficult course in the Bob Hope Chrysler Classic rotation is a bit like being the most ferocious sheep in the flock. After all, it was on the Palmer Course in 2001 that Joe Durant completed 90 holes in a Tour-record 36 strokes under par, and two years earlier it was here that David Duval charged to victory with a memorable Sunday round of 13-under-par 59.

That said, there is one hole on this course that stands above all others in difficulty and annually ranks among the toughest holes on the Tour. Number five is a par three of 233 yards that plays over water to a large but extremely difficult green. Set in the middle of nine holes where birdies flow freely, this little demon invariably trips up the field.

The Palmer Course sits at the foot of the majestic Santa Rosa Mountains in the middle of a desert, but its closing holes suddenly take on a resemblance to Venice as the All-American Canal snakes back and forth, menacing several shots. At the par-five 14th players must contend with the canal on all three swings, and the par-four 16th—nicknamed Double-Cross—calls for both the drive and approach to traverse the dastardly ditch. In the final round of the 2003 Hope, Tim Herron was tied for the lead before he suffered an unraveling quadruple-bogey 8 on this hole.

However, in 1999 it was no problem for Duval, whose approach shot nearly landed in the cup for eagle, leaving a tap-in of six inches. Duval capped his round dramatically, hitting a 5-iron second to within six feet at the lakeside 543-yard 18th hole and calmly rolling home the putt for eagle, an inward nine of 28, and a prominent place in the record books.

The Hope format is unique in that for each of the first four days of the tournament the 128 pros play not only a different course but in the

BERMUDA DUNES, 18TH HOLE

company of a different threesome of amateur partners. Then, for the final round, the field is cut to the low 70 pros and ties, who return alone to the host course (which now rotates between the Palmer Course and Bermuda Dunes).

Bermuda Dunes has been the most consistent at producing dramatic finishes. Four of Palmer's five victories came here, and sudden-death play-offs occur regularly when this is the host site. One reason may be its trio of finishing holes. Sixteen is a long but slightly downhill par four to a subtly sloped green flanked by three deep bunkers with bushes and trees at the back. It is a hole that must be played carefully, as must the 17th, a 212-yard par three to an elevated green with out of bounds ten feet beyond the putting surface.

But the real excitement comes at the home hole, a short but treacherous par five that annually pro-duces eagles, birdies, and disasters. Its tree-lined fairway is dead straight, but the tee shot must be kept left of center to allow a clear shot to the 160-foot-wide but shallow green. Those whose drives err to the right will have to hit a long, lofted

LA QUINTA, 3RD HOLE

approach, likely a fade, to avoid three clusters of palm trees that have a Shaquille O'Neal-like ability to slap away shots, and when they do, the result is rarely good, as those trees guard the left side of the largest lake on the course.

In 1992, John Cook chipped in for eagle and victory here to edge Gene Sauers, capping a four-hole sudden-death playoff in which each of them had birdied the three previous holes.

La Quinta Country Club is the longest of the Hope venues at 7,060 yards, with seven lakes adding to the beauty and challenge, but these days, with the pros diminishing and demolishing the par fours and fives with 300-yard drives, the most testing holes have become the par threes. Number three plays 202 yards from an elevated tee to a green guarded by water and sand. Proper club selection is important, because the green is two-tiered and any putt from above the hole can be an adventure. Four holes later, the assignment is a middle iron to an elevated green with sand on the left and a waterfall on the right that empties into a small lake at the front of the green. But the best hole on the course may be number 12—202 yards over a boomerang-shaped pond to a green cinched tight by bunkers. When the hole is located up front, in the narrow neck between the traps, this hole taxes its assailants for dozens of bogeys.

Indian Wells was dropped from the rotation after 2004. At just 6,487 yards, it was by far the shortest course on the Tour and it couldn't stand up to the current power game. Another course might be added eventually, but in the meanwhile, Tamarisk Country Club, which has historically been used for the tournament every third year, fills in.

Tamarisk, designed in 1952, is the second-oldest course in the desert.

The course opens with a dubious distinction— the easiest hole on the PGA Tour, a 482-yard par five where the only cause for pause is a pair of benign bunkers in the landing area. In 2002, it played to an average of 4.094, with 12 eagles and 92 birdies. Over four days the worst score on the hole was a bogey, made by only one player.

Front nines of three to five under are common at Tamarisk, but the incoming half is a bit tougher, with out of bounds in play at 13, 14, and 15, and the fast and subtly sloped greens are usually vexing. However, in the mold of the other Hope courses, opportunity returns at 18 in the form of a pushover par five. A lake guards the right side of the green, but for the pros, it is the only water hazard that comes remotely into play on the course.

SCORECARD

ARNOLD PALMER PRIVATE COURSE AT PGA WEST

HOLE	PAR	YARDAGE
1	4	427
2	5	512
3	3	180
4	4	385
5	3	236
6	5	560
7	4	439
8	4	358
9	4	456
OUT	36	3553
10	4	455
11	5	512
12	3	201
13	4	446
14	5	571
15	3	155
16	4	364
17	3	132
18	5	532
IN	36	3368
TOTAL	72	6921

SCORECARD

BERMUDA DUNES COUNTRY CLUB

HOLE	PAR	YARDAGE
1	5	538
2	4	418
3	4	377
4	3	209
5	4	432
6	4	368
7	3	176
8	5	540
9	4	389
OUT	36	3447
10	4	414
11	4	382
12	3	160
13	5	564
14	4	385
15	4	399
16	4	451
17	3	212
18	5	513
IN	36	3480
TOTAL	72	6927

SCORECARD

LA QUINTA COUNTRY CLUB

HOLE	PAR	YARDAGE
1	4	382
2	4	434
3	3	202
4	4	384
5	5	516
6	5	527
7	3	168
8	4	389
9	4	399
OUT	36	3401
10	4	405
11	5	543
12	3	202
13	5	547
14	4	469
15	3	206
16	4	454
17	4	421
18	4	412
IN	36	3659
TOTAL	72	7060

SCORECARD

TAMARISK COUNTRY CLUB

HOLE	PAR	YARDAGE
1	5	482
2	3	171
3	4	443
4	5	509
5	3	199
6	4	375
7	4	331
8	4	393
9	4	439
OUT	36	3342
10	4	407
11	3	191
12	5	550
13	4	417
14	3	225
15	4	423
16	4	404
17	4	395
18	5	527
IN	36	3539
TOTAL	72	6881

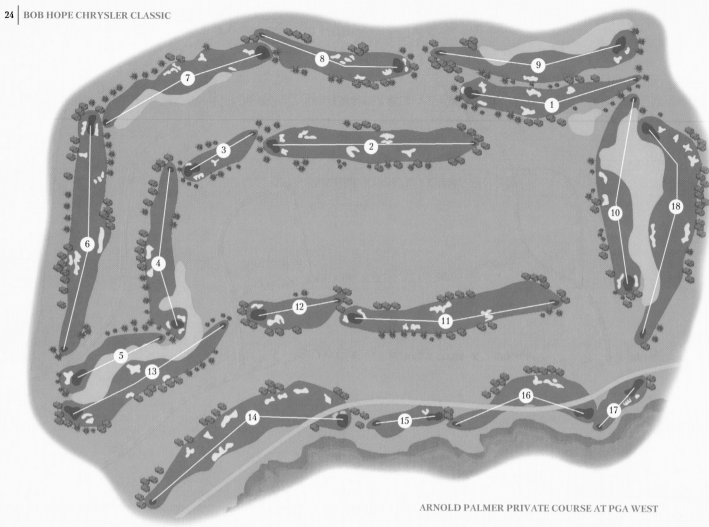

ARNOLD PALMER PRIVATE COURSE AT PGA WEST

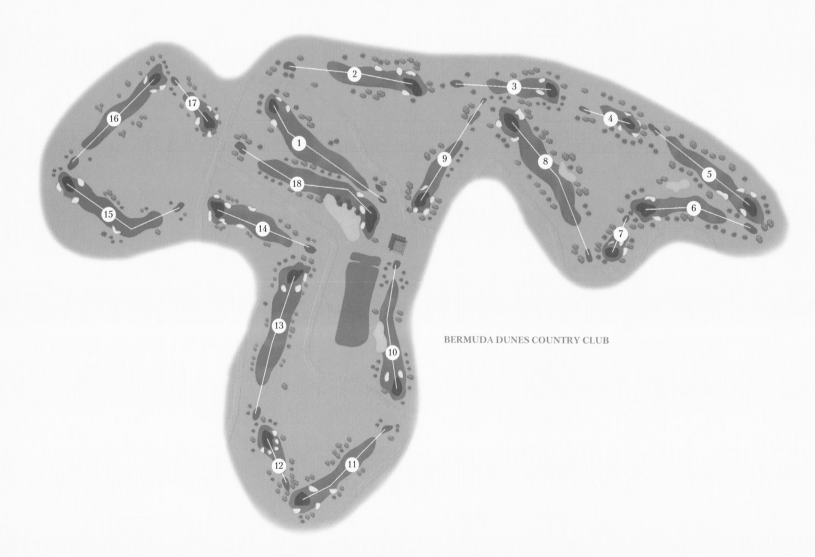

BERMUDA DUNES COUNTRY CLUB

ONLY HERE

Presidents: Dwight D. Eisenhower played in the pro-am during the 1960s, Gerald Ford was a regular during the '80s and '90s and makes his home in Palm Springs, and in 1995 Ford, George Bush, and Bill Clinton played in a historic fivesome with host Bob Hope and Scott Hoch, followed by a battalion of Secret Service agents and 25,000 spectators.

Ladies Tees: The Classic Girls—a trio of pulchritudinous local lasses clad in skin-tight teeshirts—are a tradition dating back to the days when the tournament had a Classic Queen. Debbie Reynolds, Jane Powell, and Jill St. John were among them.

Lake Bing/Phil: Bing Crosby and Phil Harris were such regulars at this event that a water hazard on the first hole of Indian Wells, which was used for the tournament from 1960 through 2004, is named after them.

The cast of stars who have played here also includes Frank Sinatra, Dean Martin, Burt Lancaster, Kirk Douglas, Desi Arnaz, and continues to this day with David James Elliott, Matthew McConaughey, and Justin Timberlake.

Magnetic South: Local knowledge holds that all putts in this tournament break toward the city of Indio, a notion that's of only marginal help when you're standing in the middle of a green in the middle of a course in the middle of the desert.

Eagles: No tournament produces as many threes on par fives, an average of nearly 70 per year over the last decade, more than twice the number at most other Tour events.

PLAYING TIP

When to Gamble

Each of the Bob Hope courses ends with a reachable par five. Most of the pros can get home on these holes with long irons, and even an amateur with good distance will have a chance for an eagle putt. But with water guarding each of these greens, you need to know how to weigh the risks against the rewards.

Make an honest assessment of your ability. You may be able to hit a 3-wood 240 yards, but the last twenty of those yards are probably bounce and roll, so if the shot you're facing calls for a carry of more than 220, you should lay up. If you're a slicer, your tendency is to miss long shots to the right, so when water or other trouble is on that side, think twice about taking a gamble. Vice versa if you have a hook.

If the do-or-die shot comes at the last hole, don't ruin a good round by taking a foolish chance. If you're one up in a match, or even all square, don't put the outcome at risk. On the other hand, when an honest self-appraisal tells you that your worst shot won't hurt you badly, that's the signal to go ahead and try for your best shot.

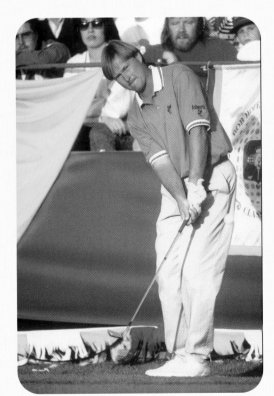

JOHN COOK, 1992 AND 1997 WINNER

DAVID DUVAL, 1999 WINNER

PHIL MICKELSON, 2002 AND 2004 WINNER

ABOVE (TOP TO BOTTOM): 7TH AND 13TH HOLES
RIGHT: 11TH HOLE

Remember the episode of Tiger and the boulder? It produced a rare moment of bizarre golf television and a classic photo for the Monday sports pages—random gallery members leaning their collective might into a massive desert rock in order to move it out of their hero's line of play.

The scene of that silliness was the TPC of Scottsdale, and if you were to form an opinion based on that incident alone, you might reasonably conclude that this is one ruggedly daunting golf course.

Nothing could be further from the truth. This is, in fact, the site of the second-lowest 72-hole total ever posted on the PGA Tour, Mark Calcavecchia's 256 in the 2001 Phoenix Open (the score broke a 46-year-old record before being bettered in 2003 by Tommy Armour III's 254 at the Valero Texas Open). It's a place where 60 has been shot more than once, where all the par fives are reachable in two, and one of the par fours has produced another unlikely moment—the Tour's only albatross hole-in-one.

Don't blame the designers, Tom Weiskopf and Jay Morrish. They crafted exactly what was requested of them, the first Stadium Course that could be used 51 weeks a year as a playground for rank-and-file golfers of the greater Scottsdale area. The land they were given was a barren tract of the Sonoran Desert, nestled beneath the McDowell Mountains. The course they created, however, is not a desert course, despite the ubiquitous saguaro cacti and mesquite trees. It's closer to a parkland layout, with broad, friendly fairways and lakes in play on six holes, or perhaps a links course, with 72 strategically placed bunkers and massive faux dunes shouldering most of the holes.

Weiskopf added 127 yards with several new tees in 2004, but the TPC of Scottsdale is still a good place for Tour players to remove the winter kinks from their swings and let out the shaft with impunity. Calcavecchia has won three titles here—in three different decades—and his secret may be that he approaches the course not as 18 holes but as three segments of six.

The opening holes are relatively non-taxing, and many players get off to fast starts—but few as fast as Bruce Lietzke, who once played the par-five third and par-three fourth in a total of four strokes, an eagle followed by a hole-in-one.

The meat of the course, according to Calcavecchia, is holes seven through 12, a stretch that includes the longest par three and the two longest par fours. "If you can play those holes in under par, you're picking up ground," he says. The par-three seventh plays 215 yards to a green fronted by a steep bank and flanked with sand. Those who escape that hole unscathed will have to reach back for a big drive at the 470-yard eighth, a dogleg left around patches of desert scrub. A large swale guards the right side of this green, complicating the lengthy second shot. But the hardest hole on the course is probably number 11, a 469-yard par four with a lake running the length of the left side of the fairway.

In the final round of the 2002 Phoenix Open, Chris DiMarco had a four-stroke lead until he double-bogeyed number 11 and then bogeyed 12 and 13 to lose it all. To his credit, DiMarco came back with a pair of birdies on two of his next three holes to right the ship and gain a one-stroke victory.

It is over the finishing stretch that birdies are made. When Calcavecchia set his scoring record, 16 of his birdies came over the final six holes—that's 16 birdies in 24 chances. The easiest hole for the pros is number 13, a par five with a Weiskopf/Morrish trademark, a split fairway. It's 595 yards long but often plays downwind, and can be shortened even more by the player who goes boldly for the smaller right-hand fairway, cutting off 40-50 yards. This is the hole where, in 1999, Tiger's ball came to rest behind a boulder. Appealing to a rules official, he was told that because the boulder was not embedded it was a loose impediment, and if he could get members of the gallery to move the big rock, it would be permissible under the rules. Sure enough, about a dozen spectators volunteered to help move the one-ton boulder out of the young feline's path, giving him a clear shot to the green. Very grateful, Tiger shook each spectator's hand and thanked them all for their assistance.

The star of the course, however, is the other inward par five, number 15, a classic risk-reward hole. The hole, which plays along the edge of a lake and culminates at an undulating island green, has been stretched from 501 to 558 yards. It has always yielded a variety of scores from three to seven, but now eagles will be harder to come by.

Number 16, a par three of 162 yards, may not be the toughest hole on the PGA Tour, but it is without question the loudest, as 20,000 spectators

LEFT: 16TH HOLE **ABOVE (TOP TO BOTTOM):** 15TH, 17TH, AND 18TH HOLES

fueled by various adult beverages gather in the grandstand and hillside to the right of the hole. Many of them place bets on where the tee shots will finish, and all of them begin hooting and hollering the nanosecond a player's clubhead meets ball. The most raucous explosion came on Saturday in 1997, when Woods came to the tee and knocked a 9-iron in for a hole-in-one. The crowd roared from the moment he hit the shot until he picked it out of the cup.

For sheer drama, however, few holes can match number 17, a driveable par four of 332 yards. Many of the Tour studs go for it, but only a shot that is hit string-straight with the proper distance will settle on this green, which drops off quickly to water on the left and rear and to sand on the right. Through the first 14 Phoenix Opens played at Scottsdale, this hole produced every score from two to seven. Then, in round one of the 2001 edition, Andrew Magee did the deed. Magee's tee shot bounced on the green while the group ahead was still putting out. The ball rolled past Steve Pate and then caromed off the putter of Tom Byrum, who was lining up a birdie attempt. From there it rolled directly into the hole. As far as anyone knows, this is the only hole-in-one ever scored on a par four in PGA Tour competition.

Number 18 is a classic finisher in the tradition of Stadium Courses, a lengthy doglegging par four with a lake lapping at the left side of the fairway and an immense spectator mound on the right.

In 1999, steps were taken to make this golf course tougher. The rough was grown to six inches, banks were shaved so balls would roll toward the water and sand, and more than a hundred trees were planted. The result? Two years later, Calcavecchia fired his 256, setting or tying seven scoring records.

But hey, that's okay. The Phoenix Open has a proud history of rewarding players who can post low numbers. It was here that Jack Nicklaus won by posting his first 29 for nine holes (1964), that Arnold Palmer charged to victory three years in a row (1961–63), and that Johnny Miller won by 14 strokes (1975).

RIGHT : TIGER WOODS EVENTUALLY RECEIVED HELP FROM THE GALLERY IN MOVING THIS BOULDER IN 1999.

OPPOSITE TOP: MARK CALCAVECCHIA, THREE-TIME WINNER

OPPOSITE BOTTOM: VIJAY SINGH, 2003 WINNER, 16TH HOLE

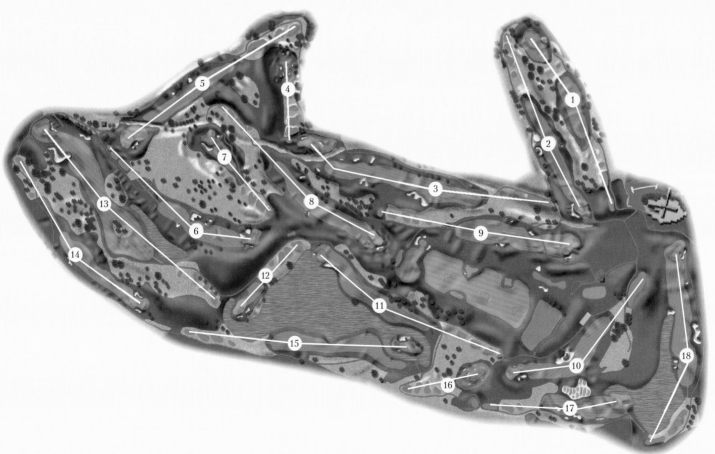

ONLY HERE

Nocturnal Ornithology: The PGA Tour's most notorious hospitality center is The Birds Nest, a pulsating nightspot that sets up shop each year about a mile from the course and rocks with live music until the wee hours. Tickets to the "VIP section" go for $150 a night. No sane Tour player's wife will let her husband go to this tournament without her.

Big Numbers: Few, if any, other tournaments can match this one at the turnstile. There is no limit to the ticket sales, plenty of room to park, and the golf course was built to handle the traffic. In a week when the weather is good, over 500,000 Arizonans will come out.

55 T-Birds: Until the event became the FBR Open in 2004, the Phoenix Open successfully resisted the temptation to take on a corporate title sponsor for 71 years. Instead, they depended on the hard work and salesmanship of the Phoenix Thunderbirds, a group of 55 community leaders who still run the tournament with a mission to promote the Phoenix area through sports while wearing snappy blue velvet tunics and silver medallions.

A Pioneer: Ted Rhodes, the first black athlete ever to perform in a PGA Tour event, made history when he played and made the cut in the 1952 Phoenix Open.

PLAYING TIP

If It Feels Right, It's Wrong

On a long-hitter's paradise like the TPC of Scottsdale, everyone is tempted to reach for a bit more distance, and there are some ways to pre-program some extra yardage as you take your address position. The key is to avoid doing what comes naturally.

First, don't widen your stance. A wide stance may feel stable and powerful, but once your feet get more than shoulder-width apart, you're limiting your ability to make a full backswing. If anything, narrow your stance a bit.

Second, don't tighten your grip pressure. Again, this feels powerful, but it only makes your arms tense and inhibits a free-flowing swing. Instead, grip the club a bit more lightly than usual.

Third, don't move your hands forward. This move, which de-lofts the club, looks and feels aggressive, but it encourages a weak, wristy pick-up in the backswing, which reduces your swing arc and saps you of power. You're better off positioning your hands a bit in back of their usual address position. This will set you up for a one-piece takeaway into a full, powerful backswing.

SCORECARD

HOLE	PAR	YARDAGE
1	4	410
2	4	416
3	5	554
4	3	175
5	4	453
6	4	431
7	3	215
8	4	470
9	4	464
OUT	35	3588
10	4	403
11	4	469
12	3	195
13	5	595
14	4	476
15	5	558
16	3	162
17	4	332
18	4	438
IN	36	3628
TOTAL	71	7216

PEBBLE BEACH GOLF LINKS
POPPY HILLS GOLF COURSE
SPYGLASS HILL GOLF COURSE

AT&T Pebble Beach National Pro-Am, California

ABOVE: PEBBLE BEACH, 4TH HOLE **RIGHT:** PEBBLE BEACH, 5TH HOLE

Should you need any further evidence that golf has become America's pastime, here it is: Just 25 years ago, the green fee at the Pebble Beach Golf Links was $30—now it's $395.

Unless, of course, you play during a certain week at the end of January or beginning of February, in which case you get a special rate—$10,000 for the week. But if you have that kind of the money to throw around, this is a dandy time and place to throw it. This is the AT&T Pebble Beach National Pro-Am—the ultimate golf fantasy game.

Indeed, the number of people salivating to pay that hefty fee far exceeds the 180 spots that are available. And why not—this is the one chance a year to play big-time golf in the world's most breathtaking natural surroundings while trading shots, quips, and stock picks with every golf-playing luminary from Tiger Woods to Bill Murray.

The AT&T was born in 1937, and its father was Bing Crosby. A member and several-time club champion at Lakeside Country Club in Los Angeles, Crosby got the idea of staging a pro-am event for Lakeside members as a chance to get the average hacks together with a few of the pros. Back then, Bing owned a home on the course at Rancho Santa Fe near San Diego, and it was there that the first Crosby clambake was held in a deluge of rain, an appropriate beginning for the event that has become notorious for its inhospitable weather.

The tournament stayed in Southern California for five years before it was discontinued during World War II. By the time it reappeared in 1947, Crosby was a member of the Cypress Point Club on the Monterey Peninsula. He moved the event there and there it has stayed, rotating first among Cypress, Pebble Beach, and Monterey Peninsula,

PEBBLE BEACH, 7TH HOLE

and now among Pebble, Spyglass Hill, and Poppy Hills. The tournament was known as the Bing Crosby, National Pro-Am, or simply "The Crosby," until 1985, when his widow Kathryn withdrew the family name because of what she deemed "over-commercialization."

The Crosby was the first tournament to employ more than one course, and it was also the first of the big celebrity pro-ams. Under its unique format, an amateur partners the same professional for three days, playing three different courses. After the third round a cut is made of both the pros and the pro-am teams, and the survivors

foresight not only to acquire the 5,300 acres then known as Del Monte Properties but to devote the most breathtaking 200 of them to a golf course.

The golden age of golf course design was about to dawn, and the five marquee architects—C.B. Macdonald, Alister Mackenzie, Donald Ross, George Thomas, and A.W. Tillinghast—were all in or near their primes. But Morse chose none of them for the creation of Pebble Beach, opting instead for a pair of local boys, Jack Neville and Douglas Grant. Neither had ever designed a course, but both were top players, each a California State Amateur Champion. Morse reasoned

PEBBLE BEACH, 8TH HOLE

return on Sunday to battle it out for the individual and pro-am titles.

For most of the pros, this is a love-hate event. They love the beauty of the Monterey Peninsula but hate the weather, which in late January can be more suited to duck hunting than golf. They love rubbing elbows with the movie stars, athletes, and moguls, but hate partnering with them for a series of six-hour rounds. Most of all, they love Pebble Beach, but hate the other two tracks.

The Pebble Beach Golf Links is, plain and simple, the most spectacular championship golf course in the world. Much of the credit goes to its developer, Samuel F.B. Morse, namesake nephew of the telegraph inventor, who in 1919 had the

that if they could play that well, they had to be able to design a course. He was right.

"It was all there in plain sight," said Neville. "The big idea was to get as many holes as possible along the ocean. It took a little imagination but not much." Today, fully half of Pebble's holes—six on the front nine, three on the back—play along the edge of the Pacific.

The first of them arrives at number four, a short, uphill par four that climbs along the edge of a cliff to the smallest green on the course—and that makes it one of the smallest in golf—perched above Stillwater Cove, a surpassingly beautiful inlet where sailboats float, sea lions bark, and otters (and golf balls) splash constantly in the surf.

When the U.S. Open came here for the fourth time in 2000, the players were greeted by a brand-new hole at the par-three fifth, designed by Jack Nicklaus. Formerly, this had been a lackluster babe in the woods, played uphill to a blind green wedged between two thickly wooded areas. The new hole, on land acquired by the Pebble Beach Company at great expense, is a seaside star, playing 188 slightly downhill yards along a ridge above the sparkling waters of Stillwater Cove and culminating at a slender, angled green that is protected by three bunkers. Instantly, the weakest hole on the course became one of the strongest.

Lee Trevino once said, "If you're five over par when you get to the sixth tee at Pebble Beach, it's the best place in the world to commit suicide." This is where the course shows its gorgeous teeth, smiling and sneering at its attackers, coaxing and conning them to play their best or suffer the worst.

Number six is the easiest of the next five holes—all played along the sea—and there's nothing easy about it. A par five that reads 513 yards on the card, it can play two hundred yards longer in a headwind. From an elevated tee, the drive is played to an immense valley of fairway. On the hillside to the left is a massive bunker dotted with grass islands, and to the right are the cliffs, dropping 50 feet to the cove. At about the 350-yard mark, the fairway swoops steeply uphill to a headland, the highest point on the course, where it levels off for the last hundred yards of the hole.

The next seven full swings must be made with the Pacific Ocean in sight, in play, and constantly in mind. Number seven is one of the most famous and photographed holes in the game, a 106-yard par three that plays downhill to a green squeezed onto a tiny spit of land, a green which at its narrowest point is only eight steps wide and shrinks with every gust of wind. It's the shortest hole in major championship golf, but yard for yard it may be the hardest in the world. Under normal circumstances, it's a three-quarter wedge shot, but circumstances on this tee are rarely normal. During one Crosby, Eddie Merrins, "The Little Pro" from Bel Air, made an ace by slugging a 3-iron into the face of a gale. And on another day, Sam Snead was so intimidated by the wind that he putted his ball down a dirt path to the hole. In the windblown final round of the 1992 U.S. Open, Tom Kite missed the green with a 6-iron but then holed out a 50-foot pitch shot for a birdie two that launched him to victory.

It's hard to conceive of a more difficult trio of consecutive par fours than the eighth, ninth, and 10th holes at Pebble. Continuing the route along the cliffs, hole eight calls for a blind drive uphill to the plateau shared with number six. It then angles dramatically to the right 180 yards across a 100-foot-deep chasm filled with rocks, thick grass, and the encroaching sea. Nicklaus calls the approach over this gorge "the greatest second shot in golf." The small green slopes sharply from back to front and is the fastest on the course.

JACK NICKLAUS AND TOM WATSON, PEBBLE BEACH, 9TH HOLE

AN OVERVIEW OF PEBBLE BEACH. 10TH HOLE IN FOREGROUND

The hardest hole on the course is number nine, a 466-yard par four whose fairway tumbles steeply from left to right, toward the sea. (You can understand why the fade-playing Trevino recommended hari-kari.) But those who seek to avoid the perils of the right risk a battle with rough and bunkers on the left. The green sits on the brink of the cliff and people have been known to hit putts off the edge and onto the beach below. In the 1963 Crosby, Dale Douglass took a 19 here. You read that correctly—19.

Number 10 is 20 yards shorter than nine, but it tilts more precipitously toward the cliffs. Hit a tee shot down the right-center of this fairway and there's a better than even chance it will end up on the rocks. Moreover, the green is even more precariously perched than the one at nine. Into a wind, like all of the seaside holes, this one becomes a bear. "The year I won the Crosby," says Ken Venturi, "on Sunday I needed a driver, a 3-wood, and a hard 6-iron to reach that hole."

After 10, the course moves inland and begins its homeward loop through stands of oak, cypress, and eucalyptus. The outstanding hole in this stretch is number 14, a classic three-shot par five that sweeps from left to right and concludes with an uphill pitch to the most fiercely contoured green on the course. The left side of the green is four feet higher than the right, and is protected by a gaping bunker collared with kikuyu grass. In the 1977 PGA Championship, Danny Edwards took six putts here. Before 1967, this hole was a bit more difficult owing to the presence of a large cypress tree on the right side of the fairway, but in the final round of the Crosby that year Arnold Palmer, one behind Nicklaus and gunning for the lead, went for the green in two and struck that tree, the ball bouncing out of bounds. He replayed the stroke, with the same result. That night, a storm hit the area; lightning struck the tree, uprooted it, and blew it to the ground. What Palmer couldn't accomplish, Mother Nature did.

Number 17 is a par three that can play anywhere from 170 to 218 yards, depending on tee and pin position, and call for anything from a 9-iron to a driver, depending on wind direction. The wide but shallow green is cinched at the waist, creating a two-tiered hourglass target with the left side higher than the right. The right-front area is open to the fairway, but the rest of the green is guarded by bunkers of various shapes and sizes.

In the 1951 Crosby, singer Phil Harris sank a lengthy putt here to clinch the pro-am title for him and his pro partner, Dutch Harrison.

"Exactly how long was that putt?" someone asked him that evening.

"I don't know," said Harris, "but I'd like to have that much footage on Wilshire Boulevard."

"Was it a hundred feet?" he was asked.

"Hell," said Harris, "it *broke* that much."

The hole is closely identified with each of the first two U.S. Opens held at Pebble. En route to victory on Sunday in 1972, Jack Nicklaus struck a majestic 1-iron into the wind that hit the flagstick and stopped inches away. Ten years later, Nicklaus looked to be on the verge of an unprecedented fifth Open title until at this hole Tom Watson turned apparent disaster into victory, pitching in from rough to the left of the green for a birdie that gave him the lead. He added a birdie at 18 to edge Nicklaus by two.

The 18th at Pebble Beach is the grandest of all grand finales, a beautiful beast of a par five that curls 543 yards along the ocean in a glorious counterclockwise crescent. Credit for this hole has traditionally been given to H. Chandler Egan, the two-time U.S. Amateur Champion turned architect who made myriad improvements to Pebble Beach prior to its hosting of the 1929 Amateur. However, recently uncovered evidence shows that it was in fact British architect Herbert Fowler who had the inspiration to move back the tee and transform what was a 379-yard par four into the most famous three-shotter in the world.

A good tee shot finishes near a pair of pines in the right-center of the fairway, well clear of the ocean on the left. The hole is reachable in two—Roberto DeVicenzo did it way back in the 1961 Crosby. In those days, however, both the player and the following wind needed to be strong. Nowadays, one out of two will do. Those who lay up, while avoiding the sea on the left, will not want to stray too far right either, as a lone tree stands sentinel at the green, all but blocking an attack from that side. That tree had been a noble Monterey pine until shortly after the 2000 U.S. Open, when it died—a victim of the pitch canker fungus that has laid waste to thousands of pines on the peninsula. Within a year, however, a 400,000-pound, 65-foot cypress was transplanted from the first hole, and the strategic challenge of number 18 was restored.

Despite its grandeur, Pebble Beach is the easiest of the three courses that host this event. The hardest, by far, is Spyglass Hill. Indeed, with its course rating of 75.3 and slope of 148, Spyglass is generally regarded as the toughest course on the entire PGA Tour. The late Jim Murray, gifted columnist for the Los Angeles Times, said it best when he wrote: "If it were human, Spyglass would have a knife in its teeth, a patch on its eye, a ring in its ear, tobacco in its beard, and a blunderbuss

PEBBLE BEACH, 17TH HOLE

PEBBLE BEACH, 18TH HOLE

in its hands. It's a privateer plundering the golfing main, an amphibious creature, half ocean, half forest. You play through seals to squirrels, sand dunes to pine cones, pounding surf to mast-high firs. It's a 300-acre unplayable lie."

When Spyglass first became one of the tournament venues in 1967, the pros were less than receptive. Said George Archer, "This course is built right around my game. It touches no part of it." And the irrepressible Lee Trevino added, "They ought to hang the man who designed this course. Ray Charles could have done better."

The man who designed Spyglass was Robert Trent Jones, long the dean of American golf course architects and the most prolific practitioner in the history of his profession. He envisioned the course as his crowning achievement, a chance to blend the sea, the dunes, and the forest into one exhilarating package—and, to a great degree, those early reviews notwithstanding, he succeeded.

The most memorable holes are the first five, along the sea, and the most acclaimed hole on the course is number one, a 595-yard par five that cascades downward from the clubhouse toward the ocean in a gentle leftward sweep. In keeping with Jones's penchant for bigness, the fairway is broad, and the enormous plateau green is guarded in front by an equally enormous bunker. Beyond it all is the pounding blue Pacific. This is one momentous start.

A short par four follows, its second shot steeply uphill to a green surrounded by bunkers and ice plant, an insidious succulent that grabs golf balls and holds them tight—hitting out of it is a bit like hitting out of a vat of caramel. Number three plays downhill and straight at the sea to a green surrounded by more ice plant. The hole is only 152 yards, but the steepness of its descent makes it a difficult shot to judge. Add a stiff wind, and this becomes the hardest of the short holes on the course.

The finest hole, from a design standpoint, is number four. A short (370-yard) dogleg left, it fits its terrain so beautifully you'd think it had been in place for centuries. Playing parallel to the sea, it winds downhill as the fairway tilts away from the higher ground on the right toward the ocean at its left. As on a links hole, there are no trees, just rough edges of untouched sand and scrub. The green is ingenious—just a few yards wide but 50 yards deep, three-tiered, tucked between a pair of dunes, and angled diagonally to the play of the hole—a green that wouldn't work on most holes in the world but is perfect for this one. Pin position dictates the strategy—when the flag is at the rear of the green, it should be attacked from the right side of the fairway, at the front from the left.

After another strong par three the course heads upland and inland, and its character changes completely. The rest of the round is spent battling a series of long, difficult par fours, with only occasional relief. Number eight is billed as the longest hole under 400 yards. It plays awkwardly uphill, bending left while falling off to a row of pines on the right. A strong draw is almost mandatory here if the green is to be reached with anything less than a middle iron. This is the number-one handicap hole on the course.

Only one par four on the back nine is less than 407 yards—and at tournament time, those are often rain-soaked yards, offering little bounce and roll. So it's a long slog home, especially at the uphill 13th, where even some of the pros need woods to get home, and at the 16th, a tree-lined 462-yard brute named Black Dog that was so difficult they had to tone it down a few years ago, its green lowered and enlarged to accept a greater percentage of approach shots.

Tall trees encroach on the last two holes as well, both par fours. The truth is, you're not out of the woods at Spyglass until you exit the parking lot.

In 1991, when tournament officials replaced Cypress Point with Poppy Hills on the roster of host courses, they knew they had an uphill battle. One of the most revered courses in the world, Cypress had brought great pleasure to the pros for the four decades it had been a tournament venue. Now, in place of a 70-year-old course came a mere four-year-old; in place of a highly exclusive enclave of 250 patrician members came a public facility owned by the Northern California Golf Association; in place of a course measuring a modest 6,506 yards came a bold layout that was longer than either Pebble or Spyglass. Johnny Miller said at the time, "It's like replacing Bo Derek with Roseanne Barr."

Well, maybe Katherine Hepburn with Anna Nicole Smith. Poppy Hills is the creation of Robert Trent Jones, Jr., namesake son of Spyglass's designer. While Jones the younger, known as Bobby, has his own imaginative eye, he shares his father's penchant for expansiveness—and that was surely one reason the NCGA chose him as their designer. They needed a golf course that could accommodate heavy play. Among other things, that meant large greens with multiple pin placements.

Jones gave them just that—greens that averaged well over 6,000 square feet, almost twice the size of the tiny targets at Pebble Beach—and he invested those greens with plenty of slope and movement, to break down each surface into smaller targets. Indeed, the whole feeling at Poppy is one of movement—slopes, hills, ravines, knolls, and plenty of doglegs. It's an angular, assertive course, and in its early years it jarred the Tour players, just as Spyglass did. Dave Stockton called it "the only course I've ever played that had a double dogleg in the men's room," and three-time AT&T champion Miller moaned, "There's no way I can play it without three-putting at least four greens."

After a few years some refinements were made, with the result that today Poppy Hills is tolerated by most of the pros and actually venerated by a

OPPOSITE: SPYGLASS HILL, 4TH HOLE **ABOVE (TOP TO BOTTOM):** SPYGLASS HILL, 1ST HOLE; POPPY HILLS, 5TH HOLE

few. Unlike its two sisters, it is set completely on high, densely forested ground that resembles Pinehurst more than Pebble Beach. The ocean comes into neither play nor view.

Indeed, water appears on a couple of occasions, the first of them at number five, a 426-yard par four with a pond extending from the right side of the drive zone to the green. In 2003, it played as the fourth-hardest hole on the Tour, excluding major championships, tagging the pros for more

double and triple bogeys than birdies.

Another lake comes into view as the golfer reaches his tee shot at number 10, an up-and-over-the-hill par five where the option on the second shot is to play safely to the right or go for the green with a lengthy carry over the lake.

There are five par fives at Poppy Hills as well as five par threes, so pace and variety are constant. Never does one play three holes in a row of the same par. Jones's 4-3-5 finish begins with a brutish dogleg par four at 16, where both the tee shot and approach must find elevated targets. Number 17 provides a break, with a short down-hiller to an ample green set in the Monterey pines, but the home hole is an audacious double dogleg. If it's not the signature hole, it is certainly the hole that epitomizes Poppy Hills, taunting the pros to hit a powerful draw from the tee and then an equally powerful fade to an enormous green that falls sharply from left to right.

Many of the game's best players have won this event, but three names stand out from the others. First is Mark O'Meara, who has five AT&T Pebble Beach titles to his credit, a remarkable record considering his career victory total is only 16. Second is Jack Nicklaus, who won three times and sandwiched a victory in the 1972 U.S. Open at Pebble between two of them. Nicklaus also won the 1961 U.S. Amateur at Pebble Beach. The third is Tiger Woods, who came from seven strokes back with seven holes remaining in 2000—including a hole-out approach for an eagle two at the 15th—to score a victory in his sixth straight PGA Tour event. Then, four months later, he returned for the U.S. Open and dominated that championship as no player ever has, winning by an unconscionable 15 strokes.

ABOVE: BING CROSBY AND BEN HOGAN, 1956
BELOW LEFT AND RIGHT: KEVIN COSTNER (LEFT) AND BILL MURRAY ARE PRO-AM REGULARS.

VIJAY SINGH, 2004 WINNER

ONLY HERE

Weather: Over the years, the competition in this event has been cancelled for rain, sleet, snow, and wind. One sunny day per tournament week is about standard, two is a blessing, four a miracle.

Confusion: With play spread over three courses for the first three days, this tournament can be difficult to follow, both in person and on television.

Star Power: It's not just the quality but the variety of celebrities who annually unsheathe their games here. Where else can you sit under a tree and watch successive three-putts by Clint Eastwood, Emeril Lagasse, Charles Schwab, Ray Romano, John Elway, and Alice Cooper?

Animal Attraction: Deer roam freely on all three courses, and at Pebble you'll also see walruses, sea lions, otters, several kinds of seabirds, and in the distance the occasional spouting whale.

PLAYING TIP

Overcoming Ice Plant

The Monterey Peninsula is one of the few places in the world where a golfer encounters *Mesembryanthemum crystallinum*, the dreaded, snagging succulent known as ice plant.

When your ball settles in this stuff, the situation doesn't look bad. The ball invariably is sitting up—almost perched, in fact. But the truth is, you're doomed. Ice plant veterans take glee in betting the uninitiated they can't extricate themselves on the first swing.

The first advice on ice plant is to stay out of it. The second is to give strong consideration to declaring the lie unplayable, taking a one-stroke penalty, and dropping free of the stuff. If you do choose to play, use a wedge—and only a wedge—play the ball well back in your stance, and chop down and through with all your might. If you move the ball, consider it an achievement, if you get it back into play, a miracle, and if you approximate your target, an accident.

DAVIS LOVE III, 2003 WINNER

TIGER WOODS, 2000 WINNER

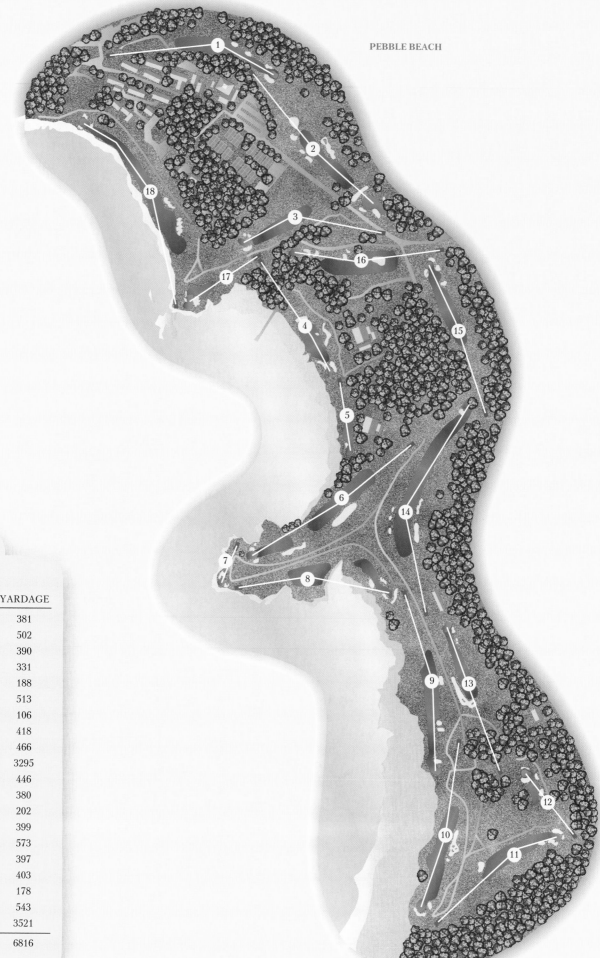

PEBBLE BEACH

SCORECARD

PEBBLE BEACH

HOLE	PAR	YARDAGE
1	4	381
2	5	502
3	4	390
4	4	331
5	3	188
6	5	513
7	3	106
8	4	418
9	4	466
OUT	36	3295
10	4	446
11	4	380
12	3	202
13	4	399
14	5	573
15	4	397
16	4	403
17	3	178
18	5	543
IN	36	3521
TOTAL	72	6816

SPYGLASS HILL

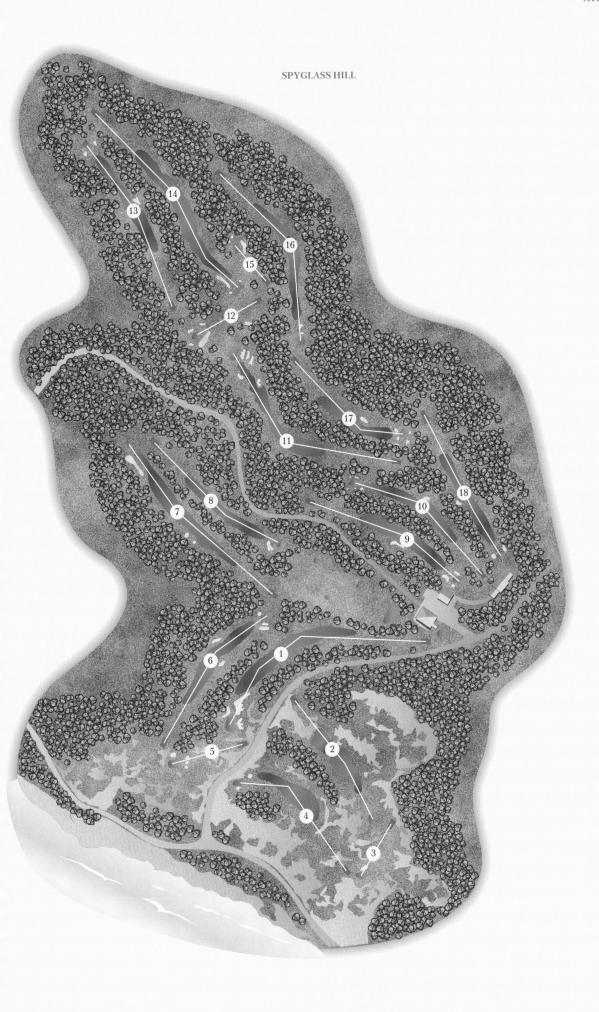

ABOVE: SOUTH COURSE, 3RD HOLE **RIGHT:** NORTH COURSE, 5TH HOLE

The Buick Invitational usually attracts a moderately strong field of competitors, but over the next few years surely every one of the world's top-ranked players will pay at least one visit here. Why? In 2008, the South Course at Torrey Pines will host the U.S. Open. For the first time since Riviera Country Club in 1948, our national championship will return to Southern California.

On the heels of its 2002 success at the Black Course of New York's Bethpage State Park—the first true daily-fee course to host the Open—the United States Golf Association decided to go public again, this time on the West Coast. The obvious choice was Torrey Pines, crown jewel of the formidable San Diego municipal golf network.

San Diego officials had pursued this plum, investing more than three million dollars in a transformation of the course by golf architect Rees Jones, the "Open Doctor" who renovated Bethpage as well as several other U.S. Open sites. Bunkers were redefined, new tee boxes introduced, some greens moved closer to hazards and all redone, and more than 600 yards added to the back tees, which now extend to a whopping 7,607 yards (the course plays at 7,568 for the Buick Invitational). Three years ago, Torrey Pines South was among the easiest of the 56 courses on the Tour. Today, it is among the most difficult.

The first evidence came in the 2002 edition of the Buick Invitational, when the average score for the pros was 73.15, two and a half strokes harder than it had been a year earlier. Even Tiger Woods struggled, shooting a five-over-par 77 in the second round—15 strokes higher than the 62 he fired while winning the Buick in 1999.

But the South is not the only course on which this tournament is staged. Back in 1973, when rain and hail soaked the course and forced a delay of the first round, officials decided to send half of the field off the adjacent North Course in order to insure completion of the tournament. The North has been a sort of silent partner to the South ever since, co-hosting the Thursday and Friday rounds. All competitors play one round each on the North and South before heading to the South exclusively for the weekend.

On Thursday evening, the tournament leader is almost always a player whose opening round was on the North. Although it has the same par of 72 as the South, the North is a full 700 yards shorter and plays nearly four strokes easier than

its big sister (although not for long, as architect Jones is scheduled to do a redesign in 2005).

One strength shared by both courses is a spectacular natural setting, on a cliff high above the Pacific. Several holes have direct views of the ocean, and others snake along the edge of a huge canyon that falls to the beach. The toughest of the canyonside holes may be number 11 on the North, a par four where the bunker to the right is a haven compared to the sheer drop on the left. Those who find the fairway will still face a challenge, for this 467-yarder plays to the smallest green on the course. Even for the best players in the world, bogeys outnumber birdies here.

Many Tour pros like to return to the practice tee after their rounds, while others head straight

for the parking lot. At the North Course, however, if a player isn't careful, he can visit either of those places before his round is through, as the par-five final hole plays past the driving range on the left and a lotful of Buick courtesy cars near the green, both out of bounds. That said, this hole is reachable in two by every player in the field, and therefore yields plenty of red numbers.

When Johnny Miller won here in 1982, he became the first player to win every PGA Tour event held in California. His victory came in part because of his performance on hole number four of the South, a par four whose left side runs along the brink of the canyon, with the sea 300 feet below. Miller birdied it all three times he played it, but the hole is much more difficult now

OPPOSITE TOP TO BOTTOM: SOUTH COURSE, 5TH AND 12TH HOLES **ABOVE:** SOUTH COURSE, 18TH HOLE

that Jones moved the fairway and green closer to the canyon. He also moved the green closer to trouble on the third and 14th holes, transforming them into dramatic and difficult tests.

The canyon returns on the right side of the seventh hole, menacing both the tee shot and approach. Then it's relatively smooth sailing until number 12, a 477-yard par four that also plays uphill and usually into the wind off the ocean. Tall trees and thick rough line both sides of the fairway, a bunker on the right catches fades that fade too much, and another on the left snags draws that draw too much, making the approach to this sand-flanked green even more difficult.

Jones added more than a hundred yards to the length of number 15, where trees left and right make for the stiffest driving assignment of the day. It may also be the most demanding second shot, at least from the standpoint of club selection, since the angled green is two tiered, with the uphill putts very slow and the downhillers like lightning.

The par-three 16th now plays 227 yards uphill and into the prevailing wind to a relatively narrow, back-to-front-sloping target with sand on both sides and the insidious canyon awaiting a severely pulled or hooked shot.

The canyon gets one last shot at spray hitters on the tee of number 17. In the sudden-death playoff for the 2001 Buick title, both Phil Mickelson and Frank Lickliter dispatched their tee shots into the depths. Mickelson won the

hole and the tournament when his double-bogey six edged Lickliter's triple-bogey seven.

Number 18 is an ideal tournament finishing hole, a just-reachable par five with a pond protecting the front-left of the green. On Sunday in 1975, Bruce Devlin spent so much time—and money—there that the tournament organizers put his name on it. The Australian was only three strokes off the lead when he played six shots from the near shore of the pond in an attempt to blast his ball onto the green. With a closing 11, Devlin toppled into a tie for 30th place, but won immortality. The next year, Devlin was ceremoniously rowed out into the center of "Devlin's Billabong" to christen the plaque that stands there to this day.

NORTH COURSE, 6TH HOLE

TIGER WOODS, 1999 AND 2003 WINNER

NORTH COURSE, 3RD HOLE

ONLY HERE

Fly Boys: During the afternoons, golf is accompanied by an aerial ballet as dozens of hang gliders and paragliders launch themselves from the La Jolla cliffs, swooping and swerving in the offshore breeze. On most days, fighter jets and helicopters from the nearby Miramar Marine Corps Air Base also can be seen. However, during tournament week the Top Guns agree to divert their flight patterns.

Home Boys: Phil Mickelson, who as a kid was a standard bearer at the tournament, won his first event as a pro here and is the only three-time champion. Former USC roommates Craig Stadler and Scott Simpson both have won here, and nine of the last 13 winners through 2004 grew up in California.

More Home Boys: This is one event where most of the gallery members know how the putts break. The Torrey Pines courses host over 100,000 rounds a year—the courses close at 1 p.m. the Wednesday before tournament week and open bright and early the Monday after. For local residents it's a great deal—their weekday green fee is just $29 for the North and $40 for the South.

Special Species: The *pinus torreyana* trees that line the fairways are the rarest native pine in the United States. The five-needled Torreys are found only along the California coast near San Diego and on nearby Santa Rosa Island.

Weird Weather: Despite San Diego's reputation for having the best weather in the U.S., this event has seen some wild conditions. Jack Nicklaus played through a monsoon and double-bogeyed the last hole to win in 1969. When Fuzzy Zoeller won in 1979, he had to take refuge from a hailstorm. In 1993, the winds blew so hard on day one that the average score on the South Course was 79, and on more than one occasion play has been cancelled because of fog.

PLAYING TIP

Digging Out of a Divot

With over 100,000 rounds per year, the fairways of Torrey Pines suffer literally millions of divots. Most get replaced and repaired, but occasionally your otherwise perfect drive will settle into one of these insidious little scrapes. It's a bad break, but in most cases you can handle it. The key is to minimize impedance of the divot by attacking sharply downward on the ball. To do so, play the ball well back in your stance—at least two inches to the rear of its usual position. As you swing, focus your eyes on the front half of the ball. These two adjustments will help you to hit down steeply and trap the ball. The result will be a low-flying shot, similar to a punch.

PHIL MICKELSON,
THREE-TIME WINNER

SCORECARD

TORREY PINES SOUTH		
HOLE	PAR	YARDAGE
1	4	452
2	4	387
3	3	198
4	4	471
5	4	453
6	5	560
7	4	462
8	3	176
9	5	613
OUT	36	3772
10	4	405
11	3	221
12	4	477
13	5	541
14	4	435
15	4	477
16	3	227
17	4	442
18	5	571
IN	36	3796
TOTAL	72	7568

TORREY PINES, SOUTH COURSE

SCORECARD

TORREY PINES NORTH

HOLE	PAR	YARDAGE
1	5	520
2	4	326
3	3	121
4	4	429
5	4	412
6	3	206
7	4	400
8	4	436
9	5	548
OUT	36	3398
10	4	416
11	4	467
12	3	190
13	4	469
14	5	507
15	4	397
16	4	338
17	3	172
18	5	520
IN	36	3476
TOTAL	72	6874

TORREY PINES, NORTH COURSE

JOHN DALY, 2004 WINNER

She is the doyenne, the dowager belle of the pro Tour ball. Seventy-eight years young, she continues to stand tall and proud, and despite the occasional nip and tuck, her beauty and charm remain. The hostess with the mostest, a certified original, she is Riviera.

Designed in 1926 by George C. Thomas and brought to fruition by his construction foreman, Billy Bell, Riviera was born when members of the Los Angeles Athletic Club decided to expand their facilities to include golf. Thomas, a Philadelphia aristocrat/autocrat and a genius at course design, had transplanted to Southern California, where his imaginative work at the Bel Air and Los Angeles Country Clubs had caught the eye of the LAAC members.

When they summoned him to their chosen site, a 240-acre tract of the Santa Monica Canyon, Thomas took one look at the property—a dry riverbed wedged between two abrupt hills, its poor soil choked with pine, eucalyptus, sycamore, and cacti—and told his clients he could build them a course but it wouldn't be a very good one.

He lied. Bolstered by the largest budget for any golf course to that time and aided by a crew of more than 200, Thomas and Bell transformed that overgrown canyon into a golf Eden so natural in its corridors and contours that it seemed to have been there all along.

At the same time it was overwhelmingly difficult. On opening day in 1927, no one broke or equaled par. In fact, after six months the best score anyone had mustered was a 73, two over. Then one of the club's glitterati members, Douglas Fairbanks, posted a $1,000 prize for a one-day tournament. The event attracted a talented field, and Willie Hunter, the likable Scot who had won the 1921 British Amateur, did the deed with a round of 69.

Golf course rankings existed even back then, and almost immediately Riviera jumped onto the National Golf Foundation's list in third position, behind Pine Valley and Pinehurst. Today, more than 75 years later and despite the blossoming of thousands of spectacular courses around the country, Riviera retains its lofty position, ranking 22nd among *GOLF Magazine*'s Top 100 Courses in the U.S.

Riviera first hosted the Los Angeles Open (now Nissan Open) in 1929, the fourth year the tournament was played, and although the event has wandered to numerous courses over the years, it returned in 1973 for a long run that seems as if it will continue forever. As such, Riviera is the oldest course still in use on the PGA Tour.

It has endured because it offers a series of 18 discrete challenges, each requiring a balance of physical and mental skill. The course begins literally on the edge of a cliff, with the first tee hard by the clubhouse and overlooking the entire property 75 feet below. A tree-lined par five of just 503 yards, it yields many more birdies than pars and is annually the easiest hole in the Nissan Open.

It is followed immediately, however, by three of the hardest. The Riviera members play hole number two as a par five. For the pros, it's a 463-yard four. A slight dogleg right with out of

bounds left and trees to the right makes for a highly challenging drive, and the lengthy approach is no easier, a long iron into a narrow and heavily bunkered green.

A great part of the genius of George Thomas lies in his minimal yet brilliant bunkering, and no greater example exists than hole number three. A sizeable bunker protects the right side of this green, calling for an approach from the left side of the fairway. However, any player who wants that angle will have to negotiate a large fairway bunker in the left side of the drive zone. This hole also plays directly into the wind to a shallow green that slopes from front to back.

Any pro who is bogey-free when he comes to

the tee of number four will be delighted to exit the next green in the same way. The fourth hole plays 236 yards, the last 30 of them over a sprawling expanse of sand sculpted by Billy Bell. Ben Hogan, a man not given to lavish praise, called this "the greatest par three in America."

It must be admitted that Hogan had something of an affinity for Riviera, having won two L.A. Opens and a U.S. Open here in the span of 18 months. It was here also that scenes were shot for *Follow the Sun*, the biopic of Hogan's life. The course is still known by many as Hogan's Alley.

Since Hogan's heyday, however, Riviera has undergone a series of updates and refurbish-

8TH HOLE

16TH HOLE

13TH HOLE

ments, most recently in 2002, when Tom Fazio restored the original Thomas characteristics to six holes that had been severely damaged by floods in 1939. At hole number five, that meant a new tee on a small hill to the right and rear of its previous location. This single change added 25 yards to the hole, brought the wind into play, and effectively transformed the preferred tee shot from a draw to a fade.

There is not another par three in the world quite like number six at Riviera, for the simple reason that the center of this green is occupied by a bunker. Heresy? Perhaps, but for three quarters of a century no one has complained, least of all Mike Reid, who in the 1986 L.A. Open

played the hole in a total of seven strokes—a hole-in-one on Thursday followed by three straight birdies.

The Fazio changes have turned hole number seven into the toughest tee shot on the course. It calls for a fade, but in the center of the landing area is a hump the size of a school bus. Hit the left side of it, and the ball may carom into a bunker, hit the right and it could kick into the old river bed—or barranca as it is now known—which is out of bounds.

Thirty-eight yards have been added to the ninth hole, bringing Thomas's well-placed fairway bunkers back into play for today's pros. The clubhouse sits atop a hill above this green, and

18TH HOLE

the hole plays subtly but unrelentingly uphill, making its 458 yards play even longer.

No hole at Riviera gets more attention or accolades than number 10, a par four of just 315 yards. For almost every player on the PGA Tour, its green is within reach from the tee, but few try, because of Thomas's ingenious green complex. The target is just 3,000 square feet and only nine paces wide at its narrowest with bunkers left, right, and beyond. Only a superbly pinched wedge will hit and sit on this green.

An additional 50 yards of Fazio-provided length have made number 12 the most difficult hole on the course. Dozens of eucalyptus trees line the hole, but the tough part is the approach, which must avoid a large sycamore just short of the green on the left. Called "Bogey's Tree," it's named after one of Riviera's stellar early members, Humphrey Bogart.

A new tee means the barranca has returned dramatically into play at the leftward doglegging 13th, where the dreaded ditch menaces the left and newly extended back of the green.

The 16th is the shortest hole on the course at 166 yards, but its green is so small that it's a challenging tee shot even with a short iron. The putting surface is ringed by high-lipped bunkers from which an up-and-down is no small feat.

One of Thomas's beliefs was that a golf course should finish with a formidable par four, and at Riviera that credo finds its fullest expression. This is a finisher in every sense, 475 yards of unrelenting challenge. For the first time in 17 holes there's a major elevation change to deal with, and this time it's uphill all the way. The tee shot is blind to a plateau fairway that banks like a raceway turn. Then it's uphill again, steeply uphill to a kidney-shaped green that nestles in an amphitheater below the imposing Spanish-style

clubhouse. That amphitheater has often been called natural, but the truth is that Bell's crew moved vast amounts of earth to create this, perhaps the first stadium golf hole.

The most unforgiving spot on the course may be the steep uphill bank to the left of this green, particularly when the pin is also cut on that side. The resulting shot can be as short as 10 feet but with a sharp slope, snatching kikuyu rough, and a green like waxed marble, most players—even Tour players—fail to get up and down.

In 1974, Dave Stockton hit what he called his "greatest shot ever" on this hole. Tied for the lead, Stockton hit a 247-yard 3-wood from a downhill lie in the rough that stopped 12 feet from the pin. He made the birdie putt for a one-stroke victory. In 2001, Australia's Robert Allenby hit an even better shot. Playing 18 in the first hole of a sudden-death playoff that involved six players—the most in Tour history—Allenby laced a 3-wood through a driving rain to within five feet of the flag and then made the putt to give him a 7-0 record in playoffs internationally.

SCORECARD

HOLE	PAR	YARDAGE
1	5	503
2	4	463
3	4	434
4	3	236
5	4	434
6	3	199
7	4	408
8	4	433
9	4	458
OUT	35	3568
10	4	315
11	5	564
12	4	460
13	4	459
14	3	176
15	4	487
16	3	166
17	5	590
18	4	475
IN	36	3692
TOTAL	71	7260

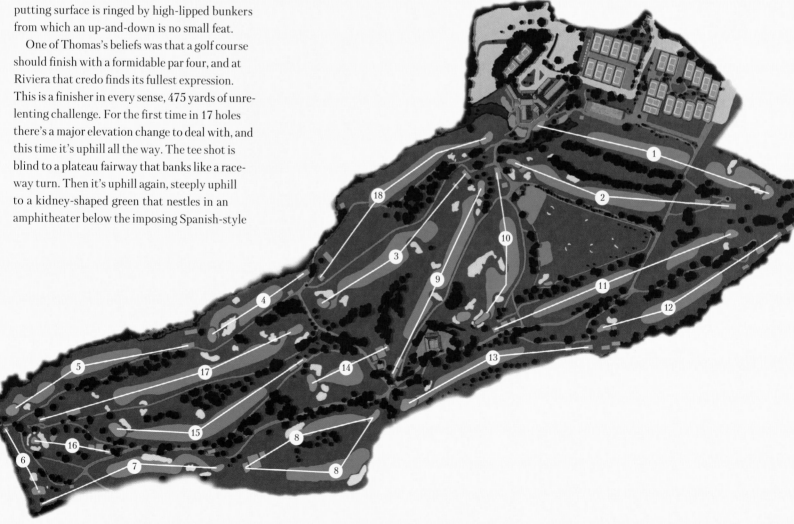

ONLY HERE

Kikuyu: An African weed that grows densely throughout the course, kikuyu is actually ideal for fairways, perching the ball high atop its stiff leaves. But in the longer fringe and rough, it grabs and swallows the ball, making crisp contact on the next shot all but impossible. Nowhere on the Tour is chipping more difficult than at Riviera.

Glitterati: Early Riviera members included Mary Pickford, Basil Rathbone, W.C. Fields, Spencer Tracy, Johnny Weissmuller, Burt Lancaster, Gregory Peck, Dean Martin, and Jerry Lewis, and it was as a young equestrian member here that Elizabeth Taylor learned to ride a horse for her starring role in *National Velvet*.

Media Event: When the L.A. Open was played here in 1929, it made history by becoming the first golf tournament ever to be broadcast on radio.

Historic Firsts: When Babe Zaharias appeared for the 1938 L.A. Open, she became the first woman to play in a men's pro tournament. Jack Nicklaus played his first pro event here in 1962 and finished tied for 50th, earning $33.33. Tiger Woods played his first Tour event here as a 16-year-old amateur, missing the cut on rounds of 72–75.

Major Moments: Riviera has hosted three major championships—the 1948 U.S. Open and the 1983 and 1995 PGA Championships.

PLAYING TIP

The Flip Shot

The snagging kikuyu grass that encircles the greens at Riviera calls for a shot that is able to fly over the fringe yet stop relatively quickly. Neither a chip nor a flop, it's best described as a flip shot.

It's played similarly to a longer pitch shot. Take your club of choice—ideally either a pitching or sand wedge—and address the ball with an open stance, your feet close together and your toes, knees, hips, and shoulders aligned to the left of the hole. If you have a very short shot and want to make the ball climb fast and drop softly, build a bit more loft into your setup by turning the face of the club open a few degrees and at the same time opening your stance a bit more.

The swing should be short back and short through. You can get good results from either a wristy motion that chips at the ball (for tight lies) or a stiff-wristed action that glides the club under the ball (for fluffy lies). Practice both methods and you'll be able to handle anything.

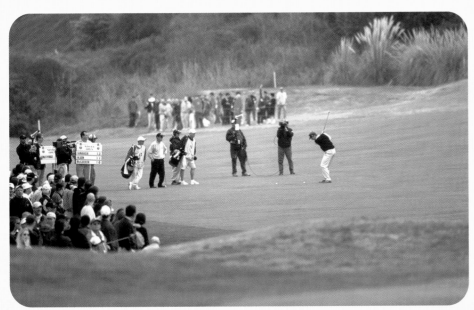

18TH HOLE

BEN HOGAN WON THREE TIMES AT RIVIERA. IN 1948, HE PLAYED THIS SHOT FROM THE BUNKER IN THE MIDDLE OF THE 6TH GREEN.

ROBERT ALLENBY, 2001 WINNER

6TH HOLE

8TH HOLE

As Bobby Jones once observed, there is golf and there is tournament golf, and the two are not remotely alike. Jones at the time was referring to the pressure of championship golf, but another fundamental difference separates those who play for pay on the PGA Tour from the rest of us: They play medal and we play match.

Except for the occasional club championship or local invitational tournament, weekend golfers tend to compete against one another on a hole-by-hole basis. Whether in one-on-one matches or as pairs within a foursome, the format embraced by at least ninety percent of casual players is the three-part nassau—a point for the front nine, a point for the back, and either one or two points for the entire 18—and the points go to the player or team that wins the most holes.

Conversely, except for the biennial Ryder Cup and Presidents Cup matches, the pros play almost exclusively stroke-play events, where the player with the lowest score wins. In the entire 10-month calendar of competition, there is just one exception, but it's a big one: the WGC-Accenture Match Play Championship.

The Accenture is one of the four World Golf Championship events launched in 1999 as a way to broaden worldwide competition, and is conducted jointly by the International Federation of PGA Tours: the Asian PGA, European Tour, Japan Golf Tour, PGA Tour, PGA Tour of Australasia, and Southern Africa Tour. The format for the event is single-elimination match play, in four brackets of 16 players each. Eligibility is limited to the top 64 players in the Official World Golf Ranking on the eve of the tournament, and players are seeded into round one according to their places on the Ranking: The number-one ranked plays his first match against the player ranked 64th, the number-two player against number 63,

and so on, with each pair of seeds adding up to 65.

The first-round matches are played Wednesday, second-round on Thursday, and the third on Friday, which gets the field down to eight players. Both the quarterfinals and semifinals take place on Saturday, leaving Sunday for the championship match of 36 holes along with an 18-hole consolation match between Saturday's losers.

Given the unfamiliarity of the format, strange things have happened in the brief history of this event. The first four champions were Jeff Maggert, Darren Clarke, Steve Stricker, and Kevin Suther-

land, prior winners of a collective three events on the PGA Tour, as the big-name players tended to be eliminated quickly. In 2002, Tiger Woods lost his opening match to 64th-seeded Peter O'Malley. A year later, however, Tiger returned to the form that won him three straight U.S. Amateur Championships (at match play) and won here in dominating style. He repeated in 2004.

However, if the format is uncomfortable for most of the pros, the venue certainly is not. Host course La Costa Resort and Spa has been a Tour site since 1969, and is consistently one of the play-

BELOW (TOP TO BOTTOM): 18TH AND 16TH HOLES   18TH HOLE

ers' favorite stops. For 30 years, it was the venue for the Tournament of Champions, where the only way to gain entry was to win a tournament on the previous year's Tour. When that event changed names and moved to Hawaii, La Costa was designated as the more-or-less permanent home of the match play championship. Only once since its inception has the event not been held here—in 2001, when it moved to Australia—and that proved to be an unhappy experiment as many eligible players elected not to make the lengthy trip Down Under.

However, despite the familiarity with La Costa, none of the players were ready for the configuration that greeted them in 2003, when tournament officials decided to flip-flop the front and back nines. The main reason for the switch was to bring the final holes closer to the clubhouse, especially 18, which culminates at the base of a spectator hill where hundreds have a good view of the action—a questionable move in a match-play event given the fact that the majority of the matches never make it to the last hole.

The change also deprived this tournament of one of the tougher finishing stretches on the Tour. Former holes 15, 16, 17, and 18 were known as The Longest Mile, where homeward-bound players routinely left a trail of bogeys and worse. Now, those holes have become the pivotal stretch in the middle of the course.

Number six is the easiest of the four at 378 yards, with the challenge really beginning at number seven, a par four dogleg right of 423 yards, its corner protected by a large pine tree. The approach is played into the prevailing wind to a severely undulating green. The par-five

eighth, at 569 yards, is unreachable on most days to most of the field, and those who go for it had best swing bravely, as a lake runs down the entire right side of the hole, and even slightly pushed or faded shots tend to wander into watery graves.

Another reason for the flopping of the nines was the difficulty of the ninth (former 18th hole), a 467-yard brute where the pros are happy to find the fairway, find the green, and grind out a work-manlike four. There was thus little opportunity for a birdie to win or tie a match.

The new trio of finishing holes does provide greater variety and the potential for added excite-ment, beginning with the pond-guarded par-three 16th, a hole made famous in the 1997 Mercedes Championships. Tiger Woods and Tom Lehman were tied for the lead after 54 holes when the last round was rained out. Officials decided to settle the tournament with a sudden-death play-off between the two of them. It began and ended at this hole—the only one dry enough to play—when Tiger striped his 188-yard tee shot two feet from the cup.

Six holes at La Costa were lengthened in 2002, and none of them more dramatically than the 17th, which was stretched from 398 yards to 483, becoming the longest par four on the course. Formerly a 3-wood and a flip wedge for the long hitters, this dogleg right now has almost everyone approaching with middle irons.

The new finishing hole certainly favors the power players. A 558-yard par five, with a creek twenty yards short of the green, it will also pro-vide food for thought for those whose matches come down to the wire. Players who are one down will have a chance for not only birdie but eagle, while those with a one-hole lead will have to decide how staunchly to protect it. Without question, it is a wonderful match-play hole. Unfortunately, less than twenty percent of the Accenture matches ever make it that far.

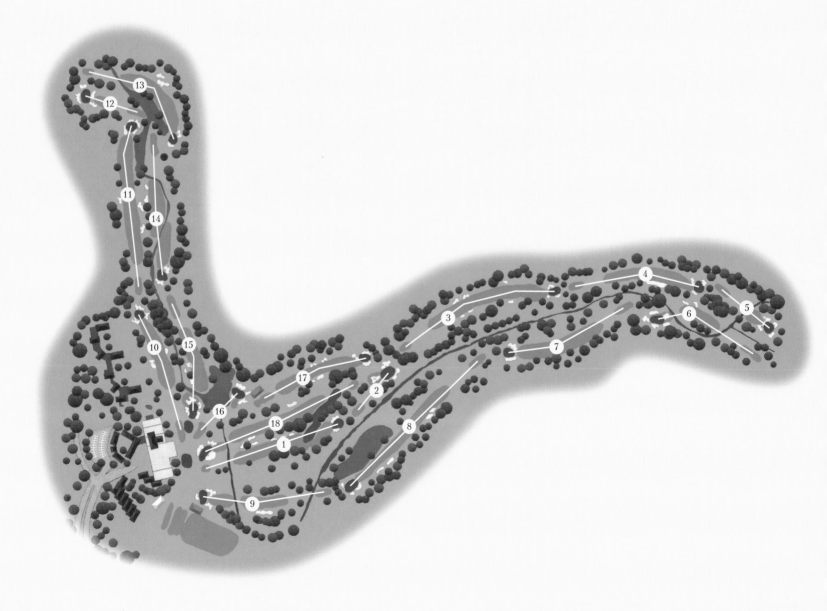

ONLY HERE

Gimmes: Since the only scores being posted are wins and losses, short putts—and long putts, if they are meaningless to the outcome of a hole—are conceded.

Men in Waiting: In addition to the 64 players competing, three alternates—the next three highest-ranked players on the World Rankings—are asked to "stay in the neighborhood," lest one or more of the competitors withdraws at the last minute.

Upsets: Over the first five years of the event, the lower-ranking player won the majority of first-round matches.

Fast Rounds: All play is in twosomes. Occasionally, one or even both players don't finish play on a hole, and most matches never get to the final hole. This is the only tournament where the pros actually play their rounds at a less than glacial pace.

PLAYING TIP

Match-Play Strategy

Plotting your moves in match play can be challenging. You don't want to become obsessed with your opponent and yet you can't ignore him. In most situations, you should simply play your game and play the golf course, but in some instances that's just plain foolish. For example, if your opponent has made a birdie on a hole and you face a 60-foot putt to tie him, there's no point in trying to lag up close for a par. Here are a few general strategies.

When you're ahead, don't let up. Don't be conservative unless that is your nature and a conservative game is what got you on top. And never get ahead of yourself, daydreaming about your next opponent or your acceptance speech. Keep concentrating on one shot at a time.

When you're behind, don't panic, especially if it's early in the match. Stick to your game plan—don't try for hero shots. Stay calm, stay focused, and don't act as if you've already lost. Looking strong when you're down can rattle your opponent as he wonders what it takes to shake you. Above all, keep a positive frame of mind, because good things rarely happen until you think they will.

SCORECARD

HOLE	PAR	YARDAGE
1	4	450
2	3	180
3	5	575
4	4	450
5	3	204
6	4	378
7	4	423
8	5	569
9	4	467
OUT	36	3696
10	4	412
11	5	526
12	3	187
13	4	386
14	4	446
15	4	365
16	3	188
17	4	483
18	5	558
IN	36	3551
TOTAL	72	7247

TIGER WOODS, 2003 AND 2004 WINNER

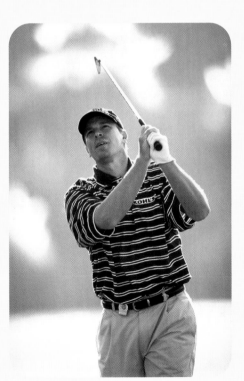

STEVE STRICKER, 2001 WINNER

KEVIN SUTHERLAND, 2002 WINNER

4TH HOLE

9TH HOLE

It's in the middle of the Sonoran Desert, but it couldn't be further from a desert course. Stroll the fairways of the Omni Tucson National Golf Resort and Spa, and except for the occasional stray saguaro you'd swear you were in Illinois or Kansas rather than Arizona. Built in 1960, before the era of environmental restrictions, the home of the Chrysler Classic of Tucson is a lush, tree-lined, lake-dotted oasis and a longtime favorite among the Tour players.

Their affection is understandable. From the time it joined the Tour rotation in 1965, this has been a course that yields low scores. It's where Johnny Miller shot 61 in 1975 en route to a 25-under-par total in one of the three straight years he won this event, and where the average winning score is nearly 20 under par, placing it among the most obliging venues on the Tour.

Why? For one thing, Tucson National is always in great condition, especially its bentgrass greens—among the first and still among the best in the Southwest. At tournament time they roll fast and true, and just as important, they are relatively flat. That translates into lots of birdies. At 7,109 extremely flat yards, this par

72 is not long by today's Tour standards, and three of the four par fives are reachable by the pros with irons—which means not only birdies but eagles. The Bermuda rough, which when thick and green can engulf balls and twist clubfaces, goes dormant and brown in winter, posing comparatively little threat. Finally, the Tucson weather is usually accommodating—warm, dry, and generally windless. It all adds up to low numbers.

Although it began as a private course, the National, as it is known to locals, is now part of the Omni Tucson National Golf Resort and Spa, which includes three nines—the Orange, Gold, and Green, with the Orange and Gold used as the tournament course.

Each nine saves its best for last. The home hole on the Orange (the tournament front nine) is a dogleg right of 440 yards with one of the course's ten lakes at its inner elbow. Strong, bold (and occasionally, foolish) players will try to carry or skirt that water while the safer route is down the left side of the fairway, leaving a lengthy approach to an elevated green protected by sand and mounds. Four here is a very good score.

Those who make par at nine will do well to hold their ground at the tournament 11th, a par four that the resort guests play as a five. It requires an accurate shot from the tee, to avoid water on the right, then a short or middle iron to a green guarded by a pair of bunkers.

Five holes later, one of the longest holes on the PGA Tour awaits. Number 15 is a gargantuan 663 yards. However, as a telling reflection of the distance today's professionals are hitting the ball, this is the second-easiest hole on the course, yielding more birdies than pars.

The best test at Tucson National comes at 18, a hole that annually ranks among the toughest on the Tour. A par four of 465 yards, it calls for a tee shot threaded between lakes right and left. The green is well protected by a bunker in the left front, so the approach must either be drawn through the opening on the right side or lofted to the green, where the reward for success will be a birdie putt on one of the most steeply sloped surfaces on the course.

It's a hole that has produced both triumph and tragedy. Arnold Palmer has won the Tucson

Open on this green and also lost it here with a closing triple-bogey seven. In 1977, Bruce Lietzke came to the tee with a one-stroke lead and three-putted to drop into a sudden-death playoff. An hour later, on the fourth hole of the playoff, he returned to 18 and sank a birdie putt of nearly 100 feet to win. And in 2003, Frank Lickliter saw agony and ecstasy all in one hole. Also leading by one stroke, he hit his drive into the water. Then he took a penalty drop and hit a 5-iron four feet from the hole to save his par and victory.

10TH HOLE

18TH HOLE

JOHNNY MILLER, FOUR-TIME WINNER

SCORECARD

HOLE	PAR	YARDAGE
1	4	410
2	5	495
3	4	377
4	3	170
5	4	395
6	4	426
7	3	202
8	5	528
9	4	440
OUT	36	3443
10	5	501
11	4	431
12	3	182
13	4	406
14	4	405
15	5	663
16	4	427
17	3	186
18	4	465
IN	36	3666
TOTAL	72	7109

ONLY HERE

First-Timers: In recent years, this event has been played during the same week as the WGC-Accenture Match Play Championship. With the game's 64 top players competing there, the field at Tucson includes a mix of rookies, aging veterans, and players who did not have strong seasons the previous year. As a result, this has been victory number one for four of the last five winners through 2004. Back in 1991, it was also the coming-out party for Phil Mickelson, who won here as an amateur while attending Arizona State.

Name Games: Since its inception, this tournament has seen numerous shifts in title sponsorship, with the result that its name has changed a dozen times.

Conquistadors: The organizers of this event are the Tucson Conquistadors, a group of civic-minded businessmen who have used this event to raise over $10 million to promote amateur athletics among Tucson's youngsters, especially the disadvantaged and handicapped.

PLAYING TIP

Desert Weapons

Some desert courses have a local rule that allows you to lift your ball out of the wasteland with no penalty. Others give you the option of dropping at a penalty of one stroke or playing the ball as it lies on the desert floor. When you're tackling one of those "play it as it lies" courses, you might want to designate one club as your desert weapon, one club that will do the dirty work, take the abrasion and abuse on behalf of the other 13. You might even bring along an old club for this purpose. Most of the shots will be recoveries—short punches back into play—so any middle iron will do.

However, if you should find yourself in a desert area near the green, don't reach automatically for a middle iron, or for the wedge. From a tight, sandy lie, even the best players have a good chance of scuffing or blading an iron shot. Instead, give some thought to banging the ball out with a putter. You'll almost always hit this shot squarely, and if the area between you and the green is open and closely mowed, a firmly struck putt is the best ploy.

Think of Florida golf resorts and the first word that comes to mind is Doral. Now well into its fifth decade, the Doral Resort and Spa, just north of Miami, has become a sort of nouveau grande dame, its 696 guest rooms and 90 holes of golf recently refurbished to the tune of $40 million.

Doral also is the first thing the pros think of when the Tour concludes its West Coast segment each February. Its tournament—now known as The Ford Championship at Doral—is the third oldest on the PGA Tour to be played continuously on one course, and has long been stop number one on the Florida circuit.

Doral's five courses are designated by color—Blue, Gold, Red, Silver, and White—and the host venue since the beginning in 1962 has been the Blue, known universally as The Blue Monster. In the early years it was just that—

6,900 fearsome yards, splashed with eight water hazards and more than a hundred sprawling, white-sand bunkers. Back then, any player who could finish 72 holes in red figures was assured of a nice payday. Says Raymond Floyd, "When I walked off that course after playing it the first time [in 1963] I thought I'd just played the hardest golf course in the world."

Those, however, were the days of persimmon woods, wound balls, shaggy fairways, and players whose level of fitness was, well, let's say Ray Floyd was a good example. A drive of 275 yards was considered mammoth. Today, a drive of 275 is still mammoth, but only on the LPGA Tour. Among the men pros, it's not even average. A dozen or more players routinely belt it out there 300 yards and more. Doral began to feel the power pinch in the 1980s, as winning scores for

the tournament got lower and lower. In 1993, when Greg Norman humiliated the Monster with a four-day total of 265—23 under par—the folks at Doral called in the same Ray Floyd and asked him to make the course as tough as he remembered it.

Floyd added several new back tees, stretched the yardage nearly 200 yards, changed the rough grass from friendly rye to gnarly Bermuda, reshaped the greens, and installed 30 new bunkers—wide, deep, steep-faced bunkers, including a "beach bunker" alongside the lake at the 18th hole. The reviews? Terrible. The pros hated the bunkering, especially that beach bunker—and, even more importantly, the resort guests (who pay dearly to play the course the other 51 weeks a year) found the Saharan revisions far too penal. So in 1999, Doral's resident teaching professional, Jim McLean, was brought in to undo Floyd's work and return the bunkers to the way they were in the original design by Dick Wilson.

The pros' assault resumed after the bunkering was made less harsh, so five holes were lengthened in 2004, bringing the total yardage to 7,385. Still the Blue is more of a shotmaker's course, a place where the challenge is not to pummel tee shots but to thread them between sand and water, to maneuver them around doglegs, under the wind, and away from the grasping rough.

Three years before he set the 72-hole record at Doral, Greg Norman established a new 18-hole mark with a Sunday 62 that included eight birdies and an eagle. It took him from seven strokes behind into a four-way sudden-death playoff which began at hole number one, a par five then playing 515 yards, where Norman hit a 2-iron second shot to the back of the green and chipped in for eagle and victory. His record has since been surpassed—a 61 by Stephen Ames in 2000—but the tournament has never seen a better final round by a winner.

Except when it's playing dead into the wind, Doral's straightforward opener yields more birdies than pars. Statistically, this is the easiest hole on the course. Things get a bit tougher at number three, a twisting mid-length par four with water down its entire right side. Then comes the first of Doral's fierce foursome of par threes—236 yards with water once again awaiting even the slightest miss to the right. When

2ND HOLE

4TH HOLE

LEFT: 8TH HOLE **ABOVE (TOP TO BOTTOM):** 10TH, 12TH, AND 18TH HOLES

played into a stiff wind, this may be the toughest par three on the PGA Tour.

The next birdie opportunity comes at the par-five eighth, but this is a hole that can also produce bogeys and worse, especially now that it has been stretched to 563 yards. It typically plays into the wind, and over the last 250 yards water squeezes in from both sides. Those who gun for this green in two had best be both strong and straight.

Two of the first three holes on the inward nine are par fives and the other is a short four, giving players a chance to gain some ground before facing a gauntlet of tough closing holes. The test begins with 13, another bruiser par three—245 yards with a trio of hungry bunkers at the green. Number 16, a dogleg par four of 372 yards, calls for strategy and finesse. Under the right condi-

tions a strong driver can opt to fly the huge bunker that defines the elbow of the dogleg, but most will try to play carefully to the corner and then wedge to a narrow, sand-choked green that slopes inhospitably from front to back. Floyd made some major changes on this hole (which were undone), but it's a wonder he touched it at all, since it was here in 1980 that he chipped in to beat Jack Nicklaus in sudden death.

Number 18 is one of the most famous finishing holes in golf, and for years it was also one of the most feared. Since 30 yards were added in 2004, to make it 473, that fear has been restored. Before the change, the once dangerous tee shot between sand and water seemed of little concern to the titanium-wielding limberbacks on the Tour who blasted over everything to an area where the fairway widens and attacked the green

with short irons. Now the water is back in play on the left, and so are the bunkers and trees on the right if players bail out in that direction. The second shot, with more water and sand to contend with, also becomes scarier when it is with a longer club, especially when a headwind blows and the pin is back left, on the edge of the lake.

Still, it can be conquered with two great shots, as Craig Parry showed in the very year the tougher 18th was unveiled. On the first hole of a sudden-death playoff with Scott Verplank, Parry followed a solid drive with a 6-iron from 176 yards that found the hole for an eagle two and victory. It matched Robert Gamez's blow at the 1990 Bay Hill Invitational for the longest winning shot in Tour history, and was, by far, the longest shot ever holed to win a playoff.

GREG NORMAN, THREE-TIME WINNER

CRAIG PARRY WON IN 2004 THANKS TO A PLAYOFF EAGLE ON THE 18TH.

SCORECARD

HOLE	PAR	YARDAGE
1	5	529
2	4	376
3	4	438
4	3	236
5	4	394
6	4	442
7	4	428
8	5	560
9	3	169
OUT	36	3572
10	5	551
11	4	402
12	5	603
13	3	245
14	4	460
15	3	175
16	4	372
17	4	419
18	4	467
IN	36	3694
TOTAL	72	7266

ONLY HERE

Local Knowledge: Doral's grainy bermudagrass greens take some deciphering, particularly as these are the first such greens the pros see each year. Since 1990, every champion but three has been a Florida resident.

The Reel Tournament: For the past two decades, the pros have had an informal after-hours competition to see who can hoist the biggest fish out of the Doral ponds, with the winner getting free lodging for the week. Andy Bean, who has won the golf tournament three times, has won the fishing title twice.

Swing Planes: The Doral course is smack on the approach route to Miami International a couple of miles away, with the result that each round is punctuated by numerous cacophonous take-offs and landings.

PLAYING TIP

Bermuda Shorts

Most golfers know that bermuda is tougher to putt than other grasses, but it is perhaps even more vexing as a rough grass around the greens, where too soft a swing barely moves the ball and too aggressive a hit produces a jumper that flies well beyond its target.

The best way to control short shots from bermuda is to close the face of your club—turn the toe about 30 degrees toward the ball. (This is in direct contrast to the open-face shot that is played from other grasses.) When the clubface is closed, it will be less likely to be snagged by the gnarly bermuda leaves. You'll hit a low ball that jumps out of the grass and runs most of the way to the hole. It's a very simple shot; practice it for a few minutes and it will become a permanent part of your southern-clime game.

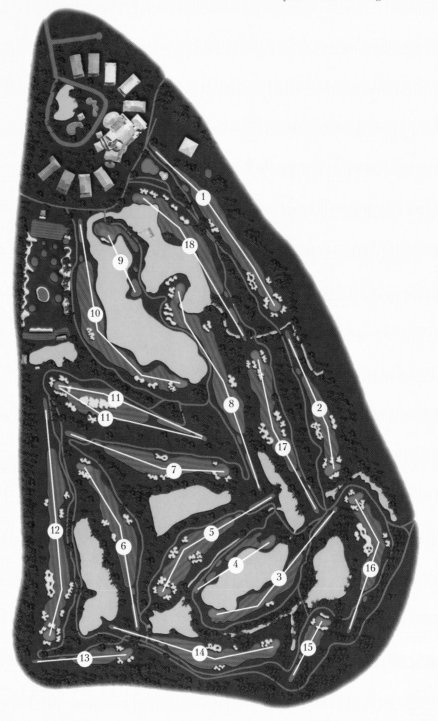

Honda has a well-deserved reputation as one of the most dependable, unfailingly consistent automobiles in the world. Oh, that The Honda Classic could boast the same.

Although the sponsor itself has been true to form—Honda is the second-longest-running sponsor on the Tour—its tournament site is ever-changing in a long series of false starts, sputters, and stalls. The move to the Sunrise Course of the Country Club at Mirasol in 2004 marked the sixth switch of venue in the past 20 years. It's as

if the tournament has taken a cue from its original host, Jackie Gleason, whose signature line was "And away we go."

The tournament started in 1972 at Gleason's home course, the Inverrary Country Club in Lauderhill, Florida, and there it had a solid 11-year run, with Jack Nicklaus, Johnny Miller, Tom Weiskopf, Lee Trevino, and Hale Irwin among the champions. Then came an ill-fated move to the TPC at Eagle Trace, a residential community course that the pros, led by Greg

Norman, vilified, saying it wasn't designed to be played from the back tees in a strong March wind. (In other words, it embarrassed them.) That marriage lasted eight years (until all the homes around Eagle Trace had been sold), whereupon the tournament shifted to Weston Hills Country Club for four years, producing a quartet of solid champions—Corey Pavin, Fred Couples, Nick Price, and Mark O'Meara.

All the while, a new home—the TPC at Heron Bay—was being readied by the PGA Tour. The

1ST HOLE

Honda was due to move there in 1996, but when the construction schedule fell behind, they had to find an alternative. An attempt to stay at Weston Hills ended because a bar mitzvah had been scheduled for that week, and the boy's father refused to move the event without sufficient compensation, so it went back to Eagle Trace.

When Heron Bay did take over in 1997, the Tour thought they'd finally found a permanent home for the Honda, but once again the players reacted strongly in the negative. This time they felt the Mark McCumber design was dull. As a result, the event failed to attract the top stars. The Tour refused to spend money on alterations to the course, so in 2003 another move was made, this time to the Mirasol community, where for one year the tournament was played at the Arthur Hills-designed Sunset Course before turning 180 degrees to the Sunrise Course.

Who knows, maybe this is indeed home. Certainly it promises to be a modern test of golf for today's players—a par 72 of 7,416 yards that can play much longer in those spring breezes. And yet, according to Fazio, length is not the challenge of Sunrise.

"These days, you can't build a course long enough to challenge the Tour players," he says. "A lot of people said the changes I made at Augusta National, adding distance, were intended to 'Tiger-proof' the course. The truth is, you can't thwart those guys with sheer distance because they all hit it a mile—even an 8,000-yard course wouldn't be daunting to them."

3RD HOLE

So how did he put some sting into Sunrise? "It's not your typical south Florida course," he says, referring to the man-made lakes that dot most of the neighboring tracks. "There are water hazards, but not many forced carries. Instead, I've tried to create lots of angles for the pros—doglegs, canted greens, elevated tees and greens, and subtle bumps and humps in the fairways. We've also created greens that will allow the Tour officials to tuck their pin placements into some very elusive spots, where the penalty for a missed shot will be severe."

Part of the course also plays alongside a nature conservancy, adding both charm and challenge. The character of Sunrise becomes apparent at the par-four first hole where a wetland runs across the fairway, meandering rightward so that any pushed or sliced shot will be out of play. The elevated green has a Pinehurst No. 2-style roll-off that rejects errant approaches, sending them 50 feet or more from the target.

The severity of the greens, many of which feature that inverted-saucer effect, drew criticism from some pros when they got their first look at the course in 2004, though by the end of the week many had warmed to the layout. It may have helped that the Tour's field staff, uncertain

10TH HOLE

16TH HOLE

17TH HOLE

18TH HOLE

SCORECARD

HOLE	PAR	YARDAGE
1	4	383
2	4	435
3	3	246
4	4	424
5	5	562
6	5	564
7	4	389
8	3	196
9	4	445
OUT	36	3644
10	4	369
11	3	221
12	5	588
13	4	473
14	4	470
15	3	185
16	4	486
17	5	556
18	4	424
IN	36	3772
TOTAL	72	7416

about how the course would play, shied away from the hardest hole locations.

One of the most difficult greens on the course is at the par-three third. While the hole is listed at 246 yards, the Tour elected to play it from a forward tee at about 160 yards in 2004 because hitting and holding the green is such a challenge.

Number 16 is another hole that gives the pros pause on the tee. Two bunkers and a lake wait in the drive zone of this par four, with more sand and water at the green. The hole is 486 yards, and plays into the prevailing wind. Any bogeys made there, however, can be neutralized at the next hole, a downwind par five of 556 yards, where the only caveat is to favor the right, as a lake borders the entire left side of the hole, lapping near the edge of the angled green.

The tournament does not finish on the Fazio course but on the 18th hole of the Sunset Course, which returns to the clubhouse and offers more room for spectator viewing and corporate skyboxes. The pros, however, may feel a bit tight on the tee as water lurks both left and right en route to the well-bunkered green of this 424-yard par four.

Sunrise is slated to host the Honda for three years, but tournament organizers are hoping that this will at last be a long-term parking spot.

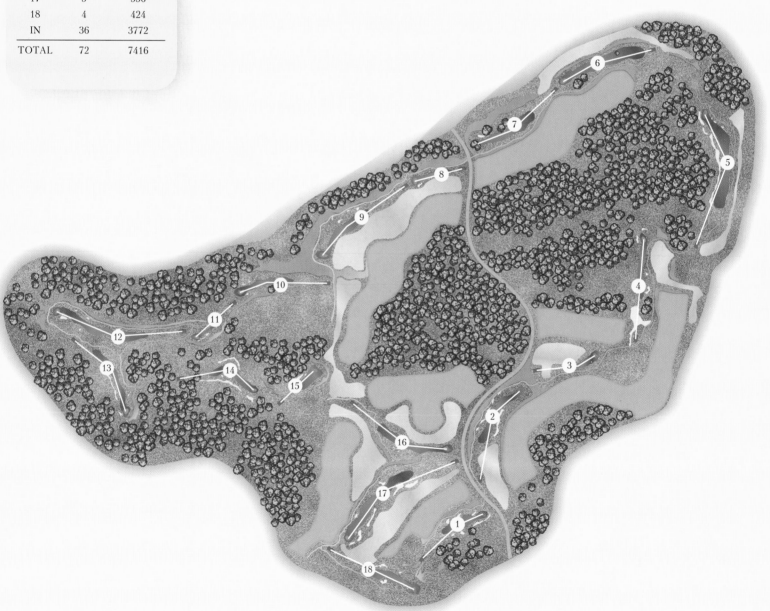

ONLY HERE

The Other Pros: The headquarters for the PGA of America—the guys who give lessons and work the pro shops—is across the street, along with the PGA National Resort, site of a PGA Championship and a Ryder Cup.

Notable Locals: While the Tour's current stars opt to live in the Ponte Vedra and Orlando areas of Florida, the older guys seem to prefer warmer climes. The greater Palm Beach area is at least part-time home to Hall-of-Famers Jack Nicklaus, Ray Floyd, Greg Norman, Nick Price, and Gary Player.

PLAYING TIP

Beware Sucker Pins

When you know an architect like Tom Fazio has designed greens to accommodate "elusive" pins, you need to keep your golf wits about you. Particularly when you have a wedge in your hand, there is a powerful temptation to shoot aggressively at a pin that is cut near sand, water, or other peril. More often than not, you should resist that urge—you have more to lose than to gain.

The pros refer to these situations as sucker pins, and if they rarely shoot at them, then the average player should be even more prudent. Play safely to the fat of the green, accept the probability of two putts, and save your aggressive tactics for a more vulnerable target.

In only two instances should you consider shooting at a sucker pin: 1) when you have no choice—your back is to the wall in a match and you must deliver, and 2) when the situation strongly favors your shot pattern— in other words, when the pin is on the extreme right of the green and the fade is your bread-and-butter shot, so you can let the ball drift across the width of the green and seek out the flag.

NICK PRICE, 1994 WINNER

TODD HAMILTON, 2004 WINNER

COREY PAVIN, 1992 WINNER

Between them, Arnold Palmer and Jack Nicklaus have played in more than 1,200 PGA Tour events. That's over 85,000 holes—a combined 20,000 miles walking the fairways of competitive golf.

In March of 2003 they each played one more time, at Arnold's Bay Hill Invitational. Palmer, age 73, invited his longtime friend and rival, age 63, and after a bit of deliberation, Nicklaus accepted. It was the 318th time—and in all likelihood the final time—that golf's two national treasures both played in a regular Tour event.

Fittingly, it was also a Palmer-Nicklaus pairing—an exhibition match back in 1965—that first brought Arnold to Bay Hill. So struck was he on that day by the Dick Wilson golf course and surrounding terrain that he bought the place. Four decades later, after much tweaking and tinkering by Arnie and his design partner Ed Seay, Bay Hill is a golf course in the Palmer image—strong and bold, instantly engaging, but a relentless adversary.

At 7,239 yards, Bay Hill is medium-long by modern Tour standards but its firm fairways and greens often are played in a brisk March wind that can make the course both longer and tighter. In addition, six water hazards and over a hundred bunkers testify to proprietor Palmer's love of gambling, scrambling, heroic golf. In most rounds,

BAY HILL CLUBHOUSE

most players will face at least one situation when they will have to make a decision—either cut their losses and play out safely or, in the style of Arnie, hitch up their pants and go for broke.

Also like Arnie, Bay Hill rivets your attention immediately. Hole number one spent most of its life as an unprepossessing par five. Now, it's a daunting, tree-lined right-to-left dogleg four to a sand-throttled green—441 yards of rude awakening. Perennially the toughest opening hole on the Tour, it is followed by a par three that is perennially the toughest second hole on the Tour, a 218-yarder that plays slightly downhill to a fiendish two-tiered green with bunkers on all sides. On this course, a par-par start is excellent, even by the game's best players.

Arguably no course on the Tour has a tougher quartet of par threes. They average well over 200 yards, each is tightly bunkered, and the two on the inward nine have been known to derail numerous rounds. Number 14 plays 206 uphill yards through a narrow corridor created by a pair of enormous parallel bunkers. The long green allows for several hole locations, and the difference in a tee shot to a flag in the front and one in the back can be as much as three clubs.

The other little devil on the way to the clubhouse is number 17, which plays from an elevated tee 219 yards to a green surrounded by water and sand. The green is shallow and typically firm, and when this all-carry shot is played either with or against a breeze, most shots fail to hit and hold the target. There has been more than one day in the history of the Bay Hill Invitational when not a single competitor scored a birdie here.

However, just as he did in his charging-to-victory days, Arnold Palmer saved his best stuff for last. The 18th, a par four of 441 yards, was totally redesigned by Arnie, and it is a finishing hole in every sense. The blind tee shot is played over the crest of a small hill, and hitting the invisible

1ST HOLE

ABOVE: 14TH HOLE **OPPOSITE:** 17TH HOLE

fairway is paramount because of what awaits on the other side of that hill, namely a boomerang-shaped amphitheater green fronted by a rock-bound lake with thick rough and bunkers beyond. Those who fail to hit the fairway often will not even attempt a shot at the green, opting instead to lay up short and left and take their chances with a one-putt par. In many years, this hole has ranked as the toughest on the PGA Tour.

It was here in the final round in 1990 that rookie Robert Gamez hit one of the most spectacular shots in history, a 176-yard 7-iron that went into the hole for an eagle two, giving Gamez a one-stroke victory over luckless Greg Norman. It's safe to say that this was the longest winning shot in the history of professional golf, at least until Craig Parry matched it to the yard at Doral in 2004.

18TH HOLE

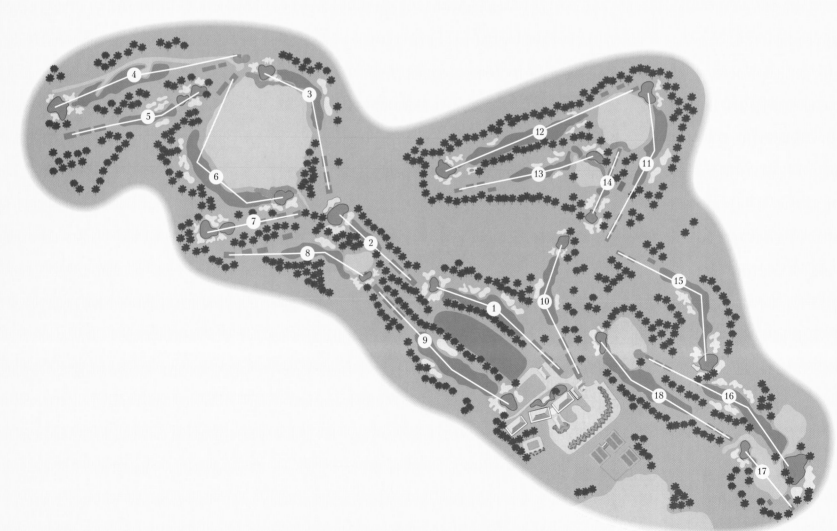

ONLY HERE

Resident Experts: Since Arnold Palmer and Disney World came here, more than a million people have taken up residence in the Orlando area, including several dozen PGA Tour players. Typically about a quarter of the Bay Hill field is from Florida, and half of those live within a few miles of the course.

Tigermania: The most famous of the local boys is Tiger Woods, a resident of nearby Isleworth, and he clearly feels at home at Bay Hill. In 2003, Tiger became the first player since Gene Sarazen in 1930 to win the same event four times in a row. That week, despite a stomach virus that had him vomiting at several points in the final round, Woods outplayed the field by a whopping 11 strokes.

Strong Fields: This is one event that always draws nearly all the top players, and for one reason: Arnold Palmer.

PLAYING TIP

Long Shots

Bay Hill boasts the longest short holes on the Tour—a quartet of par threes that average well over 200 yards. When you play this course, be ready to tee up your long irons.

For most golfers, the long irons are the most difficult clubs to hit. But they needn't be, especially when you get to play them off a tee. The key is in two words: smooth sweep. You don't hit these clubs—you wait for impact to happen.

Long-iron play requires both practice and discipline, but you'll give yourself a head start if you address the ball so that your hands are even with it or just behind it. This probably means positioning the ball at a point roughly opposite your left instep, a bit forward of its usual position in your stance. To insure a smooth, long sweep through impact, take the club away the same way—draw it slowly back from the ball. Your takeaway should be a unified movement of the hands, arms, and shoulders, with not a hint of flippiness in the wrists. After that, just stay patient—wait for the club to finish its trip to the top of your swing, and allow the coil you've created to unwind. Don't try to hit at the ball or scoop it up. Remember, a 3-iron has more loft than a 4-wood, so there's no need to help the ball—just let yourself, and your club, make a smooth sweep.

ARNOLD PALMER AND FOUR-TIME WINNER TIGER WOODS

SCORECARD

HOLE	PAR	YARDAGE
1	4	441
2	3	218
3	4	395
4	5	530
5	4	384
6	5	558
7	3	197
8	4	459
9	4	467
OUT	36	3649
10	4	400
11	4	438
12	5	580
13	4	364
14	3	206
15	4	425
16	5	517
17	3	219
18	4	441
IN	36	3590
TOTAL	72	7239

ROBERT GAMEZ, 1990 WINNER

ABOVE: 1ST TEE **OPPOSITE:** 1ST HOLE

The Players Championship will never be regarded as one of golf's major titles, and for one reason—the number four. For as long as attention has been paid to golf performance at the highest level, four has been the number. In Bobby Jones's era it was the Open and Amateur Championships of the U.S. and Great Britain. Today it's the Masters, U.S. and British Opens, and the PGA Championship. Four championships and four only.

There's just a nice, neat, roundness to fourness—four bases in baseball, four quarters in football, four majors in tennis, four years between Olympics, the Final Four, the Four Horsemen of the Apocalypse. Let's face it, this quadrilateral is truly impregnable—it's four-ordained.

Such, however, is an injustice, because The

Players Championship today has all the markings of a major championship—the field, the tradition, and the golf course. No event on the Tour calendar brings together a stronger starting field—typically all but one or two of the top 50 players in the world.

There are no spots in this field for sponsor exemptions, there is no Monday qualifying, and there is no pro-am. The buttoned-down look and feel during tournament week is that of a major. Moreover, The Players, now into its fourth decade, can claim at least a mini-history, not to mention a roster of prominent winners. Nineteen of the 25 champions here through 2004—12 of the last 14—are winners of at least one of the four majors. Jack Nicklaus has won The Players

Championship three times, Tiger Woods once and counting.

However, if one element distinguishes this tournament, it is its venue. The Tournament Players Club at Sawgrass opened in 1980 as the first of a network of courses owned and operated by the Tour and used as tournament sites for the regular, senior, and developmental circuits. Former PGA Tour Commissioner Deane Beman conceived the TPC concept as a way of eliminating the exorbitant rental fees the Tour had been paying country clubs for the use of their facilities while at the same time creating spectator-friendly courses, designed specifically to accommodate large galleries. He called them Stadium Courses.

Today there are more than 30 such facilities in

ABOVE (TOP TO BOTTOM): 5TH, 9TH, AND 11TH HOLES

the U.S. and around the world, but the TPC at Sawgrass, which sits alongside the Tour's headquarters in Ponte Vedra, Florida, remains the ultimate stadium.

When it opened, however, it was more like the Roman Colosseum, a place where people came to watch athletes struggle, suffer, and succumb. The course that Commissioner Beman and architect Pete Dye created was simply too penal, a malevolent mélange of par-defying gambits—narrow fingers of fairway lined with marshgrass and long strips of untended sand; dozens of deep, diabolically placed pot bunkers, scores of rough-

14TH HOLE

covered knolls and craters; tall trees everywhere; and meanest of all, 18 firm, fast greens, contoured like clenched fists.

When The Players Championship moved here in 1982, the Tour pros universally panned the course, the most colorful remark coming from J.C. Snead who pronounced it "90 percent horse manure and ten percent luck." Beman and Dye listened, and over the next few years they changed and softened every hole. Today, while still a very difficult course, it is also a fair test that wins near unanimous praise from both pros and amateurs.

The reworked Sawgrass doesn't taunt and intimidate so much as it teases, challenging its assailants to take the tightest, boldest line from the tee in order to get the best angle to the green. At the first hole, that angle is from the right side of the fairway, but to reach that position the player must flirt with a massive waste bunker and a water hazard. Those who drive safely down the left will face a more perilous second shot, over bunkers that guard the left entry to the green.

A similar risk-reward decision is posed at number five, the longest par four on the course at 466 yards. A big drive down the right side will cut a few yards off the slight dogleg right and leave the most open path to the long and slender green, but even a slight push or fade will find a deep bunker and a big miss will vanish into a marsh.

Back-to-back at the eighth and ninth holes are the most difficult par three and par five on the course. Number eight plays 219 yards to a green protected by numerous bunkers and grassy pits. The green, large and severely sloped, is as difficult to putt as it is to hit and hold.

Back in the 1980s, almost none of the players tried to reach the 583-yard ninth hole in two. With today's volcanic balls and drivers, however, many give it a go, and the results are invari-

ABOVE: 16TH HOLE **OPPOSITE:** 17TH HOLE

ably entertaining for the spectators who assemble on the greenside mounds. Only a surgically straight shot of 280 or so yards will find this, the smallest green on the course. All others will descend into variegated peril—chocolate-drop mounds, thick fescue, gnarly ground cover, vertical-walled bunkers, and grasping tree limbs, leaving a shot that in most instances is far more difficult than the one that preceded it. A few eagles are made here each year, along with a few unmentionables.

The par-five 11th hole is strategic architecture at its best. At 535 yards, it tempts players to have a go in two, but a pond fronts this green as does a bunker that is so deep and steep-faced it's entered and exited by stepladders. But those

who opt to lay up will have a further decision as architect Dye offers two options, on either side of the pond. The left fairway leaves a clear alley to the green but to get there the second shot must cross water. The laying up pros tend to make their decision based on pin position; if the hole is cut on the right side of the green, they tack left, if on the left, they angle right.

Many of Pete Dye's holes look more difficult off the tee than they actually are, but such is not the case at the 14th. The narrow fairway is two-tiered and banks toward a paralleling bunker on the left with water beyond. To the right is an immense, thickly grassed mound. The green is long and slim, and cinched by more sand and grass bunkers. This is annually a hole that takes

more than one player out of contention in the Sunday stretch run.

One reason the TPC at Sawgrass remains the paragon of stadium courses is the theatrical quality of its three finishing holes. On this course, even a four- or five-stroke lead is not safe over the last thousand yards. Numerous players have stumbled home with a trio of bogeys or worse. At the same time, players have occasionally risen to heights they'd never dreamed of, as virtually unknown Craig Perks did, sinking two chip shots and a lengthy birdie putt to win the title in 2002, his only Tour victory.

The fun begins with a par five of 507 yards that calls for a draw from the tee and then a gentle fade into the green—the key word being gen-

tle, as any ball that even rolls off the right side of the green will drop into a lake. As with the 11th, those who choose to lay up must plot their shots carefully, as a large tree left and short of the green plays havoc with any approach from the left side. Anyone who wants a simple pitch for the third shot must first be brave enough to challenge the lake on the right. The green has two tiers and slopes quickly toward the water. Even the pros have occasionally putted into the lake.

According to Johnny Miller, number 17 is what every great golf course needs, "a hole that makes your rear end pucker." In a comparatively short time, this little devil with an island green has become the most famous par three in the world. It is only 137 yards long, and the green is large, but there is zero margin for error. Except for a tiny pot bunker at the front-right, there is no place to land the ball but green—or water. It's an intimidating shot under any cir-

cumstances, but when the wind blows, it's doubly daunting. Back in the 1984 Players, 64 balls hit the water on a single blustery day, and the hole played to an average of 3.79, the highest score ever recorded for a par three on the Tour. And those are the pros. Each year, between 120,000 and 150,000 balls are recovered from the watery depths.

The course concludes with a brilliant and dramatic dogleg par four where the choice from the tee is simple—blast a brave drive down the left side, in defiance of the bordering lake, and the result will be a straightforward shot to the green; or bail out to the right and face possible tree problems and a more difficult angle of approach. The lake runs along the entire left side of the hole while grassy humps and hollows lurk on the right, just beneath an enormous spectator mound with tiered seating for 40,000 people.

CRAIG PERKS, 2002 WINNER

DAVIS LOVE III, 1992 AND 2003 WINNER

SCORECARD

HOLE	PAR	YARDAGE
1	4	392
2	5	532
3	3	177
4	4	384
5	4	466
6	4	393
7	4	442
8	3	219
9	5	583
OUT	36	3588
10	4	424
11	5	535
12	4	358
13	3	181
14	4	467
15	4	449
16	5	507
17	3	137
18	4	447
IN	36	3505
TOTAL	72	7093

ONLY HERE

Masters Maneuvers: One of the ways to qualify for The Masters is by achieving a position among the top ten on the money list or the top 50 in the World Ranking through The Players Championship, and with that tournament only a couple of weeks after this one, a subplot always develops at Sawgrass, with several players trying to gain or hold positions on those lists.

Trophy Engraver: A silver engraver sits hard by the 18th hole, dreading a victory by Per-Ulrik Johansson or Jose Maria Olazabal. His job, after the winning putt is holed, is to engrave the victor's name on the trophy in the ten minutes or so before it is presented.

Membership Privileges: Since this club belongs to the Tour players, each member of the field has his name on not only a locker but on a prime space in the club parking lot.

PLAYING TIP

Sand Savvy

No course has a greater variety of sand peril than the TPC at Sawgrass, but the most distinctive are surely the massive fairway bunkers. The sand base in these bunkers is typically shallow and firm, so you rarely see a bad lie—the ball sits up just as it does on a fairway, allowing you to make clean contact. Nonetheless, you should take care. Use one club more than from a fairway lie and keep your swing compact, with a bit less lower body movement than normal. A slightly wider-than-usual stance will help keep the legs quiet.

If you often hit fat or topped shots from these lies, try setting up in a slightly open stance, with your feet and body aligned left of the target. This "slice stance" facilitates a more downward impact, so you'll be less likely to hit behind the ball (for a fat shot) or up and over it (for a top). The open stance will also encourage a slightly higher trajectory, which will help you fly the ball over the bunker's lip. Just expect a bit less yardage, along with some left-to-rightward drift.

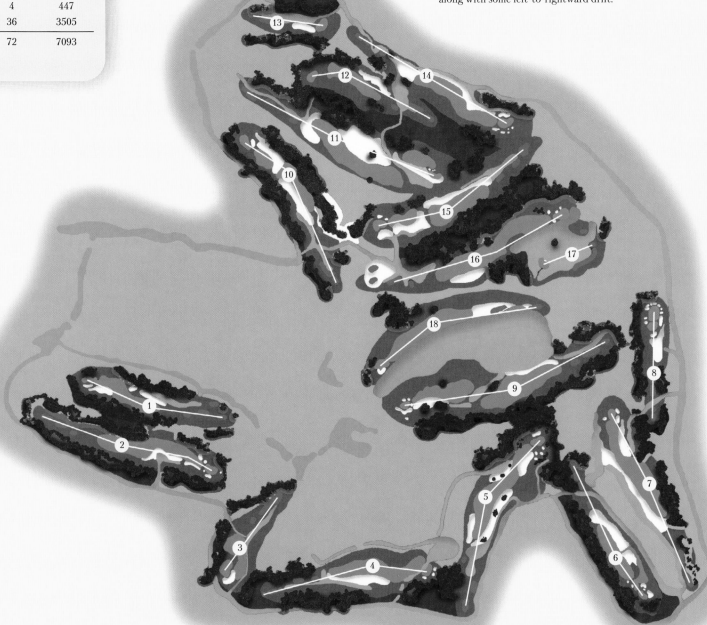

ABOVE: 3RD HOLE **RIGHT:** 10TH HOLE

During his career as a professional golfer, Greg Norman was perhaps best known for the victories that slipped from his grasp. Sometimes it was a lightning bolt from another player that brought down the Great White Shark—the dramatic hole-outs by Larry Mize in the 1987 Masters and Bob Tway in the 1986 PGA Championship were as improbable as they were decisive—but just as often it was Norman himself who failed to capitalize on opportunities. In 1986, for instance, he led each of the four major championships after three rounds but won only the British Open. And then there is his most colossal collapse of all—the 1996 Masters—where he began the final 18 with a six-stroke lead over Nick Faldo, only to lose to him by five.

In his second career as a businessman, however, Norman has shown himself to be strategically adept, a man who knows a prime prospect when he sees it and also knows how to take full advantage. His various enterprises—from clothing to yachts to wines—have all been extremely successful, and as a golf course architect he has channeled his competitive energy into a fast rise to the top ranks, with highly regarded courses all over the world.

There is perhaps no better example of Norman's skill as a designer—or his ability to convert opportunity into triumph—than the TPC at Sugarloaf. When in 1995 he was given the contract for this course—his first solo design in North America—Norman's assignment was to produce a layout suitable for a private residential club, with no hint of tournament play. Soon after construction began, however, Sugarloaf caught the attention of the PGA Tour. The BellSouth Classic had

outgrown the Atlanta Country Club, where it had been played for thirty years, and the Tour was in search of a new, more spacious facility. In almost no time, Sugarloaf Country Club became known as the TPC at Sugarloaf, and Norman was told to adjust his course to accommodate the world's best players.

Sugarloaf suddenly had become not simply Norman's debut but a step onto the game's number-one stage, and he took the challenge seriously, making more than two dozen personal visits. Yardage was added, bunkers were repositioned, greensites were tweaked for improved spectator viewing, and the result is a course that has won raves both from the Tour players who tackle it once a year and the club members who enjoy it the other 51.

Set on lush, rolling terrain just northeast of Atlanta, Sugarloaf blends Norman's own strong convictions on golf course design with elements of the classic courses he has seen and played, especially the original links of the British Isles where he won two British Opens.

"Some golf courses can really touch a part of you and make you feel energized or inspired," he says. "That's how Augusta National feels, and I get the same sensation at Sugarloaf. There's a similar beauty and awe about it." Like the home of the Masters, this is a parkland course—part of a 1,500-acre private estate that was once used for the breeding of Tennessee Walking Horses. Three streams and three natural lakes come into play, and—again like Augusta—the terrain often moves dramatically up and down, with

towering pines and oaks lining and defining most of the holes.

"The initial walk-through told us we had something special," says Norman. "The land flowed and the corridors were just there." As a result, he and his associate, Jason McCoy, crafted a routing plan that made full use of the natural features while disturbing them as little as possible.

The scenic first nine begins to crescendo at the seventh hole, a beautiful but bruising par four of 458 yards. If the tee shot is straight as well as powerful it will avoid the pair of bunkers that flank the landing area, but still leave a middle iron home. The only hole on the course without a greenside bunker, it truly needs none as sweeping slopes and swirling winds supply ample challenge to the approach.

16TH HOLE

SILENCE, SOUTHERN STYLE

18TH HOLE

The hardest hole on the course is a par three, number eight, which weighs in at a hefty 248 yards. Many players will need 3-woods just to reach this target, but they had best hit a high and soft-landing shot, as the green pitches in two directions and sand waits on all sides.

Those who survive number eight with a three will be just as happy to secure a four at the ninth, a tightly tree-lined, rightward-doglegging par four that is the toughest driving hole on the course. The approach is also daunting as the right side of this green drops off into a creek.

Water runs down the entire left side of number 12, but the most intimidating sight from the tee is a pot bunker in the right-center of the fairway. Those who can avoid the water and sand will face a short-iron shot to a green guarded by a creek to the front and right.

Then it's a walk uphill to the tee of tantalizing number 13, a 310-yard par four where the pros have a chance to make eagles or make fools of themselves. This slight dogleg left is driveable, but any shot that goes too far left will find one of the deepest bunkers on the course, or worse yet, a runoff area—one of several on this course—with the next shot a menacing little uphill pitch over that same bunker. The less bold player will hit a fairway wood or iron from the tee, then pitch on, but since this green slopes away from front to back, only a crisply struck shot will stop near its ball mark.

The home hole at BellSouth's former site, Atlanta Country Club, was a mid-length par five with the choice of playing safe or going for broke with a lengthy second shot across a lake. It was a hole that produced agony and ecstasy aplenty, and the 18th at Sugarloaf is cut from the same cloth. This is the hole that underwent the greatest change for the sake of the pros, originally a straightaway par four that was lengthened a hundred yards and rerouted as a dogleg right par five. The landing area is two-tiered, and those who take the bold route to the lower level will be rewarded with a bona fide but terrifying shot at the green, all 200-plus yards of it over water.

SCORECARD

HOLE	PAR	YARDAGE
1	4	434
2	3	144
3	4	389
4	5	558
5	4	418
6	5	569
7	4	458
8	3	248
9	4	465
OUT	36	3683
10	5	608
11	3	189
12	4	434
13	4	310
14	4	453
15	4	406
16	3	179
17	4	455
18	5	576
IN	36	3610
TOTAL	72	7293

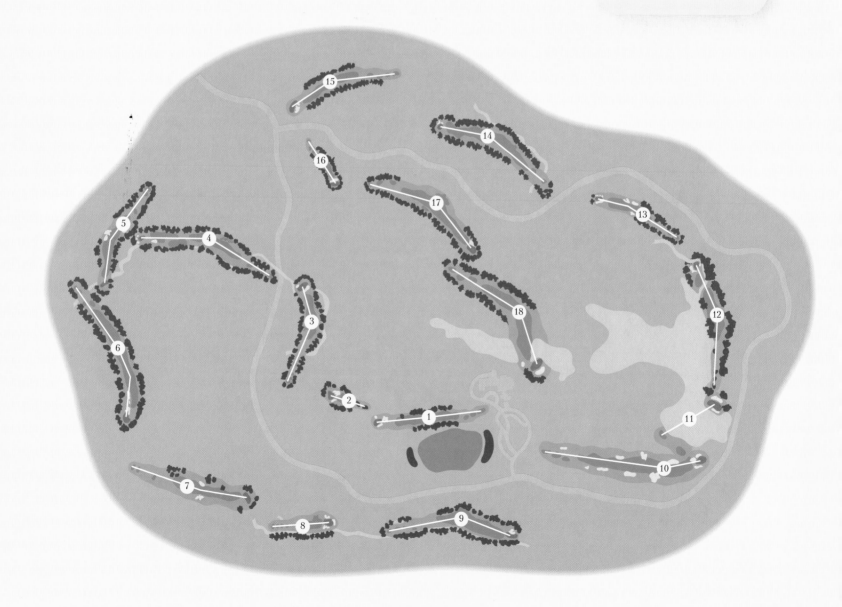

ONLY HERE

Revetted Bunkers: Greg Norman used his bunkers sparingly—there are only 63 on the course—but he introduced a new look in American golf architecture: sod wall bunkers, similar to those at St. Andrews and Muirfield in Scotland.

Defenselessness: This tournament has been on the Tour schedule since 1967, but no player has ever won it back to back.

Rebel Quells: At most events gallery marshals quiet the crowds by raising paddles that read "Quiet, Please." Here, those paddles say "Hush, Y'all."

PLAYING TIP

Get Your Head Straight

The TPC at Sugarloaf has some extremely tight driving holes, but on virtually every course there is at least one tee where accuracy is vital. Many players live in fear of such shots, and that is of course wrong because fearing leads to steering and steering leads to veering. Calmness and confidence are what you need.

Assuming you have sound fundamentals, the best way to encourage a smooth, positive swing is with mental preparation. Get your mind off the consequences of a poor shot and focus instead on a positive result. Pick a specific spot on the fairway where you'd like your ball to finish, and then visualize your ideal drive flying, bouncing, and rolling to that spot. If you can stay focused on that vision, there will be no room in your mind for negative thoughts.

Another mental trick is to pretend you're standing on the tee of a very easy driving hole, a hole where you always hit a good shot. The best time to do this is in the last few seconds before you take the club back. After all, your ball on the tee looks the same as it does on that easy hole—so tell yourself that's where you are. This positive focus will help you to produce a confident swing and a straight drive.

GREG NORMAN DESIGNED THE COURSE.

PHIL MICKELSON, 2000 WINNER

10TH HOLE

Every great and enduring golf course is a work in progress. However, surely no course in the world has seen as relentless or rigorous revision as the Augusta National. Virtually since the moment it opened, more than 70 years ago, the home of The Masters has been in perpetual evolution. About the only thing that hasn't changed is the azaleas.

In response to ever stronger players and better equipment, Augusta's stewards have persistently tweaked and toughened their track to the point that the course today bears little resemblance to the one originally crafted by Alister Mackenzie and Bobby Jones. What was conceived as an examination in strategy and shot planning—a thinking man's course—now rewards muscle as much as mind. A course that once allowed, and occasionally even encouraged, low-running approach shots today calls for a sustained aerial attack. What began as Jones's homage to the capricious Old Course at St. Andrews, now more closely mimics the meticulously punishing tests of the U.S. Open.

It is the last two decades or so that have brought the most marked change, with the greens transforming from bermudagrass to faster-running bent, new bunkers and trees tightening the drive zones, and in 1999 the historic unveiling of a "second cut," Masters parlance for the 1 ⅜-inch semi-rough that now lines the fairways.

However, no year witnessed a more comprehensive overhaul than 2002 when fully half of the holes were lengthened and tightened by architect Tom Fazio. The result is a meaner and

leaner Augusta, nearly 7,300 yards from the championship tees. Four of the par fours are at least 460 yards, with two of them, back to back, at 490 and 495.

Blame it on Tiger. In 1997, he turned the Augusta National into his personal pitch-and-putt course, breaking the scoring record with a 72-hole total of 270—eighteen under par. Four years later, he capped his second Masters victory—and a "Tiger Slam" sweep of the four majors in 12 months—by slugging a drive at the 18th

hole that left him just 75 yards to the pin. When Tiger and his colleagues returned a year later, that 18th hole had been lengthened by 60 yards.

To Fazio's credit, many of the changes did allow the strategic character of the holes to be retained. The par-four first is perhaps the best example. There are only two bunkers on the hole—one in the right side of the landing area, the other at the left front of the green—but in this minimalism was Mackenzie's strategic genius. The bold route from the tee, to the right

ABOVE: 11TH HOLE RIGHT: 12TH HOLE

and near the bunker, left an open shot to the green, while a more cautious tee shot to the left side of the fairway left the player with sand to carry on the approach.

By the turn of the 21st century, however, most of the players in the Masters field were pummeling their tee shots blithely over that bunker, leaving short irons home. Fazio, in moving the tee back 25 yards and extending the far end of the bunker 15 yards toward the green, created a 300-yard carry—a shot that few players will try except when the hole plays downwind—and thereby restored the original strategy to the hole.

Today one par four at Augusta remains under 400 yards—well under 400—but it remains one of the most vexing assignments on the course. Hole number three is a slight dogleg right that measures just 350 yards from the tips, but its raised green is fiercely fast and falls off steeply to the front and back, making it a difficult target to hit and hold. In 2003, Tiger's quest for an unprecedented third straight Masters title begin to unravel here on Sunday when he tried to drive the green and wound up with a double bogey. Moments later, the 54-hole leader Jeff Maggert met a bizarre disaster—a triple bogey that included two penalty strokes when his bunker shot caromed back and struck him in the chest.

13TH HOLE

15TH HOLE

One major change remained after the 2002 overhaul and a year later Masters officials addressed it when they made number five—an uphill dogleg that is the hardest par four on the front nine—even harder by lengthening the hole by 20 yards and moving the fairway bunkers 80 yards forward, narrowing the landing area. A hooked tee shot on this hole will tumble down a steeply forested bank into an area where, three-time Masters Champion Jimmy Demaret once quipped, "they may not find you for three days."

No hole on the outward half of Augusta has seen more of a metamorphosis than number seven. Having begun its life as a 340-yard approximation of the home hole at The Old Course, complete with a Valley of Sin fronting the green, it is now a tightly tree-lined 410-yarder, its green raised 20 feet above the fairway and surrounded by a quintet of deep bunkers.

There's an old saying that The Masters doesn't really begin until the last nine holes on Sunday, and there's no question that the inward side of the Augusta National—even after all the alteration and toughening—still provides high drama,

as it did in 2004 when Phil Mickelson charged home in 31 strokes to edge Ernie Els. Except perhaps for the last nine at the TPC at Sawgrass, no finishing stretch gives players a better chance to take the stage as either a hero or a goat.

The adventure begins with the two longest back-to-back par fours in the world, 495-yard number 10 and 490-yard 11. Both holes play downhill, 10 precipitously so, but most players will still need middle and long irons—and accurate ones—to earn birdie putts on these greens. A large bunker guards the right side of number 10, where the surface slopes from right to left toward a deep swale. The original course design called for the nines to be the opposite of what they are today, with this hole as the first.

The drive on 11, once wide-open, has been made more difficult by the addition of trees planted to the right of the fairway in 2004. The approach to this hole is one of the most daunting on the course, with a bunker right of the narrow green and a pond to the left. The 11th is best remembered for the pitch shot Larry Mize hit in a sudden-death playoff in 1987. After his approach

16TH HOLE

finished nearly 20 yards right of the green, Mize, a native of Augusta, bumped his ball back onto the surface and into the hole for a spectacular birdie that stole the title from Greg Norman. (In 2004, however, the playoff format was changed so that only the 18th and 10th holes will be used.)

Jack Nicklaus calls the 12th hole the toughest tournament hole in golf. Gary Player calls it the toughest par three in golf. And who knows what Tom Weiskopf calls it—in 1982 he took a 13 here, the highest single-hole score in Masters history. It's the shortest hole on the course—just 155 yards—but this is 155 yards of compressed architectural guile, an ingenious combination of perils seen and unseen. First there is Rae's Creek running in front of the diagonal green. There is one bunker in front and two more beyond—

backed by dense vegetation—and in between is the shallowest and fastest putting surface on the course. The green is shaped like a footprint, and at its instep, just beyond the front bunker, it is just eight paces deep. But the most intimidating element is the invisible demon, the wind. Although the tee and green are shielded, the shot to the hole passes through 100 yards of air space where it is buffeted by the northwest breezes swirling down the fairway of number 13. Accurate club selection here requires a combination of experience, patience, skill, and guts.

The 13th hole, a majestic par five, is probably the most famous hole on the course and certainly the most photographed. It was envisioned by Alister Mackenzie at almost the first moment he laid eyes on the property. The dogleg follows the

path of the little creek on its left side, winding right to left for 510 pine- and azalea-lined yards. At about the 500-yard mark, the creek takes a right turn, passing just in front of the billowing green. Two bunkers and a swale protect the left side of the green, with two more bunkers beyond. The hole is very reachable for every player in the Masters field, but anyone who hopes to get home in two will require at least two things—precision on the tee shot and courage on the approach.

The accessibility of 13 to even medium-length hitters reflects Bobby Jones's disdain for long and unreachable par fives where, in his words "you don't start playing golf until the third shot." Another example is the 15th hole, 500 yards long with the last 250 of them steeply downhill to a broad, shallow green fronted by a

18TH HOLE, JACK NICKLAUS IN 1986

pond. Beyond the green is more water while a sizable bunker lurks on the right.

A good drive here leaves players with an opportunity and a decision, whether to gun for the green in two, most commonly with something between a 5-iron and a 3-wood, or to lay up and hope for a pitch-and-putt birdie. It was here that Jack Nicklaus made his big move on Sunday in 1986, striking a 4-iron to 15 feet and then sinking the putt for eagle. With a score of 30 on the homeward nine, Nicklaus won his record sixth green jacket, at the age of 46.

However, the hole at Augusta National that is most closely identified with Nicklaus surely is number 16. Originally a short, undramatic par three, it was reworked in 1947 by Robert Trent Jones and today plays 170 yards across a long

pond to another menacingly sloped target. Hitting this green is not good enough; one must be able to hit the correct sector of it or be prepared to three-putt. A ridge, nearly two feet high, climbs diagonally across from right-front to back-rear, slicing the kidney-shaped surface into two peanut-shaped tiers. Three bunkers add difficulty to the tee shot and a shot that lands in the large one at the right-rear rarely converts into a par.

Nicklaus nearly holed his 6-iron tee shot here in the final round in 1986, and back in 1975 this was the scene of the most dramatic putt of his career, a slope-climbing 40-footer for birdie that jumped him out of a tie with Johnny Miller and Tom Weiskopf and into green jacket number five.

In the overhaul of 2002, the hole that saw the greatest transformation was unquestionably

number 18. The championship tee was moved 60 yards back and five yards to the right, and the fairway bunkers—added in 1967 when the club thought the hole needed some teeth—were enlarged by 10 percent and flanked on the left with trees. Carrying those bunkers now requires an uphill drive of 320 yards—which means that the next time Tiger uses a sand wedge to approach this green, he'll be hitting his third shot. Nonetheless, as Mickelson showed in 2004, it's still possible to win with a birdie on 18, and it's a more impressive feat for being harder earned.

ONLY HERE

The Jinx: There is no pro-am tournament at The Masters but on Wednesday afternoon a competition takes place on the club's adjacent Par 3 Course. Since that event started in 1960, no player has won the Par 3 Contest and gone on to victory on the big course in the same week.

Glass with Class: A pair of Waterford goblets goes to anyone who scores an eagle during Masters competition. Crystal vases go to those who shoot the lowest scores in each round.

Patrons: Tickets to The Masters are not available to the general public. Instead there is a patrons list, comprised of long-standing season ticket holders who are entitled to keep buying tickets each year until death. As patrons "depart," new ones arrive, elevated from a waiting list reputed to be several thousand salivating souls long.

Juniper, Camellia, and 16 Others: Each of the holes is named after a tree or flowering shrub that proliferates within its confines, a reminder that this course lies on the site of a former nursery.

PLAYING TIP

Thinking Man's Golf

In describing the challenge of the Augusta National, Bobby Jones wrote: "There is not a hole out there that can't be birdied if you just think; and there is not a hole out there that can't be double-bogeyed if you stop thinking."

With its broad fairways and generous greens, Augusta might lull Masters competitors into sloppy play were they not aware of the need to seek the best sectors of those fairways and greens, to anticipate the shots that will ensue, as in a game of chess or billiards.

This is a strategy that can serve you well on any golf course. To use it, play each hole backwards in your mind, starting at the green. If, for instance, the pin is on the right side of the green, or if there is big trouble to the left, you'll have the best chance of success if you approach from the left side of the fairway, keeping the trouble more or less at your back. Likewise, to get your ball to that left side, you should tee up on the right side of the teeing area, so that you can hit directly away from the less desirable right side. In this sense, the technique is similar to bowling. To pick up a spare on the 10 pin, you approach from the left and roll the ball across the alley; to get the seven pin, you approach from the right.

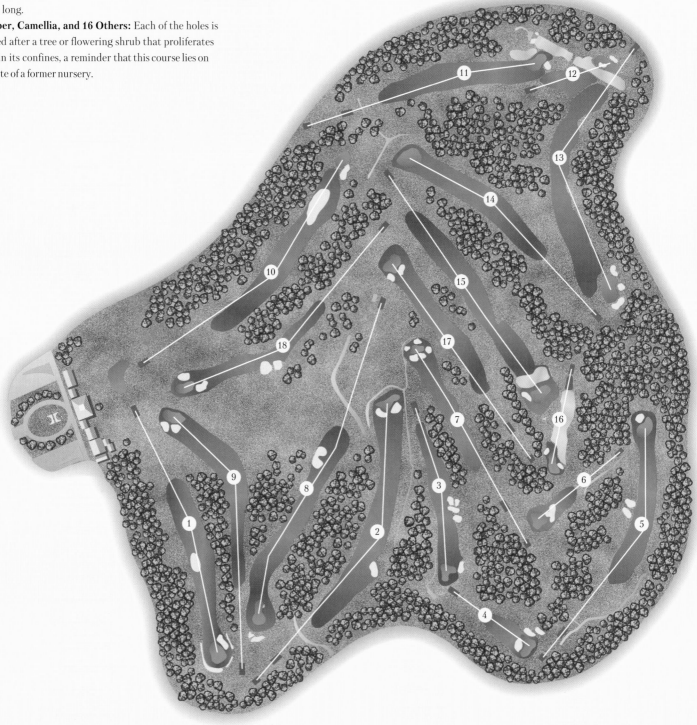

PHIL MICKELSON, 2004 WINNER

TIGER WOODS, 1997 AND 2001 WINNER

SCORECARD

HOLE	PAR	YARDAGE
1	4	435
2	5	575
3	4	350
4	3	205
5	4	455
6	3	180
7	4	410
8	5	570
9	4	460
OUT	36	3640
10	4	495
11	4	490
12	3	155
13	5	510
14	4	440
15	5	500
16	3	170
17	4	425
18	4	465
IN	36	3650
TOTAL	72	7290

LARRY MIZE, 1987 WINNER

The three keys to success on the Harbour Town Golf Links at The Sea Pines Resort are the same as the three keys in real estate: location, location, location. With its slender fairways snaking through 300 tree-clad acres of marshland on South Carolina's Hilton Head Island, this is one course where power is not nearly as important as precision, where controlled shotmaking and a well-oiled short game go a very long way, and where success is largely a matter of mind over muscle.

In 1969, when then-unheralded Pete Dye unveiled his creation to the world of golf he warned "it's different, but then so was Garbo." In an era of bigness in golf architecture—runway strip tees, sprawling ink-spot bunkers, and greens large enough to have their own zip codes—Harbour Town broke all the rules, yet instantly won the unanimous praise of pros and amateurs alike. That year, Arnold Palmer won the inaugural Heritage Classic. Jack Nicklaus—who consulted on the course design—has won here as have Tom Watson and Johnny Miller (twice each), Hale Irwin (three times), and Davis Love III (five times). Today, the MCI Heritage remains one of the most popular events on the tour. Despite its timing—one week after The

4TH HOLE

Masters—it attracts a consistently strong field and invariably produces a high-profile champion—17 of the 25 winners through 2004 here are also holders of at least one major championship.

The contrast with Augusta National may be one reason for the tournament's popularity. "It's a great week to enjoy yourself and just play golf," says Love. "The course obviously is a lot more friendly, but still a good test, the pressure is not as bad, and it's just a nice atmosphere to enjoy the game."

After a week of high pressure, the players come to Hilton Head to kick back, enjoy some low-country hospitality, and play a golf course that makes entirely different demands from those of Augusta National: punches under the wind, cuts over mammoth oaks, splashes from bunkers and thrashes from pampas grass, careful chips from clinging rough and just plain impossible straight shots.

Most of the landing areas are ample but the encroaching trees often give tee shots a claustrophobic look. On almost every hole the terrain and placement of hazards encourage the player to work the ball from left to right or right to left. The late PGA champion and television commentator Dave Marr, after playing a particularly

9TH HOLE

13TH HOLE

10TH HOLE

15TH HOLE

11TH HOLE

ABOVE (TOP TO BOTTOM): 16TH. AND 17TH HOLES
RIGHT: 18TH HOLE

frustrating round at an early Heritage, captured the essence of Harbour Town with a comment to one of the tournament officials. "I never complain about pin placements," Marr said, "but you certainly have put the fairways in some strange places today."

The wise strategy is to find the fairway and hew to the best part of it, for the greens at Harbour Town are tiny—about 4,000 square feet, which is about a thousand square feet smaller than average. And when you miss one, par can be as elusive as Garbo.

Ken Venturi, while he was an announcer with CBS, repeatedly credited Harbour Town with having the "best set of par threes on any golf course," and it's tough to argue with that. The first and most difficult of them is number four— 200 yards from the back tees with a lagoon running down its entire left side and circling around the back of the green. Three holes later, the assignment is only five yards shorter and this time the green is encircled entirely by sand. As if that weren't sufficiently intimidating, a half dozen trees lean into the airspace from tee to green, leaving precious little room for error.

But the toughest stretch of the course is the middle, beginning with the 470-yard eighth hole, a leftward dogleg with trees on both sides. A 50-yard-long bunker runs along the left side near the green, and many players will be relieved to find it, as just a yard or two further left is the lagoon. Two strong and carefully played shots will be needed to find and hold this green. The short par-four ninth presents another challenge in accuracy. Even amateurs tend to use long irons and fairway woods from the tee to thread a shot between tall pines that crowd the fairway. Then it's a wedge to a heart-shaped green with a pot bunker at the back.

The inward nine starts with three killer par fours, each over 430 yards but demanding accuracy even more than length. A lake to the left of the fairway haunts the tee shot at the right-to-left dogleg tenth while chutes of trees must be threaded at 11 and 12. The finest par four on the course is arguably number 13, just 373 yards, where the drive must be positioned to the right side of the fairway to set up the second, a field goal between two encroaching oaks. A large U-shaped bunker, its front face fortified with cypress planks—awaits a misplayed approach shot.

Thirty years ago Lee Trevino called the 571-yard 15th at Harbour Town the best par five he'd ever seen. "It's so long it doesn't favor the long hitters," he said. "Even King Kong couldn't get on that green in two." These days, it's reach-

able to many players, but those who want to be sure of a par wait to attack the tucked-in-a-corner green with a wedged third shot.

All of the holes at this golf course are challenging to play and pretty to look at, but the last two are something special both visually and strategically. Seventeen, a 185-yard par three, plays directly over water and is guarded by a 90-yard-long bunker that is bulkheaded with Dye's signature railroad ties. The wind invariably is in the face of the day's last pairings, as is the setting sun, making club selection difficult.

Eighteen is similar in design to the famed finishing hole at Pebble Beach, except that it is a par four instead of a five. Its 452 yards snake alongside Calibogue Sound (pronounced Calibogey) with the tee, the landing area, and the green set on small promontories. Too far left off the tee and you're in the salt marshes; too far right and you're on someone's backyard deck, out of bounds. Depending on the wind direction, the green may be reachable with a 9-iron, or unreachable with a 3-wood. There's a bail-out area to the right but steep mounds make the chipping assignment a difficult one. A tall red-and-white striped lighthouse stands to the rear of this green, adding a touch of man-made beauty to one of the most scenically splendid holes in the world.

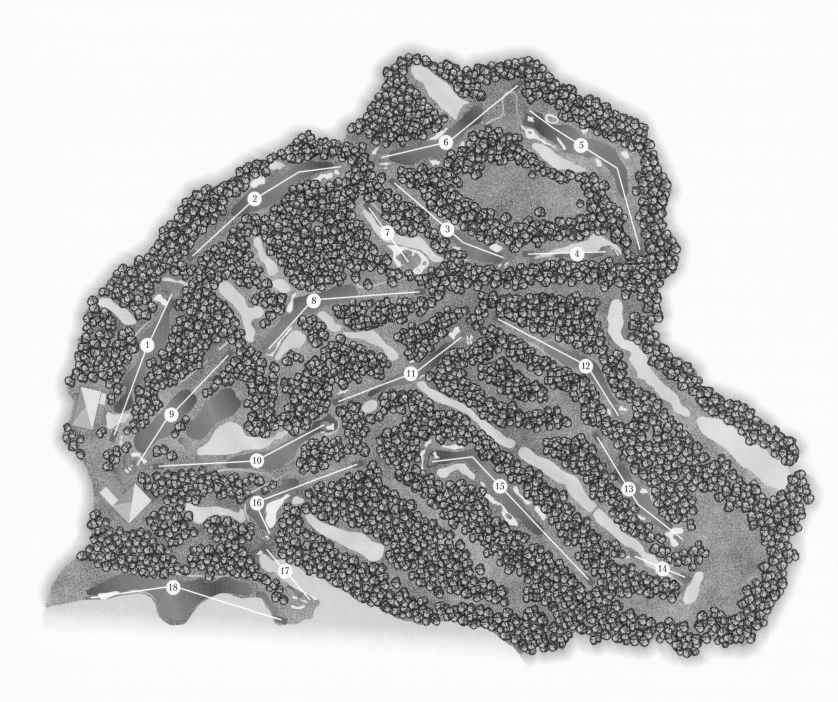

SCORECARD

HOLE	PAR	YARDAGE
1	4	410
2	5	502
3	4	437
4	3	200
5	5	530
6	4	419
7	3	195
8	4	470
9	4	332
OUT	36	3495
10	4	444
11	4	436
12	4	430
13	4	373
14	3	192
15	5	571
16	4	395
17	3	185
18	4	452
IN	35	3478
TOTAL	71	6973

ONLY HERE

Mudshots and Plankies: With lagoons and marshes in play on half the holes, and bunkers fortified with enough wood to build a barn, improvisation is the name of the game. At number 13, for instance, more than one Tour player has saved par from the bunker by bouncing his shot up the face of the cypress planks and onto the green.

History: Harbour Town sits near the site of the oldest golf club in South Carolina and arguably in the United States. The South Carolina Golf Club was formed by Scottish merchants in 1786.

Faux Scotland: In keeping with the heritage theme, each champion receives a tartan plaid jacket. When he returns to defend his title, he is led to the first tee by bagpipers, and then "drives himself in" with a ceremonial tee shot accompanied by a cannon blast, the same ritual used to welcome incoming club captains at the Royal & Ancient Golf Club of St. Andrews.

Putting Records: Since Harbour Town's greens are the smallest on the Tour, chip-and-putt pars are frequent, even for the pros. In 1989, Kenny Knox set a Tour record by taking just 93 putts over 72 holes, including one round when he needed only 18.

PLAYING TIP

Beating Bahiagrass

Rough doesn't get much rougher than at Harbour Town, where the areas beyond the straight and narrow are grown thick with bahiagrass, a rare breed of weed that drives golfers crazy.

You can't get cute with this stuff. Don't even think about finessing the ball with a soft swing. Instead, your object should be to insure clean, crisp contact. You can minimize the grab of the grass by positioning the ball a couple of inches to the rear of its usual position in your stance. This will enable you to bring the club steeply down on the ball instead of sweeping through the grass. Stand a bit closer to the ball as well—that will have the same effect.

In extremely deep lies, calling for a gouge out with a short iron or wedge, close your clubface a few degrees—as you would for a buried lie in sand. And to insure firm impact with any lie, increase your left-hand grip pressure. This will help you hold the club square and resist the grasp of the bahia.

DAVIS LOVE III, FIVE-TIME WINNER

18TH HOLE

For the better part of three decades the Houston Open and its site, The Woodlands course at the residential community of the same name, formed one of the Tour's most felicitous partnerships, annually attracting star-studded fields that delighted tournament sponsors and reaped record contributions to charity. Ultimately, however, that marriage became a victim of its own success.

During the 1980s and '90s, as both the game of golf and the American economy grew, so did The Woodlands, from a small development into a sprawling self-enclosed city. By the end of the century, the community infrastructure that had

once been ideal for hosting a tournament had become too clogged with residential traffic to comfortably accommodate the week-long circus that is a PGA Tour event. And so, in 2002 the Shell Houston Open found a new home, signing a ten-year contract with Redstone, a 1,600-acre residential community in Humble, Texas, ten minutes from the Houston airport.

The Redstone acreage included an existing golf course, El Dorado, which was renamed Fall Creek and revamped by Peter Jacobsen and Jim Hardy in time to host the Houston Open in 2003 and 2004. Although it can be stretched to over 7,500 yards, it is essentially an old-style course

that allows running approaches to many of its greens, and it debuted to widespread praise from the pros. But from the beginning Fall Creek was intended as a way station, with the tournament's ultimate home a Rees Jones course to be unveiled in 2005.

Known as the "Open Doctor," Jones has earned a reputation—once held by his father Robert Trent Jones—as the game's premier course renovator, having worked his magic on a series of U.S. Open sites, from the Country Club at Brookline in 1988 to Torrey Pines South, which will play host in 2008. But the course at Redstone is his first effort from scratch expressly for a PGA

ABOVE: 1ST TEE OPPOSITE: 5TH HOLE BELOW: 10TH HOLE (PHOTOS OF FALL CREEK COURSE)

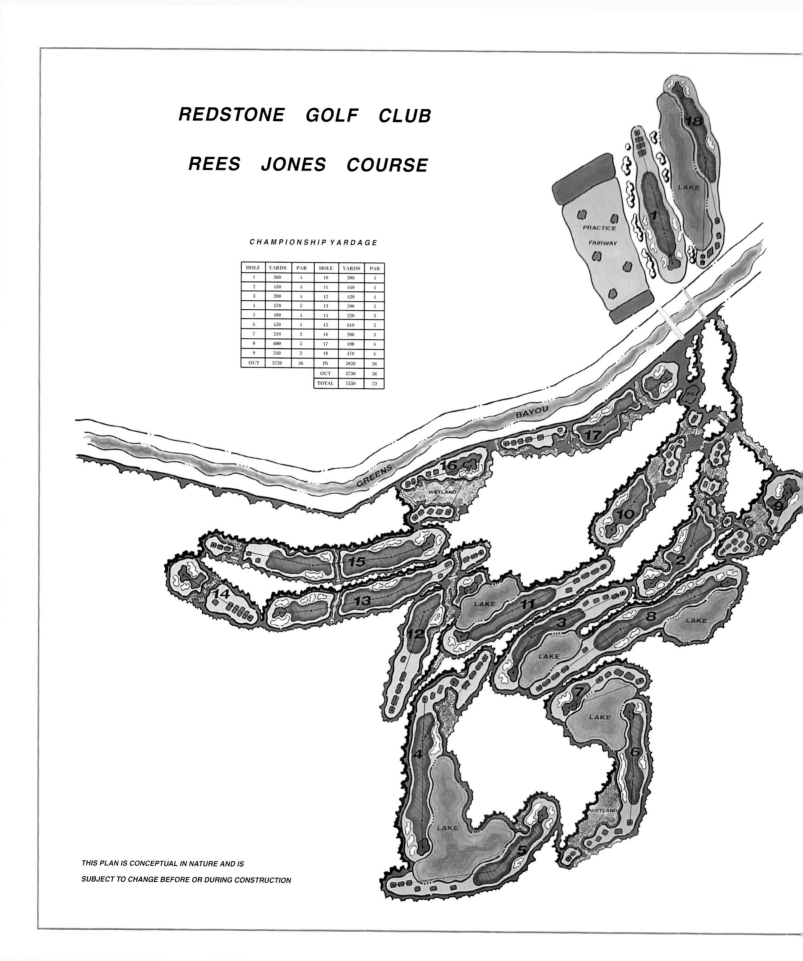

REDSTONE GOLF CLUB

REES JONES COURSE

CHAMPIONSHIP YARDAGE

HOLE	YARDS	PAR	HOLE	YARDS	PAR
1	360	4	10	380	4
2	430	4	11	440	4
3	390	4	12	420	4
4	570	5	13	590	5
5	480	4	14	220	3
6	450	4	15	610	5
7	210	3	16	200	3
8	600	5	17	490	4
9	240	3	18	470	4
OUT	3730	36	IN	3820	36
			OUT	3730	36
			TOTAL	7550	72

THIS PLAN IS CONCEPTUAL IN NATURE AND IS
SUBJECT TO CHANGE BEFORE OR DURING CONSTRUCTION

LEFT: PLAN FOR THE NEW COURSE **ABOVE:** REES JONES VISITS THE SITE WITH
PLAYER CONSULTANT DAVID TOMS AND COMMISSIONER TIM FINCHEM.

GOLF COURSE DESIGN BY:
REES JONES, INC.
MONTCLAIR, NEW JERSEY

Tour event. (During the other 51 weeks of the
year, it will be open for public play.)

Jones was given an attractive site, clad with
mature hardwoods and pines and tangent to a
wetland area that weaves in and out, and he did
little to alter it. "I would rather create a natural,
classic course that blends with its surroundings
than a course full of unnecessary gimmicks that
discourage the average golfer," he said. "My style
emphasizes definition. I work hard at giving the
golfer a concept as he stands over the ball. I want
him to see the intended target and be able to
visualize the shot."

However, Jones did bring one element into
frequent play: water. "It's the only thing that
stops those guys," he said, referring to the Tour
pros. "Distance means nothing to them any
more, they're magicians from the bunkers—
especially those with PGA Tour-prescribed
sand—and they can all chip and putt like
demons. Water is the only element of peril."

Water comes into play on nine holes at
Redstone, with wetlands on eight more. A string
of six holes from the third through the eighth all
feature water. The centerpiece of that stretch is
number six, a leftward doglegging par four that
calls for a tee shot over wetlands to a rolling fairway. To the right of the fairway a series of shoul-

dering mounds will forgive the slightly errant shot but penalize a comprehensive miss. But even drives that find position A will leave a testing approach to a green that sits beside a lake.

The back nine, if the Tour uses its full length, plays a Texas-sized 3,820 yards. Like all good tournament courses, Redstone crescendos to a dramatic finish. The fun begins at the par-three 16th, which offers a Jones gambit, two tees allowing for divergently different attacks at the green. One calls for an all-carry shot of 200 yards over wetlands, the other has the wetlands parallel right from tee to green. In all likelihood, the Tour will alternate the tees, using each one twice.

The 17th is a challenging dogleg left par four that plays a hefty 490 yards. Long hitters can cut off a bit of that distance, though, by carrying a fairway bunker on the left. Others will hit to a wider landing area, but face a long second shot to an elevated green.

Then players will take a bridge across Greens Bayou (which separates most of this course from the Jacobsen/Hardy layout) for the home hole. Water runs down the entire left side of this challenging par four of 470 yards, beckoning drives and approach shots. A large bunker to the right of the green leaves little room for bailout. The vision is for an imposing clubhouse, numerous hospitality tents, and plenty of room for spectators. Clearly, at Redstone the Shell Houston Open is looking forward to a happy second marriage.

5TH HOLE, PHIL MICKELSON

ONLY HERE

On-Site Insight: An integral part of the Redstone operation is the Dick Harmon School of Golf, run by the son of Masters champion Claude Harmon and brother of Tiger Woods's former coach Butch. Dick Harmon has been recognized by both *GOLF Magazine* and *Golf Digest* as one of the top 100 teachers in America.

An Historic 1-2-3: The first tournament hosted by the Houston Golf Association was the 1946 Tournament of Champions, predecessor to the Shell Houston Open. A trio of all-time greats occupied the top three spots, Byron Nelson winning it, Ben Hogan finishing second, and Sam Snead third.

PLAYING TIP

The Art of Laying Up

With water in near constant play at Redstone, a decision must often be made, whether to gun for the green or lay up. If you choose the latter, don't just slap an iron up the fairway. Be sure to leave the ball well short of the hazard and in a position that will allow you to make a full, aggressive next shot to the hole. If, for instance, you know that you hit a full pitching wedge 100 yards, then choose a lay-up club that will leave you about 100 yards short of the pin. Planning like this is the essence of wise course management.

17TH HOLE, MARK CALCAVECCHIA

FRED COUPLES, 2003 WINNER

SCORECARD

HOLE	PAR	YARDAGE
1	4	360
2	4	430
3	4	390
4	5	570
5	4	480
6	4	450
7	3	210
8	5	600
9	3	240
OUT	36	3730
10	4	380
11	4	440
12	4	420
13	5	590
14	3	220
15	5	610
16	3	200
17	4	490
18	4	470
IN	36	3820
TOTAL	72	7550

TPC OF LOUISIANA | *HP Classic of New Orleans, Louisiana*

Back in 1980, the PGA Tour opened the first of its Tournament Players Clubs at the TPC at Sawgrass in Ponte Vedra Beach, Florida. The architect for that project was Pete Dye, and working with an undistinguished piece of ground he created a layout that today is regarded almost universally as one of the world's best arenas for professional golf. The annual site of The Players Championship, it remains the flagship of the TPC network.

Nearly 25 years and 30 TPCs later, Dye was called upon to work his magic once again, this time on 250 acres of bayou country, hard by the Mississippi River, for the TPC of Louisiana. Beginning in 2005, this is the course that will host the HP Classic of New Orleans.

"Commissioner Finchem picked me to do this and I think I know why," joked Dye on learning he'd gotten the job. "He finds a flat site and he calls me. But I appreciate the confidence he has in me, and, what the heck, I still love digging in the dirt."

Dig he did, transforming a flat, low-lying piece of property with help from a pair of Tour players, Steve Elkington and Louisiana native Kelly Gibson. What they produced is not only a 7,500-yard par-72 golf course but a marvel of hydro-engineering, self-contained and surrounded on three sides by drainage canals.

Despite being just 20 minutes from downtown New Orleans, the setting is heavily wooded, predominantly with cypress trees, and has a mature look although it opened in 2004. The greens, flat by Dye's standards, are also relatively small—in the manner of his design at Harbour Town—but the green complexes seem much larger as the bunkers are set off from the putting surfaces, with chipping areas in between.

1ST HOLE

"We didn't want the bunkers right up against the greens," he said. "We wanted to have a different look—maybe a little optical illusion—and a different strategy to the holes."

Much as he did at Sawgrass, Dye has made extensive use of large waste bunkers here. In addition, five slender lakes wind among the holes, coming into play on a dozen or so shots.

Time will tell how this golf course sits with the pros—not to mention the amateurs who will play it as a daily-fee course—but for now the key seems to be in the pacing of the holes, Dye's genius for

creating a compelling succession of threes, fours, and fives. Each nine, in addition to having a pair of par fives and par threes, includes two short par fours, two long ones, and one of medium length. The four short fours—arguably the best holes on the course—average just 385 yards from the TPC tees while the four long ones weigh in at 100 yards longer.

Water first comes into play at number three, a par three of 224 yards with a lake menacing the right side from tee to green. All four of the "short" holes on this course measure at least 200 yards

from the championship tees and three of them are in the 220-230 range.

The same water hazard curls around to complicate the tee shot at number four. A long drive is needed on this 483-yard par four, but anyone who errs to the right will find the lake, and anyone whose approach strays left will find one of Mr. Dye's waste bunkers.

Over time, the toughest hole on the course may prove to be the sixth, a 494-yard par four dogleg left with water waiting on the inside of the corner and another waste bunker wrapping around the

4TH HOLE

8TH HOLE

18TH HOLE

front and right of the green. However, just across that water hazard is its back-nine sibling, 495-yard number 12, where the tee shot must be threaded through stands of trees, leaving a lengthy approach to an angled green tucked at the far edge of a waste bunker. The player who can get through those two brutes in even par will surely gain strokes on the field.

Another of Dye's short-but-treacherous par fours rears its head at 13, a 371-yarder that takes an abrupt left turn at about the 250-yard mark. On days when the hole plays downwind, some of the longer hitters may try to drive this green, but they will have to hit a long and accurate draw and find a very small target with sand in front and beyond.

At Sawgrass, Dye crafted a dramatic three-hole finish, threading a par five, a par three, and a par four through a watery gauntlet. He has done it again at Louisiana, beginning this time with the par four. Number 16 bends 428 yards slightly left-to-right around a stand of trees en route to a green perched at the edge of a lake. The same water hazard defines the entire left side of 17, the longest par three on the course at 230 yards. Then it's the monster finisher, 583 yards of gentle left to right bend, with water running parallel right all the way to the green. The player who can birdie this hole to win the HP Classic will have won a well-deserved victory.

CLUBHOUSE AND 18TH HOLE

ARCHITECT PETE DYE, FLANKED BY PLAYER CONSULTANTS KELLY GIBSON
(LEFT) AND STEVE ELKINGTON, DURING CONSTRUCTION.

SCORECARD

HOLE	PAR	YARDAGE
1	4	398
2	5	550
3	3	224
4	4	483
5	4	442
6	4	494
7	5	580
8	4	380
9	3	200
OUT	36	3751
10	4	399
11	5	573
12	4	495
13	4	371
14	3	220
15	4	469
16	4	428
17	3	230
18	5	583
IN	36	3768
TOTAL	72	7519

ONLY HERE

Excursions: The tourney offers fishing trips to the players, cooking classes for their wives, and paddleboat trips on the Mississippi River.

Gourmet Nights: Ask the pros who are regulars at this tournament why they attend, and most will cite its proximity to New Orleans' famed restaurants.

PRO TIPS

How to Hit the Hardest Shot

On courses such as the TPC of Louisiana, where many of the bunkers are well removed from the greens, you're apt to face the consensus hardest shot in golf—the long explosion.

Before even addressing this shot, do yourself a favor and be sure you're properly armed. Don't ever play a long bunker shot with a third, lob, or lofted wedge. In fact, the best club is a pitching wedge, or perhaps a strong sand wedge with 52 degrees of loft or less. This will give you the lower, longer shot you need.

As to technique, don't get too complicated. Assuming you have a reasonable lie, simply address this shot with a less open stance than you would a short bunker shot, while keeping the clubface slightly open. On extra long shots, put a bit more length and power into your swing. Above all, be sure to swing upward to a full follow-through.

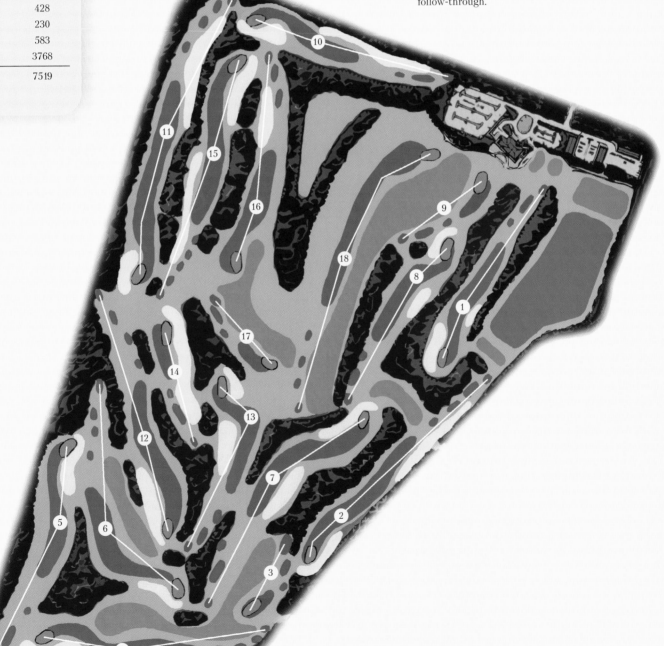

PGA Tour players, probably more than most people, are resistant to change. They're a conservative, cautious, superstitious lot who tend to bristle at the notion of anything that might upset their rhythm or alter their schedule. New tournaments on the Tour calendar therefore are met with a reservation just shy of contempt.

The organizers of the Wachovia Championship in Charlotte, North Carolina, knew that—but they also knew they had a few advantages on their side. First among those was a superior golf course. Quail Hollow boasts an exquisitely manicured parkland layout, designed by George Cobb in 1961. Between 1969 and 1979 it was the site of the Kemper Open (now the Booz Allen Classic) before that event moved to Washington, D.C. It has since been modified and updated by both Arnold Palmer (1985) and Tom Fazio (1997) and today is regarded as one of the finest courses in the state, good enough, in the eyes of many, to host a U.S. Open.

Secondly, Quail Hollow is a major outpost of golf's old boy network. The son of the club's founder—and the current club president—is Johnny Harris, a millionaire real estate developer whose best friends include Palmer (who once owned a house on Quail Hollow's 15th fairway) and Dick Ferris, longtime chairman of the PGA Tour's Policy Board. Harris, a member of the Augusta National Golf Club, also is close to Tour Commissioner Tim Finchem. With powerbrokers like that in your regular foursome, it's easy to cut through red tape. Thus, when Harris sought a week on the Tour schedule, he got not simply a slot but a prime slot, midway between the Masters and U.S. Open.

Another of Harris's cronies—a member of Quail Hollow—is Ken Thompson, CEO of the Wachovia Corporation, the nation's fourth largest financial services company. Seeking to spread the word about his company, headquartered in Charlotte, Thompson agreed to become the title sponsor and ponied up a $5.6 million purse with one million going to the winner, making this one of the ten richest tournaments in the game. That caught the players' attention, as did numerous perks and inducements including Mercedes-Benz courtesy cars for all players.

Tiger Woods did not make it for the inaugural Wachovia Championship in 2003—he was busy earning a $2 million guarantee simply for showing up at the Deutsche Bank-SAP Open in Germany— but just about every other top player entered, with David Toms the winner. With the help of 3,000 enthusiastic volunteers, everything ran smoothly. The tournament was a huge success and now seems headed for a long and successful run.

2ND HOLE

8TH HOLE

16TH HOLE

During its tenure as host of the Kemper, Quail Hollow produced a solid list of champions, including Doug Sanders, Ray Floyd, and three victories by Tom Weiskopf. However, the course tackled by today's pros is a decidedly different test. At just under 7,400 yards, it's about two hundred yards longer, but that's insignificant, given the increased distances being achieved with modern golf equipment. No, with its tree-lined corridors, multiple doglegs, subtle changes in elevation, and devilishly contoured greens, the 21st-century Quail Hollow is a test of ball control, shotmaking, and the short game, thanks to Fazio's redesign.

That said, there are holes that will require both power and accuracy and the first of them is number three, a hole that plays almost straight from the members' tees but is a 452-yard dogleg for the pros. A drive of nearly 280 yards will be needed

3RD HOLE

17TH HOLE

1ST HOLE

just to reach the turn in the fairway. From there it's a middle iron to a raised green that slopes from back to front. With thick stands of trees down both sides of the fairway, this is a hole that allows no mistakes.

Three holes later comes a short hole that is not short. From the back tees number six measures 250 yards to a green bunkered front-left and back-right, and hitting the target is only half the assignment as this putting surface has three tiers.

Number seven is a terrific tournament hole, a risk-reward par five in the tradition of Augusta National's 13th, with a creek bordering one side and crossing in front of the green. Any pro whose tee shot can avoid the bunkers right and left will likely try to get home in two here, which means the hole will produce its share of

18TH HOLE

eagles, but for those who find the creek, par will feel like a triumph.

By contrast, number 10 is a par five that few players will be reaching. Five hundred and nine-ty-one yards from the tips, it winds through tall trees on both sides, bending first from right to left and then back the other way. To leave a shot to the green the drive will have to be hit 300 yards, but two bunkers in the left side of the landing area caution against too aggressive a tack. Three greenside bunkers—the largest of them at the front—will have most players laying up to wedge-on range.

For tournament spectators, the most thrill-packed hole surely is number 14, a par four of just 346 yards. The long, narrow green is driveable but anyone who tries had better be accurate as well as strong, as the path is strewn with six bunkers and water runs down the entire left of the hole.

Quail Hollow's signature hole is the 17th, a par three of 217 yards with roughly 200 of those

yards played over a rock-walled lake which also wraps around the left and rear of the green. A gentle fade is the preferred shot, both to take the water out of play and control the touchdown on the back-to-front and right-to-left sloping green. This is the most daunting shot of the day.

Number 18, a par four of 478 yards, has the potential to become one of the most drama-pro-ducing holes on the Tour. The key element is a creek that winds up the left side of the tree-lined fairway, menacing both the tee shot and the approach, while a bunker on the right side of the drive zone and two more at the right of the nar-row, sloping green make it clear that the only safe way home is with two straight shots. Toms was fortunate to come to the 72nd hole of the inaugural Wachovia Championship with a six-stroke lead, for he needed four strokes to reach this green and then four-putted for a quadruple bogey eight.

ONLY HERE

Perks: Among the inducements used to lure players to this event: use of a Mercedes-Benz for a week; a barber shop in the locker room; free dry cleaning; a concierge to book dinner reservations; special day care for the kids; Mother's Day gifts for the wives; and even a park-ing valet for the caddies.

Happy Wednesday: The best perk of all might be the Wednesday pro-am, where the pros are paired with just two amateurs instead of the typical four. Rounds are therefore completed in four hours or less as opposed to the usual five hours and more.

More Diplomats than the U.N.: Sure it's a gimmick, but give the organizers credit for elevating their volun-teers to Marshal Ambassadors, Mobile Greeter Ambassadors, Scoring Ambassadors, Admissions Ambassadors, and Transportation Ambassadors.

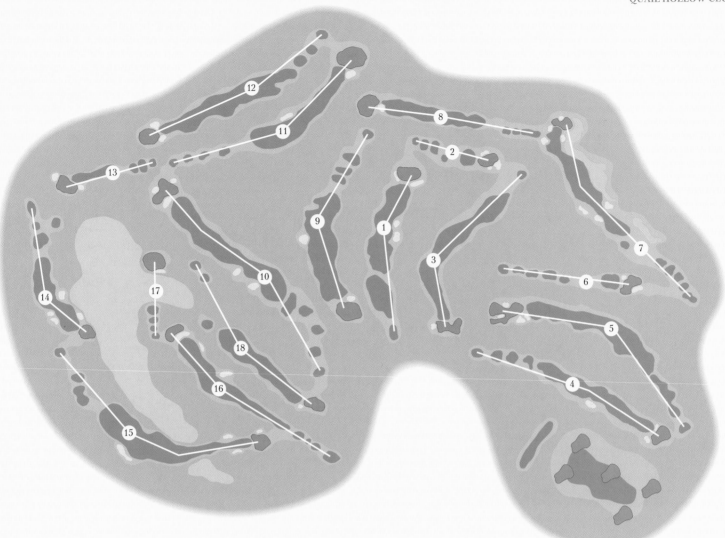

PLAYING TIP

Learn to Lob

On a shotmaker's course such as Quail Hollow, with elusive, fiercely sloped greens, you often find yourself facing a short recovery shot that must be made to stop soon after it hits the putting surface. That's a tough assignment unless you know how to hit the lob.

Golf's version of the lob is the same as in tennis, a high, soft, floating shot that thuds to earth with little spin. It is played most easily from light rough, where you can slip the face of your sand wedge or lofted wedge under the ball without fear of hitting the shot thin.

The proper technique is very similar to the sand explosion. You set up in an open stance—feet, knees, hips, and shoulders all pointing left of your target— with the ball positioned about midway between your feet. When you're extremely close to the green and need extra loft, turn the face of your club open a few degrees. As for the swing, you can play a wristy shot or hit it with quiet, almost stiff wrists, according to your personal comfort and preference. The important thing is tempo—make the slowest, laziest up-and-down move you possibly can. It is this languid tempo that creates the soft, high flight.

SCORECARD

HOLE	PAR	YARDAGE
1	4	410
2	3	178
3	4	452
4	4	458
5	5	570
6	3	250
7	5	532
8	4	343
9	4	491
OUT	36	3684
10	5	591
11	4	421
12	4	456
13	3	201
14	4	346
15	5	566
16	4	478
17	3	217
18	4	478
IN	36	3754
TOTAL	72	7438

DAVID TOMS, 2003 WINNER

TPC FOUR SEASONS RESORT LAS COLINAS
COTTONWOOD VALLEY COURSE

EDS Byron Nelson Championship, Texas

LAS COLINAS, 5TH HOLE

LAS COLINAS, 8TH HOLE

Only one player has a PGA Tour event named in his honor—Byron Nelson. That is both ironic and fitting. Ironic in that, among golf's Hall of Famers, surely no man was more modest and self-effacing than the gentleman farmer from Fort Worth whose record of 18 victories in one year—11 of them in succession—will never be equaled. And fitting in that, because of that same dignity and grace, Nelson has always engendered a special love and reverence, from the Tour players as well as knowledgeable golf fans around the world.

The EDS Byron Nelson Championship is played on two contiguous courses in Dallas, the TPC Four Seasons Resort Las Colinas and Cottonwood Valley, and both of them reflect the character of Lord Byron, who was a consultant on both designs. Resort courses, they are totally accessible with a bias toward no one. Their fairways are relatively generous, their greens are generally open and approachable, and on neither course is there a hint of flamboyance. They are fair courses, but upon closer study they are also formidable. As with Byron Nelson, familiarity breeds respect.

The tournament field is split for the first round of play, half playing the TPC and half Cottonwood, with the two groups switching for the second round. The third and fourth rounds are played exclusively on the TPC course. Each is a par 70, and although Cottonwood is the shorter by about 200 yards, it is arguably the more difficult of the two, with three or four of its holes annually ranking among the hundred or so toughest on the Tour.

Cottonwood's challenge begins immediately, with an opening par four of 448 yards, the second shot over water to a green that was designed in the shape of Texas with a single bunker the shape of Oklahoma.

Robert Trent Jones, Jr. was the perpetrator of that hole as part of his design of the original Cottonwood in 1982, but the course has since been reworked by Jay Morrish and the result is a hybrid, with holes two through ten Morrish designs, then to Jones for 11 through 18.

Cottonwood was first used as a venue for the tournament in an emergency in 1994 when heavy

LAS COLINAS, 7TH HOLE

rains forced officials to spread out the play to a second course. The next year, it became a permanent co-host. In the process, hole number three was converted from a par five to a par four (in order for the par of the course to equal the 70 at the TPC). As a result, number three is the toughest hole on the course, a slight dogleg par four of 475 yards that calls for a tee shot across a row of bunkers, then a lengthy second to a small plateau green that demands accuracy in both distance and direction.

The best and most beautiful hole on the course is number 15, a par four of 441 yards with a tee shot framed by thick stands of trees on both sides of the fairway. The hole bends sharply at about the 250-yard mark and heads directly uphill to a green that slopes severely from back to front and is also bisected by a ridge. Even the pros are happy with pars here.

Jay Morrish also designed the TPC Four Seasons course, with consultation from Ben Crenshaw before Crenshaw went on to a successful architectural career of his own. Incredibly, they completed the course in less than a year, just in time to host the 1986 edition of the Nelson tournament. Since then, numerous changes and improvements have been made—trees were planted, bunkers were added, and several holes were lengthened and stiffened to maintain the challenge for today's longer-hitting pros. Yet it

remains a course that rewards finesse more than power, and where an ability to handle the Texas winds is an important asset. Two-time Nelson champ Bruce Lietzke is fond of saying "this course is for the guy who hits it straight and putts it straight."

Most of the long holes at the TPC play downwind, and at number three that following breeze can be a big help, as this par four named The Bear stretches the limit at 490 yards. However, accuracy here is also important. The tee shot must be placed between a slender lake on the right and a target bunker on the left. The green, like all but two or three here, is generously open at the front, allowing for a bounce-on approach, but it needs to be judged carefully.

The toughest stretch is in the middle, beginning with 457-yard number eight, a slight dogleg right tightened by trees on both sides. To the left of the small oval green is the deepest grass bunker on the course, and getting up and down from it is a stern test of one's short game. The par-four 10th, one of the few holes that generally plays crosswind, forces players to drive over a lake and skirt a cluster of five bunkers to the right of the drive zone. The second shot also must avoid sand, with front-flanking bunkers this time cutting off all but a narrow entrance to the green.

Wind and wet continue to menace the path at number 14, where the tee shot must be placed

perfectly in order to leave a clear view of the green and the approach is played over a lake through swirling breezes to a perched green. This has proved to be a pivotal hole in several Nelsons.

The par-five 16th is 554 yards, not overly long by today's standards, but it winds uphill all the way. Long hitters can get home in two, but a set of cross bunkers, about one hundred yards short of the green, and a mammoth bunker at right greenside will give pause on that second swing. And those eagle and birdie putts will have to be stroked from the surface of a severely sloped two-tier green.

The most-changed hole since the original design of the course is unquestionably the 17th, a downhill par-three whose clover-shaped green now sits hard by a lake. The water is at the front-right, a large sand bunker is front-left, and back-right is a grass bunker, all of which make this the toughest 196 yards of the day, especially when the wind is up.

In terms of drama, the home hole is an anti-climax, a mid-length dogleg-left par four that climbs slightly uphill. Byron's Tree, a 50-foot-high oak, stands at the corner, forcing drives to the right, and the well-protected green is also severely sloped. Still, it's a place for lots of pars, relatively few birdies and bogeys. No fanfare, which is exactly Byron Nelson's style.

LAS COLINAS, 12TH HOLE

LAS COLINAS, 16TH HOLE

LAS COLINAS, 14TH HOLE

LAS COLINAS, 17TH HOLE

COTTONWOOD VALLEY, 15TH HOLE

BRUCE LIETZKE, 1981 AND 1988 WINNER

ONLY HERE

Playoffs: Since 1970, this tournament has produced more playoffs than any event on the PGA Tour, a total of 15.

Low Scores: Every winner from 1994 through 2003 shot all four rounds in the 60s. Sergio Garcia broke the string when he shot 71 in the final round in 2004.

Tape-Measure Blows: When the wind kicks up here, the ball can really travel, especially when those Texas fairways are hard and running fast. A 400-yard drive here is not out of the question.

PLAYING TIP

Know the Mow

Maintenance procedures can affect the way your ball reacts at impact, and you should be particularly aware of this around the green, especially on courses such as the TPC Four Seasons where the mowing patterns can vary from hole to hole.

If mowers have cut the grass in such a way that it pushes against the front of your ball, you can expect some resistance if you try to putt the ball or hit a low chip shot. The blades of grass will tend to impede impact a bit, imparting extra backspin that can make the ball skip or veer off line. In such a situation, you might want to opt for a more lofted shot that slips the ball quickly upward and over the grass.

If, on the other hand, the grass has been mown so that the blades point in the same direction as your shot—in effect, the mower has created grain in your favor—you'll have little or no resistance from the grass and you'll therefore have more options. The smartest shot might be a running chip or putt, to get the ball running smoothly toward the hole.

SCORECARD

TPC FOUR SEASONS RESORT LAS COLINAS

HOLE	PAR	YARDAGE
1	4	385
2	3	192
3	4	490
4	4	425
5	3	180
6	4	438
7	5	533
8	4	457
9	4	439
OUT	35	3539
10	4	447
11	4	347
12	4	426
13	3	183
14	4	409
15	4	475
16	5	554
17	3	196
18	4	440
IN	35	3477
TOTAL	70	7016

SCORECARD

COTTONWOOD VALLEY GOLF COURSE

HOLE	PAR	YARDAGE
1	4	448
2	3	154
3	4	475
4	4	427
5	4	417
6	4	360
7	4	400
8	4	394
9	3	188
OUT	34	3263
10	4	432
11	5	545
12	3	191
13	4	409
14	4	383
15	4	441
16	5	539
17	3	204
18	4	439
IN	36	3583
TOTAL	70	6846

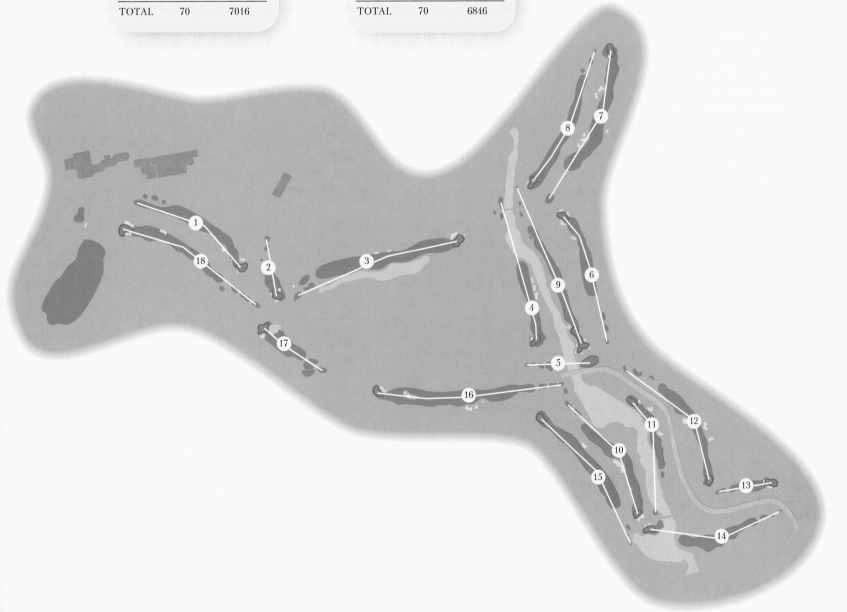

When in 2003 the world's best woman golfer decided to test her skills on the PGA Tour, the venue she chose was Colonial Country Club in Fort Worth. Annika Sorenstam knew that at Colonial, perhaps more than any site on the men's circuit, accuracy—not power—is the key to success.

A par 70 of 7,080 yards, Colonial is a test based largely around a succession of taut and bending par fours, where finding the fairway and finding the green are paramount. Designed by John Bredemus in 1933, it hosted the U.S. Open eight years later, the first course in the South to do so. In 1946 the Colonial National Invitation Tournament came here and it has stayed for sixty years, making this the longest-running continuous venue of any event on the PGA Tour.

In its heyday, Colonial was called the hardest par 70 in the world. That is no longer the case, at least for the pros, as the winning score here is routinely double digits under par. In 2003, as Annika missed the cut on rounds of 71-74, Kenny Perry set a new tournament record with a score of 261—19 under par. That said, Colonial—thanks to continuous tweaking and updating over the years by architects ranging from Perry Maxwell (1940) to Keith Foster (1999)—has retained its character as an examination in shotmaking, management, and ball control.

The front nine is generally agreed to be the tougher of the two, thanks to the "Horrible Horseshoe," a demonic trio of holes created by Maxwell just in time for that 1941 Open. The first of them is number three, at 476 yards the longest

par four on the course. (When the U.S. Women's Open was played here in 1991, it was played as a par five.) A slight dogleg from right to left, it calls for a precisely placed tee shot between a large tree and a trio of bunkers at the elbow of the dogleg, followed by a long iron that had also better be a straight iron. The PGA of America once rated this as the toughest third hole in America.

Number four is a Texas-sized par three of 246 yards that plays to an elevated green. Despite six decades of attack by the game's best players it has never yielded a hole-in-one in tournament competition, and even birdies are rare.

And number five is not simply the hardest hole at Colonial, it is consistently one of the hardest on the Tour. The 470-yard dogleg right is tightly

3RD HOLE

5TH HOLE

9TH HOLE

4TH HOLE

LEFT: 13TH HOLE **ABOVE:** ANNIKA SORENSTAM ON THE 16TH HOLE **BELOW:** 18TH HOLE

guarded by a tree-lined ditch on the left, more trees to the right, and the Trinity River to the deep right, all made more claustrophobic by the prevailing left-to-right wind. The ideal tee shot is a power fade, which the long hitters play with a 3-wood—and with courage. This leaves a long-iron approach to the fast-running, closely-bunkered green. All of which explains why the nickname for this hole is Death Valley.

Of the 82 bunkers on Colonial the most forbidding may be those to the left of the drive zone at the 402-yard ninth hole. Catch any one of them, and the next shot becomes a fearsome assignment as a pond spreads across the entire front of this green.

Any player whose starting time calls for him to begin at the tenth tee will have to make the first swing of the day a very good one, as this short but tight par four calls for a thread-the-needle tee shot through trees on both sides, followed by an approach requiring equal care.

Number 13 is only 178 yards, but the lake in front causes many shots to end up at the back of the green above the hole. A bunker was added to the left in 1999 and the back bunker, which the pros putted out of in the past, has a new higher lip to prevent that shot. Ian Baker-Finch, the 1989 champion here, is remembered for the shot he played here after his tee shot found the pond. In an act of great daring, Baker-Finch removed his shoes, socks, and yes, his trousers, wading into the drink in his boxers to blast his ball to the green.

Another scary tee shot confronts the players at number 15, a 430-yard par four with out of bounds

ANNIKA SORENSTAM

in the form of a road on the entire right side and thick trees to the left. If that path is navigated successfully, the approach will be relatively short but the target is a severely sloped, two-tiered green.

The home hole is not a particularly long or bruising one, but in keeping with the Colonial character it rewards only two well played shots. Ideally, it's a draw from the tee to avoid flanking stands of trees and fit the right-to-left bend of the fairway. On the approach a trio of greenside bunkers awaits, and a bank to the left of the green drops off steeply to a lake.

ONLY HERE

Hogan's Alley: Local boy Ben Hogan won the first two Colonials, five of them in all. In the clubhouse, a special trophy room contains many of his prizes and mementos.

Faders: It's no wonder that Hogan won here five times—and Bruce Lietzke and Lee Trevino won twice each. Ten of Colonial's par fours and fives favor a left-to-right ball flight.

Veterans: It's a course that takes a bit of studying and rewards those who learn well. Hogan was 46 when he won here the last time. Tom Watson won at age 48, Nick Price at 45.

The Wall of Fame: Near the first tee is a permanent tribute to the players who have won at Colonial. The Wall of Champions holds plaques for each of the victors, starting with Craig Wood in the 1941 U.S. Open, including every Colonial champion and Meg Mallon, winner of the U.S. Women's Open in 1991.

PLAYING TIP

The Controlled Fade

No wonder Ben Hogan mastered Colonial. No course favors a controlled fade more than this one, and no one ever controlled a fade better than Hogan.

Assuming you don't already have a fade—or its unattractive cousin, the slice—it is not a difficult shot to learn. The idea is to impart clockwise spin to the ball. To do that, it's simplest to address the ball in an open stance, with your body aligned left of the target, while keeping your clubface pointed straight at the target. This setup will encourage you to take the club away from the ball on an outside path instead of straight back, and will result in a downswing that cuts across the ball from out to in, imparting the clockwise spin that makes the ball drift from left to right. The more fade—or slice—you want, the more you should open your stance.

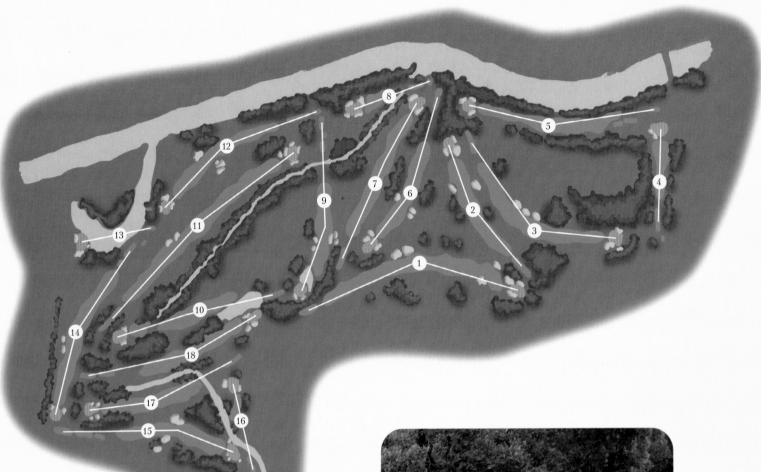

KENNY PERRY, 2003 WINNER

SCORECARD

HOLE	PAR	YARDAGE
1	5	565
2	4	400
3	4	476
4	3	246
5	4	470
6	4	393
7	4	427
8	3	192
9	4	402
OUT	35	3571
10	4	404
11	5	609
12	4	433
13	3	178
14	4	457
15	4	430
16	3	188
17	4	383
18	4	427
IN	35	3509
TOTAL	70	7080

ABOVE: THE FANS RIGHT: 3RD HOLE

Three words describe the atmosphere at the FedEx St. Jude Classic. With apologies to pop songdom's Buster Poindexter, they are "hot, hot, hot." The town is Memphis, the season is summer (though in 2004 it was switched to May for at least a couple of years) and the game is not golf, it's survivor as the pros try to outplay and outwit each other, while outlasting a fire-breathing Mother Nature.

At a site where the temperature can hit 100, keeping up one's stamina and keeping one's cool are important, but at the TPC at Southwind so is keeping the ball in play. The course, designed by Ron Prichard and with consultation by Tour buddies Hubert Green and Fuzzy Zoeller, is not long, but 11 water hazards, 50 acres of bermuda-grass rough, 100 bunkers, and several hundred tall, grasping trees testify to its reputation as a layout whose assailants must toe the straight and narrow.

Still, with the pros hitting the ball longer and scoring lower, the PGA Tour decided to redesign Southwind after the 2004 tournament, with the revamped course to be ready in 2005. In addition to lengthening some holes, accuracy will remain a premium as some water hazards will be expanded and fairways tightened. The course will become a par-70 as the fifth hole is converted from a par five to a par four.

The challenge at Southwind begins right out of the box with a slightly uphill 426-yard par four. Water waits on the inside of this dogleg left and there is a trio of bunkers to the right. The small, sloping green is set on an angle to the fairway with two more bunkers in front and one to the rear. Everyone welcomes an opening par here.

Southwind boasts a strong quartet of par threes, beginning with the picturesque 194-yard fourth, the left side of its green hugged by a rock-walled lake. Number 11 brings to mind the famed 17th at the TPC at Sawgrass, though there is a bit more margin for error.

The 12th hole will be lengthened to 410 yards, making it one of the toughest on the course because of the way it wraps around the edge of the lake. In this age of mammoth drives, some players may be tempted to bite off a big chunk of that lake, but they do so at the risk of a stroke-and-distance penalty.

A natural amphitheater gives spectators a great view of the action at the par-three 14th, but the player who stands on that tee will be looking at a tall assignment—231 yards over water to a severely undulating green.

LEFT: 14TH HOLE ABOVE (TOP TO BOTTOM): 9TH, 15TH, AND 17TH HOLES

18TH HOLE

DAVID TOMS, 2003 WINNER

SCORECARD

HOLE	PAR	YARDAGE
1	4	426
2	4	387
3	5	550
4	3	194
5	5	527
6	4	427
7	4	458
8	3	169
9	4	450
OUT	36	3588
10	4	447
11	3	185
12	4	384
13	4	430
14	3	231
15	4	385
16	5	528
17	4	464
18	4	461
IN	35	3515
TOTAL	71	7103

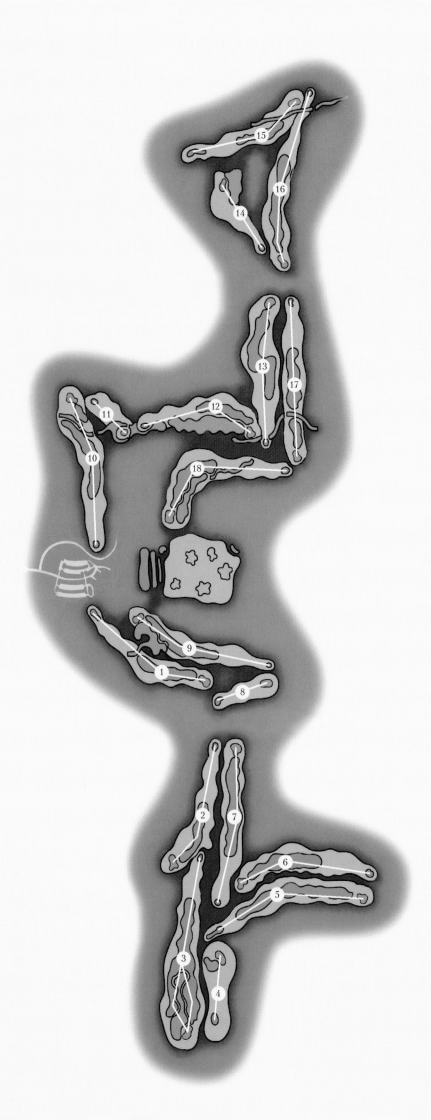

Birdies may be had at 15 and 16, a short par four and five, respectively, but the last two holes at Southwind are brutal. Number 17 plays from an elevated tee but it's 464 yards, and a player who finds rough off the tee will have a daunting second, as a creek crosses about 40 yards in front of the long and narrow green which is surrounded by five bunkers. In most years, this plays as the hardest hole on the course.

Then it's a finisher in the classic TPC mold—461 yards of dogleg left with water lapping along the left side for the last 400 yards or so. Bunkers to the right of the drive zone await anyone who gives the water too wide a berth. The medium-sized green is surrounded by another amphitheater, and the thousands of spectators who assemble here on Sunday invariably are treated to a thrill-filled show, full of both birdies and bogeys.

ONLY HERE

Hot Scoring: Each year at least one player shoots 61 or 62 here, but torrid scoring is a tradition in Memphis. It was at this event, although a different course, that Al Geiberger became the first Tour player to shoot 59.

Cold Comfort: The most coveted ticket here may be a pass to The Cool Zone, an exhibition tent where tournament co-sponsor Coleman demonstrates the full might of its air-conditioning units.

Fairwayside Barbecues: The back nine at Southwind winds through a residential community of 500 single-family homes.

PLAYING TIP

Handling the Heat

Tournaments like this one give new meaning to the term "heat of competition." But the pros know how to handle it, and their tactics are easy to adopt.

Keep dry: Carry a towel to mop up perspiration, particularly on your hands. It's also smart to take your glove off between shots so that it won't become slippery. An extra glove for the back nine will give you confidence the moment you slip it on.

Keep cool: Wear light-colored, loose-fitting clothing, and by all means, wear a hat, both for shade and to reduce the risk of skin cancer.

Keep hydrated: Don't pass up any water coolers or fountains, and if you're on a course where the opportunities are few and far between, take along some bottled water of your own. One good trick is to freeze the water overnight, so it begins the day as a solid block of ice, then melts into cold water as you play.

As far as playing strategy, remember that your muscles will be loose and elastic, the ball will be warm and resilient, and the ground will likely be hard and dry. These factors combine to suggest two things: You won't need to swing hard to get plenty of distance, and you won't need as much club as on a cool day.

ABOVE: 6TH HOLE RIGHT: 8TH HOLE

The story is a familiar one. The world's most famous golfer assembles a few friends, buys acreage near his hometown, and builds a golf course that gains instant acclaim. Then he starts an invitational tournament that quickly grows in stature, eventually to become his lasting legacy.

Bobby Jones did it in 1934 with the Augusta National Golf Club—and 40 years later Jack Nicklaus copied him, with the Muirfield Village Golf Club and the tournament that would become known as The Masters of the Midwest—The Memorial.

When Nicklaus first walked the 170-acre tract of rolling farmland near his native Columbus, Ohio, he had one goal in mind—a course that would test the world's best players. He designed it himself, in collaboration with architect Desmond Muirhead, and when Muirfield Village opened in 1974 it was both the most difficult and best conditioned test the PGA Tour had seen in many years. A decade passed before any competitor in The Memorial posted a four-round total of less than 280. Today, the course has softened and usually ranks about halfway down the Tour's toughness list. But it also ranks on both *GOLF Magazine*'s and *Golf Digest*'s lists of the Top 100 Courses.

Nicklaus and Muirhead began with a routing plan that gracefully brings into play the streams, woodlands, and other natural features of the site. Water appears on 11 of the holes, beginning at bruising number one, a 451-yard dogleg right that plays from an elevated tee. (Nicklaus has a strong preference for holes that play downhill, and at Muirfield at least half of them do.) Three bunkers guard the inside of the dogleg while trees and a creek run along the outside. The green is the largest on the course, but it's ringed with four bunkers.

Things get no easier at 455-yard number two, where the creek snakes around to menace both the tee shot and the approach. At Muirfield Village, even the pros are delighted to make a par-par start.

Number eight measures only 182 yards, and the downhill shot makes it seem even shorter, but with its narrow green virtually surrounded by sand, this hole historically ranks as the most difficult of the four par threes. But Jack saved his best hole on the front nine for last, a taut 407-yard par four where nothing but a straight tee shot will do. Too far right and trees will block the approach. Too far left and a steep, wooded hill threatens even

12TH HOLE

ABOVE (TOP TO BOTTOM): 9TH AND 14TH HOLES

worse trouble. The tilted green is spectacularly framed by a lake, a creek, a forest, and a hillside, and must often be approached from an angled lie, even after a good drive. This is a hole that calls for courage and finesse from tee to cup.

Muirfield's most photographed hole is number 12, a 166-yard par three patterned after the 12th at Augusta National, with its green set against a hillside and fronted by a pond. The winds don't swirl as capriciously as they do through the Georgia pines, and this hole plays downhill

instead of level, but its tiny, two-tiered green is far more difficult than that of its model.

Rated among the world's great short par fours is the 363-yard 14th, a slightly left-to-right dogleg played from an elevated tee to a tree-lined valley. At about the 245-yard mark, a creek emerges from the left woods to angle across the fairway and along the right side of the green. The narrow putting surface slopes sharply from left to right and back to front and is guarded by several bunkers. The longest hitters can carry the

creek where it crosses the fairway—John Daly routinely attacks it with a driver, reasoning that even a short pitch, no matter the lie, is better than a full shot to the green. But 99 percent of the pros hit irons from the tee and then trust their wedges to get them safely home. In some years this hole has produced everything from eagle to triple bogey.

Number 15 is a rarity—a dead-straight, short par five with character. The fairway rises and dips like a roller coaster through a 503-yard chute of trees, culminating at a small, sloping green that drops off steeply to the front and right. This is another hole that produces plenty of triumph and tragedy.

Architect Nicklaus has loved his golf course from day one, but there was always one hole that bothered him. "I always felt that 17 was a little blah—it had no excitement," he said. So one day in the summer of 2002 he brought out the bulldozers and, in eight hours, tore it down. The competitors in the 2003 Memorial were greeted by an entirely different hole. Lengthened from 431 to 478 yards, it is now the longest par four on the course. A long waste bunker to the left of the fairway remains, but the approach is now complicated by a deep stream-crossed valley in front of a new green which is smaller and more heavily contoured than its predecessor.

Nicklaus calls the home hole one of his most strategic, inviting players either to attack it with a long drive around the corner of the left-to-right dogleg—while risking problems with trees or a creek—or lay back with a shorter club, leaving a longer iron for the uphill approach. The green is large but two-tiered, heavily contoured and bunkered on all sides. It's a hole that has yielded several dramatic finishes, most notably 1993 when Paul Azinger holed a shot from the front bunker for birdie to win by one.

17TH HOLE

JACK NICKLAUS ON THE 18TH HOLE

18TH HOLE

SCORECARD

HOLE	PAR	YARDAGE
1	4	451
2	4	455
3	4	401
4	3	200
5	5	527
6	4	447
7	5	563
8	3	182
9	4	407
OUT	36	3633
10	4	441
11	5	567
12	3	166
13	4	455
14	4	363
15	5	503
16	3	215
17	4	478
18	4	444
IN	36	3632
TOTAL	72	7265

ONLY HERE

Masters Mimicry: Although he named the course after the site of his first British Open victory, Jack Nicklaus patterned his tournament after The Masters. From the perfectly manicured course with its wide fairways and sloping greens to its special locker room for Memorial champions only, this event has its roots in Augusta.

Memorializing: Each year the tournament's Captains Club selects an individual "who has played golf with conspicuous honor" and adds him or her to the pantheon of Memorial honorees, via an induction ceremony held on Wednesday afternoon.

Worthy Winners: Few events can claim a more glittering list of past champions. The victors include Tiger Woods (three times in a row), Tom Watson, Hale Irwin, Greg Norman, Ray Floyd, Curtis Strange, and the host himself, twice. Fifteen of the 22 winners also have won a major championship.

Easy viewing: Former Tour Commissioner Deane Beman usually gets credit for inventing stadium golf, but this was the first modern course built to accommodate large galleries. The amphitheater 18th hole alone holds more than 20,000 spectators.

KENNY PERRY, 1991 AND 2003 WINNER

PLAYING TIP

Two Collar Shots

The linoleum-like surfaces of Muirfield Village require a soft touch around the green, but when your ball comes to rest against the collar of fringe, a soft strike becomes difficult. However, there are at least two shots to try.

First is the bellied wedge. Using your putting stance and stroke, strike the ball at its equator with the leading edge of your sand wedge. The heavy clubhead of the wedge will glide through the fringe grass smoothly and unimpeded and will enable you to strike the ball solidly, without any sudden acceleration. This takes some practice, but it's a shot that's worth your time.

If you can't master the bellied wedge, you might have another option, depending on the design of your putter. If you have a model with a squared-off toe, turn the clubface 90 degrees and strike the ball with the toe of the club. The putter, when held this way, is a fraction of its normal width and thus parts and penetrates the heavy grass rather than being twisted by it.

TOURNAMENT HOST JACK NICKLAUS

The Buick Classic is the PGA Tour's only regular stop in the New York metropolitan area, but that's okay because the venue—the West Course at Westchester Country Club—is the quintessential host. Like New York itself, this golf course rewards excellence, is intolerant of mediocrity, and can be brutal to those who don't stay focused. Yes, if you can make it here, you'll make it anywhere.

One of the oldest courses on the Tour, Westchester opened in 1922 as part of an envisioned community for millionaire sportsmen. In addition to the golf, there were three polo fields (now serving as the practice range), a bridle path, a horse track, 20 tennis courts, and a beach club on Long Island Sound. The "clubhouse" was an eight-story

Biltmore Hotel, with apartments for the members and its own brokerage firm on the ground floor.

It was all unveiled to instant success, with 1,500 people signing up on opening day for an initiation fee of $25, but things collapsed a decade later when the Depression hit. The club was saved when a group of members, who had built magnificent homes adjoining the course, protected their property values by purchasing the facility. The Tour arrived in 1967, with the Westchester Classic, won by Jack Nicklaus, and the event was off and running.

Certainly, the New York market adds to the allure of this tournament, but its popularity among the players is due in large measure to the respect they have for the golf course. At just 6,783 yards

and with water only faintly in play, it seems less than formidable on paper. But consider that only 21 acres of this course are fairway while 80 acres are rough, and at tournament time in June that rough is in mid-season form—healthy and thick. Combine that with a series of tightly tree-lined, swooping par fours culminating in small greens, and the result is all the challenge a world-class player wants. In most years this ranks as one of the ten toughest courses on the Tour.

For the tournament, the first and second nines are reversed, with the result that play begins on a par three, and the second nine, where most of the challenge lies, starts with a hole that was conceived as a benign "easy four" for the members—314 yards

11TH HOLE

9TH HOLE

10TH HOLE

12TH HOLE

16TH HOLE

17TH HOLE

from an elevated tee—but is a drama-producing "do I try to drive it or not" decision for the pros. These days, depending on wind direction and hole location, about a third of the field gives it a go, hoping to arrive safely either on the putting surface or in one of the greenside bunkers. Those who miss badly to either side will find major trouble in the form of tree limbs and steep slopes, and par will suddenly look like a great score.

Immediately thereafter come, back to back, the two hardest holes on the course. Number 11, a par four of 442 yards, plays slightly downhill from the tee, but a stream crosses the fairway at the 255-

18TH HOLE

yard mark, and most of the field will play short of it, leaving a lengthy second through a chute of trees to a three-tiered green. Twelve, a par five for the Westchester members, plays down a roller-coaster fairway so that even a big tee shot leaves a downhill lie with a severely uphill approach to a green with dramatic drop-offs short and right.

The next major hurdle comes at 15 and the hurdle is a tall one, as an enormous white oak tree stands defiantly at the inside corner of this 462-yard dogleg right. The decision players face is to drive over the tree and cut off some yardage or shape a left-to-right tee shot around it. Without one of those two shots, the approach will be both long and blind, as the fairway crests before rolling downhill to the green.

The toughest par three follows, a downhill shot of 204 yards to a very narrow target cinched by deep bunkers. Then it's back up the hill for a short dogleg par four to another small green with a 15-foot-deep bunker at its front and and even deeper drop-off behind. Most players will be happy negotiating those holes with a pair of pars.

At the home hole, however, everyone steps to the tee thinking birdie. A right-to-left dogleg of 526 yards, this is one of the Tour's great finishers.

A strong draw from the tee will put the green in easy reach, but a large bunker short of the green collects more shots than does the putting surface, and the third shot from that sand is sometimes a long blast, universally regarded as the hardest shot in the game. The multi-tiered green here has been known to produce three-putt agony for the contenders. Still, more often than not, it is a closing birdie—either in regulation play or in a playoff—that produces victory. When Spain's Seve Ballesteros won this tournament in 1988 he played the hole in six under par—two birdies and two eagles.

SCORECARD

HOLE	PAR	YARDAGE
1	3	190
2	4	384
3	4	408
4	4	419
5	5	565
6	3	151
7	4	326
8	4	464
9	5	505
OUT	36	3412
10	4	314
11	4	442
12	4	485
13	4	410
14	3	154
15	4	462
16	3	204
17	4	374
18	5	526
IN	35	3371
TOTAL	71	6783

ONLY HERE

Mayor and Son: Andrew Giuliani, son of former New York mayor Rudy Giuliani and a fine high-school golfer, is a regular in the pro-am, and his father has served as the event's honorary chairman. In recent years much of the proceeds from this event have been donated to charities associated with the events of September 11, 2001.

Tiger Taming: In four appearances here, Tiger Woods has never finished better than a tie for 13th, an embarrassment in that he is a spokesman for Buick.

Gilder's Plaque: Embedded in the center of the 18th fairway is a plaque that commemorates the shot played by Bob Gilder in the third round of the 1982 event. Leading the tournament at the time, Gilder slugged a 3-wood second shot 251 yards into the hole for a double eagle. It spurred him to victory on a record total of 261—no other winner has come within six strokes of that mark.

PLAYING TIP

Putting Fast Greens

The sloping bentgrass greens of Westchester Country Club are among the fastest on the Tour, but from time to time we all encounter extra-slippery surfaces. On such occasions, there's a simple way to adjust your technique for a softer hit, without changing your actual stroke: Hit your putts off the toe of the clubface.

When you stroke a putt off the toe, you can expect a much softer impact than when you strike it smack on the sweetspot. A putt that would normally roll 30 feet will roll anywhere from 20 to 27 feet, depending on the model of putter you have. (Putters with heel-toe weighting will have less distance loss.) This softer hit will enable you to adjust to super-fast greens easily, without having to alter your stroke.

18TH HOLE

JONATHAN KAYE, 2003 WINNER

SEVE BALLESTEROS, 1983 AND 1988 WINNER

At the TPC at Avenel, the PGA Tour made a silk purse from a sow's ear. Roughly 20 minutes west of the White House, in Potomac, Maryland, this course sits smack between a housing development and a sewage plant. Perhaps in part for that reason, when it was announced that Avenel would replace venerable Congressional Country Club as host of the Kemper Open, the skeptics were numerous and vocal.

The course needed a boost—and it got one from the very highest authority. The President? No, the king. In 1986, a few months after Avenel opened, the Chrysler Cup (sort of a senior version of the Presidents Cup) was played here and

Arnold Palmer put the place on the map when, on consecutive days, he scored holes-in-one at the third hole, which then played 187 yards. With that bit of history in its pocket, Avenel was off and running.

That said, this is no Congressional, a course long and strong enough to have hosted two U.S. Opens and a PGA Championship (Congressional will host the tournament in 2005 while Avenel undergoes a redesign). Avenel, a par 71 of 7,005 yards before the redesign, boasts a great variety of holes—including a collection of par fours that range in length from 301 to 472 yards. It's a place that rewards accurate iron players more often

than long-ball hitters and where a well-oiled short game may be the most effective weapon of all.

This is also a course where players can get off to a fast start, as the par-three third (now bulked up to 239 yards) is the only bruiser among the first six holes. But things get serious quickly at number seven, a 461-yard dogleg right where the tee shot must be placed between bunkers left and dense trees to the right and the approach must avoid two very deep bunkers at greenside.

The signature hole is arguably the ninth, a downhill par three of 166 yards with Rock Run Creek protecting the front of a small, hard-surfaced green. Similar to the famed 12th at Augusta

ABOVE: 4TH HOLE OPPOSITE: 9TH HOLE

ABOVE: 12TH HOLE **BELOW:** 15TH HOLE

ABOVE: 16TH HOLE **BELOW:** 17TH HOLE

National, the tee shot must pass through swirling winds. This is a place where players tend to take three and then exhale.

The creek wends its way into the back nine, complicating the drives and approaches to the next five holes, most menacingly at number 12, a tree-lined 472-yard par four where water parallels the left side of the fairway and then crosses in front of a severely contoured green. This is the most difficult hole on the course.

Two holes after that longest of the par fours comes the shortest. The 301-yard 14th is driveable, but those who give it a go will have to negotiate the creek, which runs the length of the hole and nestles up to the front and right side of the green. Two deep bunkers gape hungrily for anyone who misses to the left. Most players will lay up with middle irons off the tee and trust their wedges to bring them short birdie putts.

The finishing stretch is a tough one, beginning at the 467-yard 15th. Players will let it all hang out off the tee, as a saddle fairway tends to col-lect drives that drift to either side. Depending on wind conditions, the approach can call for anything from a short iron to a long iron, and the two-tiered green produces plenty of three-putts.

The deepest bunker on the course lies in wait at the left-front of the green at number 16, but on this contoured, fast-running surface getting up and down can be difficult from any angle.

A lot of thought will go into club selection at 17, an elevated 195-yard par three where the wind plays a major role. A shot played with the

SCORECARD

HOLE	PAR	YARDAGE
1	4	393
2	5	622
3	3	239
4	4	435
5	4	359
6	5	520
7	4	461
8	4	453
9	3	166
OUT	36	3648
10	4	374
11	3	165
12	4	472
13	5	524
14	4	301
15	4	467
16	4	415
17	3	195
18	4	444
IN	35	3357
TOTAL	71	7005

wrong club—or the wrong swing—is likely to find the large pond at the front and right. But even those who reach the surface are not home free as this sloping green is a demon to putt, particularly when the tournament is on the line.

The home hole—a dead straight par four of 444 yards—is the least taxing of the final four, but its amphitheater setting provides a stage for high drama, often in the form of a birdie. Just ask Lee Janzen, who in 1995 played the hole five times and totaled just 15 strokes! His fifth three won the tournament in a playoff.

ONLY HERE

Water Blasts: With a shallow creek hugging several holes, half-submerged (and thus playable) lies are not uncommon.

First-Time Winners: Since this event often is squeezed on the calendar between The Memorial and the U.S. Open, the marquee players tend to skip it, leaving an opportunity for the lesser lights.

Knight Music: Anyone who has forgotten that this event is played in the backyard of the nation's capital will get a reminder at the end of the tournament when a military band marches over the rise at 18 and caps the closing ceremonies with a brief concert.

PLAYING TIP

Chipping in a Stadium

When you miss a green at a TPC course, especially on one of the finishing holes, your ball could come to rest on the downslope of a spectator mound, a lie that adds some complexity to the ensuing chip.

Downhill chips are shooters—they tend to come off the clubface lower and hotter than chips from flat lies. Therefore, you should choose a more lofted club than you normally would. You should also play the ball about an inch farther back in your stance than you would from a level lie, since on a downhill lie your club will tend to "meet the ground" earlier in its swing. For most situations, these are the only changes you need make. However, from a severely downhill lie, add a bit of extra wrist action to your chipping motion to guard against a topped or skulled shot and to insure that you get your clubface squarely down to the back of the ball.

LEE JANZEN, 1995 WINNER

RORY SABBATINI, 2003 WINNER

No tournament on the PGA Tour—and few sporting events of any kind—can claim a history like that of the Western Open, a competition that spans three centuries. First played in 1899, it is still going strong, one of the most coveted titles in professional golf.

For many years—up until World War II—winning the Western was viewed as just a step below winning the U.S. Open, and the roster of champions testifies to its enduring stature. Walter Hagen has won it five times, Billy Casper four, Tom Watson and Tiger Woods three times, and the two-time champions include Ben Hogan, Sam Snead, Arnold Palmer, and Jack Nicklaus.

"Western" is surely a misnomer for this event that has been staged everywhere from California to New York. For the last half-century, however, it has been rooted firmly in the soil of its birthplace, Chicago, and since 1990 its home has been a course known as Dubsdread, the featured layout at Cog Hill, a four-course public facility in nearby Lemont. Cog Hill is the lasting legacy of the late Joe Jemsek, who had caddied there as a boy, earning 65 cents per loop. Jemsek rose to become a fine player, a successful businessman, and the impresario of daily-fee golf in Chicago, buying Cog Hill in 1951 with the stated goal of providing a country club experience for public course players.

However, when in 1964 he added the Dubsdread course, he had another mission—to create a championship caliber layout, playable by all, but capable of testing the pros, even for a major championship. Architects Dick Wilson and Joe Lee gave him just that, not to mention a course that has consistently ranked near the top of the rankings of public courses in the U.S.

From the front tees, Dubsdread is challenging but not oppressive; from the tips, it could hold a U.S. Open. The landing areas are tight, with most holes bordered with mature trees on both sides, and the putting surfaces, although large, are heavily sloped—many with two and three tiers—and surrounded by deep, menacing bunkers. This

6TH HOLE

4TH HOLE

7TH HOLE

12TH HOLE

13TH HOLE

16TH HOLE

17TH HOLE

18TH HOLE

is a second-shot course, where the player who misses too many greens will be an endangered species.

The course is laid out in the shape of a V, with the two nines emanating from and returning to a central point in a pair of narrow loops. The first difficult test comes at number four, a 434-yard dogleg with water and sand pinching both sides of the fairway and an hourglass green surrounded by three more bunkers.

Dubsdread's soft underbelly is its par fives, all of them reachable. Tiger, in one of his three victories, played them in 12 under par for the week. The easiest of the four is hole number five, despite the 13 bunkers strewn along its 525 yards. In 1991, John Daly holed his second shot here for a double eagle.

But immediately after that easiest of the long holes comes the hardest of the short ones. Number six plays 242 yards to a two-tiered green surrounded by five sprawling bunkers.

Dubsdread's back nine is laid out across sidehills instead of from ridge to ridge in the manner of the front. As such, it is both more memorable and more difficult, particularly the stretch from holes 12 to 14, known respectfully as Death Valley.

The distinguishing feature at number 12, a downhill par three of 220 yards, is the bunker at the elbow of the L-shaped green. It is the deepest and most difficult to escape on the course. Trees and out of bounds beyond this green add to the assignment from the tee.

More OB haunts the tee shot at the next hole, a bruising 482-yard par four where the white stakes are on the right and bunkers loom on the left. The green is guarded by a ravine in front and sand on both sides. As if that's not enough, gusting Chicago winds often wreak havoc with the approach.

Another testing short hole presents itself at 14, where task number one is to avoid the six

bunkers encircling the green, task number two is to find the correct tier of this two-level target, and task number three is to coax one's approach putt across the slick slope to somewhere in the vicinity of the cup.

The signature hole may be 16, a 445-yard par four that doglegs through a banked fairway with trees right and a creek left, with all shots feeding down the slope toward the drink. The green is mercifully flat but tucked into the trees with bunkers on three sides.

The finishing hole at Dubsdread is what a final hole should be—dangerous if played poorly and rewarding if played well. Four hundred and eighty yards from the championship tee, it doglegs slightly right to a green flanked by bunkers right and a pond left, and once again everything slopes toward the water. Few titles are won with birdies here, but several have been lost with bogeys and worse.

ONLY HERE

British Open: Three berths in the British Open are determined at the Western. Two go to the two players, not already exempt, highest on a money list that includes The Players Championship and the five consecutive tournaments culminating in the Western. One spot goes to the highest finisher in the Western not already exempt. More spots used to be available at the Western, but the number was reduced when an American qualifier was added to the British Open system in 2004. A year earlier, unknown Ben Curtis finished 13th here, won one of the exemptions, and two weeks later stunned the world by winning at Royal St. George's, his first victory as a professional.

Kids: The pride of this event—and the Western Golf Association which runs it—is the Evans Caddie Scholar Program, begun by 1916 U.S. Amateur and Open champion Chick Evans. Since 1930, it has provided over 7,000 college scholarships for Chicago-area caddies. The Tour players are encouraged to use the caddie scholars this week, and many do. All proceeds of the tournament got to the fund.

PLAYING TIP

Be Your Own Teacher

Odds are, if you play Dubsdread, you'll find at least one of its more than a hundred bunkers before the round's over. Here, as on any course that's heavily bunkered, you need both competence and confidence from sand.

A great way to get them is to teach yourself—find a practice bunker and spend an hour there, experimenting with ways to alter the length and trajectory of your bunker shots. There are three things you can work on:

1) Vary your swing length. Just as with wedge shots from turf, you can control the distance of your sand shots by shortening and lengthening your swing.

2) Vary the pace of your swing. You may have noticed that the Tour pros occasionally make a soft, almost lazy swing in the sand. This is another way to take some distance off a shot, and make it land softly as well.

3) Vary the cushion of sand. When playing most greenside bunker shots, you do not hit the ball, you hit behind it, usually an inch or two. By varying the distance between the ball and the point where your wedge penetrates the sand, you can control the flight of your shots—the more sand you take, the shorter the shot you'll hit.

Take an hour and fiddle with these techniques a bit—and to vary the trajectory of your shot, experiment with the openness of your stance and clubface. You'll be surprised at how much you can teach yourself.

SCORECARD

HOLE	PAR	YARDAGE
1	4	455
2	3	167
3	4	424
4	4	434
5	5	525
6	3	242
7	4	425
8	4	378
9	5	568
OUT	36	3618
10	4	380
11	5	564
12	3	220
13	4	482
14	3	192
15	5	519
16	4	445
17	4	420
18	4	480
IN	36	3702
TOTAL	72	7320

WALTER HAGEN, FIVE-TIME WINNER

BERNARD LANGER ON THE 9TH HOLE

1ST HOLE

The TPC at Deere Run, host of the John Deere Classic since 2000, is a classic case of "local boy makes good." When the Tour decided to develop a Stadium course for the Midwest's Quad Cities area, they bypassed the usual architect suspects— Pete Dye, Tom Fazio, Rees Jones, Jack Nicklaus, *et al*,—and went instead with one of their own veteran players, D.A. Weibring.

It was a wise choice. Weibring (now a member of the Champions Tour) claimed four of his five regular Tour victories in his home state of Illinois and three of them in this very event, back when it was known as the Quad City Open and then the Hardee's Classic. Not only did he throw himself completely into the design of the TPC at Deere Run, he was involved in all phases of its creation, from financing the deal to securing the property.

And that property was something special, just under 400 acres of rolling wooded land beside the Rock River in western Illinois. Archeological evidence indicates that native Americans lived on this land as far back as 5,000 years ago. Much more recently, during the past century, it became Friendship Farm, one of the top Arabian horse breeding operations in the United States. The property was therefore well maintained, and its natural beauty provided an ideal setting for a golf course.

Weibring was wise enough to work with that property, not against it, removing less than 20 percent of the mature oaks, beeches, and sycamores, and altering almost none of the land's pitch and roll. As a result, there are dramatic elevation changes and postcard views throughout this course, with the river visible from nine of the holes. His course, although only a few years old, looks as if it's been in place for decades.

In contrast to most TPC courses, this is not a modern, target-style layout. Weibring is a confirmed traditionalist and although this is a relatively long par 71 (7,183 yards), his design places a premium on shotmaking from tee to green. Numerous doglegs, and even a few blind shots, add to the challenge along with 70 bunkers of varying shapes and depths and half a dozen water hazards. The greens are not overly undulated, but they have plenty of speed, and several are adjoined by sloped chipping areas where the club selected might be anything from a sand wedge to a 4-wood. On this course, precision and strategic shot placement are as important as power, along with an imaginative short game.

2ND HOLE

10TH HOLE

OPPOSITE: 16TH HOLE **ABOVE:** 17TH HOLE

Weibring also likes to give players plenty of options to consider, and nowhere is that more apparent than on the tee of the fourth hole, a 454-yard par four where a large oak tree stares back from the middle of the landing area, forcing a choice. To the left is a 32-yard-wide fairway with a bunker adding to the assignment; to the right, which offers a shorter, easier approach, a second fairway is just 22 yards across. Then it's uphill to one of the highest points on the course, a green that seems to float on the horizon. The tendency is to miss short, and that's a good thing because beyond this surface is trouble from which there is no recovery.

The front nine ends with the longest par four on the course, a 485-yarder where strategy and placement are again important as the tree-lined corridor narrows suddenly for the approach shot, all the way to the long and narrow green.

Hole number 14 is a par four that offers the pros an opportunity to make an eagle—or a double bogey. It plays 361 yards downhill and some players will attempt to drive it, but the small, elevated green is elusive. A miss short and left will roll into the Valley of Sin, a tightly mowed area that leaves a blind shot to the pin. A miss long will be lost down a 60-foot bluff.

The toughest hole on the inward nine is number 15, a 465-yard par four with a forced carry over a valley of gorse and a long, narrow green that is tightly protected by sand and trees. Then it's on to the signature hole at Deere Run, a picturesque all-carry par three that sits on a bluff 40 feet above Rock River. The water doesn't come into play, but two huge bunkers do.

Seventeen presents a birdie opportunity for those who can hit two long and straight shots, but the fairway of this par five dogleg left is canted and tightly tree-lined, and the raised green is guarded

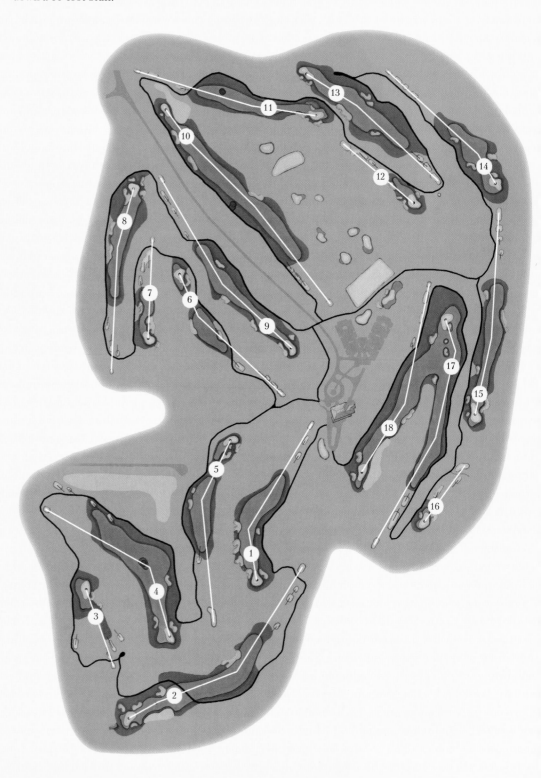

SCORECARD

HOLE	PAR	YARDAGE
1	4	395
2	5	561
3	3	186
4	4	454
5	4	433
6	4	367
7	3	226
8	4	428
9	4	485
OUT	35	3535
10	5	583
11	4	432
12	3	215
13	4	414
14	4	361
15	4	465
16	3	158
17	5	557
18	4	463
IN	36	3648
TOTAL	71	7183

in front by four bunkers and rejects even slightly errant shots into shaved-down chipping areas.

A par four at the finishing hole will be well earned, as this 463-yard dogleg right puts a premium on accuracy. Off the tee, Position A is left center, avoiding a large fairway bunker. From there it's a lengthy approach to a deep but narrow, tree-ringed green with two bunkers on the right and a slender pond on the left. There are many ways to make a mistake here.

ONLY HERE

Debut victories: During the last three decades roughly half of the champions here have been first-time winners. Part of the reason has been the event's less-than-prime dates. In its early days, it was played the same week as the British Open. The event was subsequently moved to the fall, then recently to the week before or after the British Open.

Tee History: Each hole on the course has a name and each of the names relates in some way to the historical significance of the property, from its Native American settlement through the birth of the Quad Cities, and the story of plowmaker John Deere and the company he founded.

LEFT: D.A. WEIBRING, THREE-TIME WINNER AND COURSE DESIGNER
RIGHT: VIJAY SINGH, 2003 WINNER

PLAYING TIP

One Club or Several?
At courses such as the TPC at Deere Run, where several greens are protected by run-offs and chipping areas, you need an ability to play the pitch-and-run shot. The technique is uncomplicated—just a long, rhythmic pitch shot. More complex is the question of club selection, whether to try to play all your pitches with one club—be it an 8-iron or a sand wedge—or use a gamut of weapons from the 5-iron through the lofted wedge. To a great extent this is a personal thing, but one way to choose your strategy is to consider your strengths.

Do you chip better than you putt? If so, you're probably wise to take one club and use your native touch and hand-eye coordination to adapt to the varying demands of the shots you face. If, however, you putt better than you chip, then vary your pitching clubs and keep your technique constant. You should also use your putting method as your pitch-shot technique—hit every pitch with the same type of stroke—and alter the loft and run of your shots by choosing the club that best fits the assignment.

The award for the PGA Tour course with the weirdest name surely goes to the En-Joie Golf Course. Despite its relative proximity to Montreal, En-Joie owes nothing to the French. "En" is short for Endicott, the quiet little town in upstate New York where the club is situated. "Joie" stands for Johnson, more personally George F. Johnson, the man who built the course. Together, they are Endicott-Johnson, for many years the largest shoe manufacturer in the U.S., and not coincidentally, a company based in Endicott and owned by George Johnson.

Johnson was a visionary who believed in treating his employees as if they were owners of the company. In 1927, he built them a golf course, naming each hole after a different department in the company. The 15th green was actually designed in the shape of a shoe. The local paper hailed it as "the first attempt by an industry to inject democracy into the white-collar men's game of golf."

George Johnson died more than half a century ago and the Endicott-Johnson plant has been closed for decades, but that spirit of democracy lives on in the B.C. Open, a big-time event with small-town charm. Long ago, Lee Trevino described this event aptly when he said "Most tournaments on the Tour cater to two or three big guns. At the B.C., a rookie gets the same treatment as a star."

For the past several years, the B.C. has been played the same week as the British Open, and that's probably a good fit. With most of the top players plying their trade across the pond, the Tour's working class assembles in this region known as "The Valley of Opportunity" in hopes of gaining a high finish, a big paycheck, maybe even a victory.

Certainly this is a course that can induce confidence. Although it has undergone a couple of updates in the last twenty years, En-Joie remains a short par 72 of under 7,000 yards, with a quartet of reachable par fives and four of its par fours measuring less than 380.

One of those short fours is the first hole, but the birdies here are outnumbered by bogeys, as this green slopes precipitously toward the left side where a pond awaits. It's the first of ten holes at En-Joie where water comes into play.

Number seven may be the hole where the water is most menacing, as a large pond lies to

ABOVE (TOP TO BOTTOM): 2ND, 14TH, AND 15TH HOLES **OPPOSITE:** 1ST HOLE

18TH HOLE

the right of this par three, lapping at the very edge
of the green. There's a bail-out area to the left, but
up-and-downs from that side are difficult.

A similar challenge greets players on the tee of
14, a 212-yard par three where the water on the
right will give pause, but even more intimidating
is the out of bounds to the left. Even those who
hit this green will not be home free as a ridge
through the putting surface tosses shots both
ways and complicates all putts.

Number 15 has lost its shoe-shaped green but
this 432-yard par four still packs plenty of kick.
The tee shot calls for a long carry over water,
and the approach is the most demanding on the
course, with a pond in front, two bunkers, and a
severe drop-off to the rear.

Club selection is the key at the 17th hole, a
par three of 185 yards where the green is surrounded by numerous swales and bunkers. Those
who miss this green will have a tough time making par, but so will those who hit the green but
not the correct part of it, as this putting surface
is 150 feet long.

The final tee shot on most courses is a psycho-
logically demanding one, but at En-Joie it is
made doubly difficult by out of bounds and two
large ponds to the left. Adding to the beauty of
the ponds is a waterfall that connects them, with
the cascading waters very much in play. Once in
the fairway, however, players will have a birdie
opportunity on this 419-yard par four. In 2003,
50-year-old Craig Stadler made a birdie here on
Sunday for a 63 to cap a comeback from eight
strokes behind and gain his 13th victory on the
PGA Tour. A week earlier, he won his first tournament on the Champions Tour.

CRAIG STADLER, 2003 WINNER

SCORECARD

HOLE	PAR	YARDAGE
1	4	367
2	4	379
3	5	554
4	3	175
5	5	565
6	4	433
7	3	188
8	5	553
9	4	407
OUT	37	3621
10	4	356
11	4	441
12	5	545
13	4	442
14	3	212
15	4	432
16	4	321
17	3	185
18	4	419
IN	35	3353
TOTAL	72	6974

ONLY HERE

Initial Confusion: Originally this event was known as the Broome County Open, but the B.C. in the title does not stand for Broome County. The tournament is named in honor of Johnny Hart, an Endicott boy who is the cartoonist of the B.C. comic strip. The winner's trophy is a sculpture of the B.C. character in golf action.

Square Deals: This is one town where you can still get a hotel room for $50 and a nourishing meal for $10. Best of all, the weekday resident green fee at En-Joie is just $23, the lowest of any PGA Tour site.

PLAYING TIP

Know Your Own Strength

Although En-Joie is not a long course, distance is constantly a factor—carrying distance over water hazards and bunkers—and careful club selection is vital. That begins with an accurate knowledge of your capabilities with every club in the bag. Too many golfers have unrealistic notions about their own strength—they overestimate it for two reasons: 1) They assume that every shot will travel the distance of their best shot; 2) They think of distance as the total of flight and roll. As a result, most amateurs miss greens by leaving the ball short.

To avoid this mistake and hit more greens, spend an hour or so taking some accurate readings on your distances. The best way to do this is by hitting several practice shots with each club. As you play the shots, estimate the distance that the ball rolls. Disregard your best and worst shots, and then pace off the distance to the area where the average of the others finished. (Note: The pace of the average male is a bit shorter than a yard, so unless you're over six feet tall, take big steps.) This will give you the total distance, and when you subtract the roll of your shots, you will also know the carrying distance for each of your clubs. An accurate knowledge of your carrying distance is the key to smart club selection.

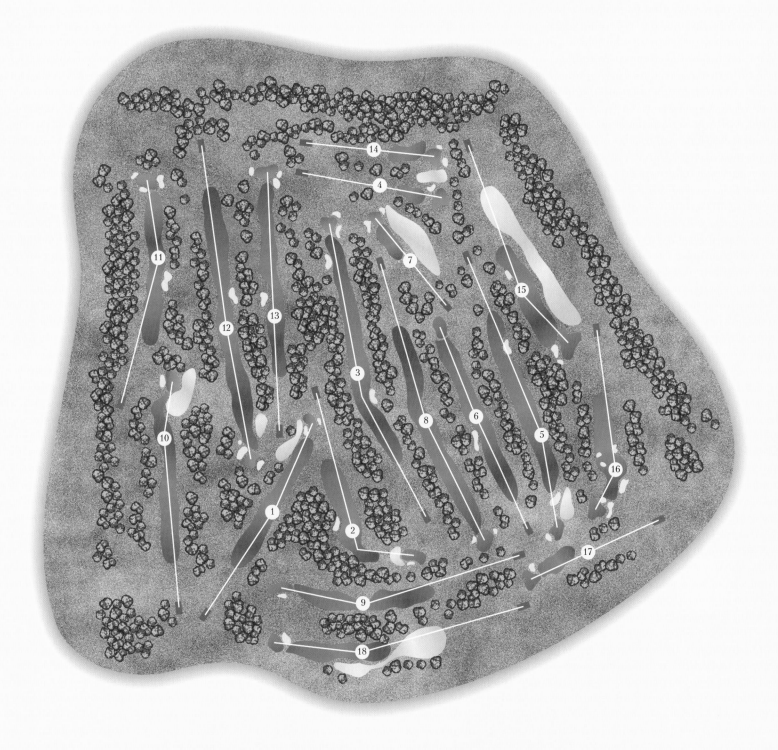

The event formerly known as the Greater Milwaukee Open is the Tour's version of the little engine that could. Against death-defying odds, it has not only survived but thrived for five decades.

Consider that over the past 20 years or so the costs of staging a Tour event have escalated exponentially. Then consider that this event is held on a public golf course in a less-than-major-market city and that it rarely has attracted more than one or two top-ten players. Yet year after year the GMO has managed to draw large crowds and raise hundreds of thousands of dollars for charity, even without a title sponsor. Then, in 2004, U.S. Bank came aboard to give the tournament a solid financial underpinning.

Maybe the tournament's success is a gather-ye-rosebuds thing, borne of the short Wisconsin playing season. Maybe it's that the PGA Tour show comes here only once a year. Whatever the reason, one thing is clear: Wisconsin fans love their golf and aren't afraid to show their support.

The GMO dates back to 1968 when Dave Stockton edged Sam Snead at the Northshore Country Club. Five years later the tournament shifted to the Tuckaway Country Club, where it remained until 1994 when tournament organizers took over Brown Deer Park, a public golf course in disrepair, and turned it into a test for the game's best players.

A test, but not a difficult test. A par 71 of just 6,759 yards, Brown Deer is a place where the pros crank up their birdie machines.

Interestingly, the tougher holes appear early, and in a true architectural oddity the first hole is the most difficult of all, a 461-yard par four that culminates in a heavily bunkered green. And there is little relief at the second hole, a dogleg left that calls for a drive through a chute of trees and over a fairway-crossing creek. From there, it's a long uphill approach to a narrow and undulating green.

Number four is a par five for the public but a four when the Tour comes to town, playing 485 downhill yards with the second shot crossing another creek. The creek is well short of the green and does not come into play unless the tee shot strays off the fairway. The rough on this course is among the thickest and gnarliest the Tour players see all year.

The last four holes allow players to finish like champions. Most of the field will go for the green at the 531-yard 15th, but its small and sloping surface will keep eagles to a minimum. Brown Deer was designed in the days of hand

1ST HOLE

mowing—well before the era of triple cutting and rolling—and as such its greens have some major humps and dips which, when shaved low, can provide for thrill-filled putting.

Holes 16 and 17 are short par fours with narrow fairways. The pros' preferred ploy here is a long iron or fairway metal from the tee, then a wedge to the green. At both holes, a forward pin is the toughest as a creek runs in front of 16 and a deep bunker shuts off the entrance to 17.

Eighteen, another reachable par five, calls for a strong and straight drive over a creek. Those who find Position A will have a good look at the green—but looking back at them will be a quintet of front bunkers, all but eliminating a run-on approach. Those who want to finish with an eagle will have to play a long second shot that flies high and lands softly.

16TH HOLE

4TH HOLE

18TH HOLE

SCORECARD

HOLE	PAR	YARDAGE
1	4	461
2	4	417
3	3	171
4	4	485
5	3	164
6	5	556
7	3	215
8	4	436
9	4	359
OUT	35	3250
10	4	461
11	3	196
12	4	381
13	4	437
14	3	188
15	5	531
16	4	371
17	4	387
18	5	557
IN	36	3509
TOTAL	71	6759

TIGER WOODS (ABOVE) MADE HIS PROFESSIONAL DEBUT IN MILWAUKEE IN 1996, HIGHLIGHTED BY A HOLE-IN-ONE. STEVE STRICKER **(MIDDLE)** AND JERRY KELLY **(RIGHT)** ARE WISCONSIN NATIVES WHO HAVE COME CLOSE TO WINNING.

ONLY HERE

Cheeseheads: Despite a climate inhospitable to golf, Wisconsin claims five pros who make their living playing the PGA Tour—Jerry Kelly, Steve Stricker, Mark Wilson, Skip Kendall, and J.P. Hayes—and all five are loyal supporters of the GMO. Kelly is on record as saying that he would be as happy to win the GMO as he would to claim a major championship. To date, no home-state boy has done the deed, though Kelly and Stricker have finished second.

Low Scores: The GMO has been a hotbed for low scoring since the tournament moved to Brown Deer in 1994. The winning score has yet to exceed 269. No 72-hole Tour event where par is at least 71 has had a longer streak where the winning aggregate was sub-270.

Veterans: With most of the prime-timers skipping the GMO, this has been a haven for experienced players trying to sneak in a late-career victory. Six of the last eight winners through 2003 have been over the age of 40.

PLAYING TIP

How to Read the Rough

Courses with rough as thick as that at Brown Deer require you to have a combination of firmness and finesse. Usually, a strong swing will be needed to extricate the ball, but even more important is an ability to read the lie. All fairway lies are fairly similar, but no two rough lies are alike.

Fundamentally, there are three kinds, which we'll call the flicker, the flyer, and the floater. The flicker is a ball that is perched on top of the grass—a lie that is almost too good. You can't bash down on it as you would most rough lies because your club will slide under the ball, producing a high, weak shot, maybe even a whiff. Instead, the key is to make a driver-like swing, with a long, low takeaway. This will help you to hit the ball on a shallow angle of attack, flicking it cleanly off its perch.

The most common lie in rough is a flyer, where the ball sits down in two- to four-inch grass. You can get the club on it easily enough, but not without allowing some grass to come between your clubface and the ball. That means you'll hit a shot with less backspin—a ball that will fly higher, bounce more actively, and roll farther than a shot from the fairway. In these situations, take at least one club less than you would from the fairway, and play the ball a bit farther back in your stance to encourage a downward impact that will minimize intervention of the grass.

The floater is a ball that sits well down in deep rough. Your only option here is to take your wedge and cut your losses by slashing the ball out as best you can, using much the same technique you'd use on a sand shot. Don't try for too much distance, because the ball will not jump out of this lie, but will float lazily.

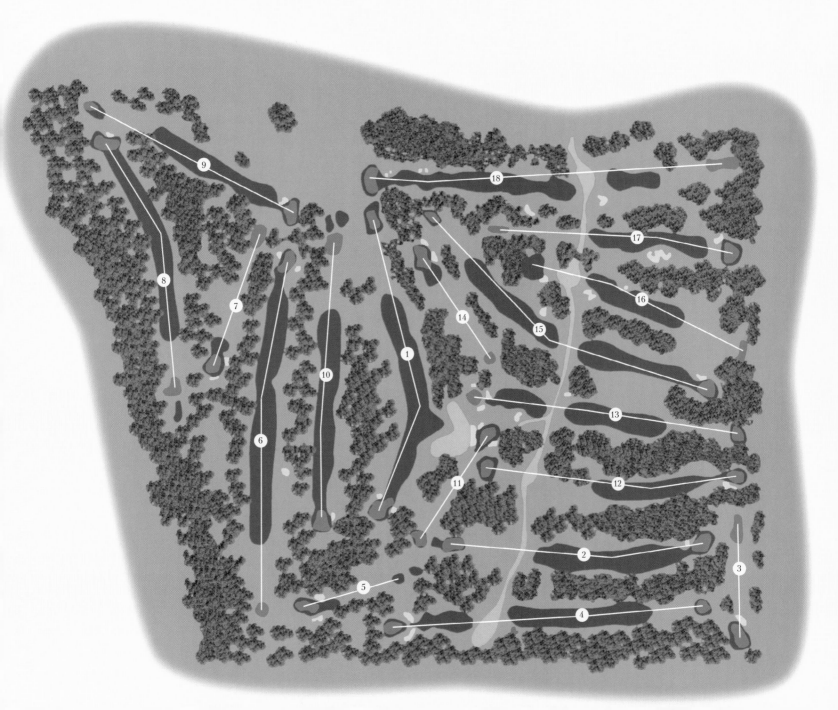

16TH HOLE

13TH HOLE

Should you ever have an urgent need to converse with PGA Tour Commissioner Tim Finchem, here's how to do it. Call the Tour headquarters, ask to speak to the Commissioner, and when they say "Who's calling, please?" say it's Roger Adams.

Roger Adams is the General Manager of the Buick Division of General Motors. That makes him Tim Finchem's biggest customer, the guy whose phone call the Commish will always take.

With the addition last year of the Buick Championship (formerly the Greater Hartford Open), Buick now has its own grand slam of events (the other three are the Buick Invitational in California, the Buick Classic in New York,

and this event, the Buick Open, in the backyard of the company's Detroit headquarters). Collectively, their purses total nearly $20 million. And as if that's not enough to command the collective attention of America's golfers, consider that the company's spokesman-in-chief is Tiger Woods.

Buick is not only the largest sponsor on the Tour, it is the longest standing. The first Buick Open Invitational took place in 1958. With $9,000 and a new car going to the winner, it was the richest tournament on the Tour. Billy Casper claimed the prize, his three-under-par 285 total at Warwick Hills Country Club edging Arnold Palmer by a stroke.

Today, the venue for the Buick Open is still Warwick Hills, but these days a score of 285 won't crack the top 50 (although it will still earn about $10,000). When it debuted, this course was described by Sam Snead as "just a long walk." It was in fact the longest walk on Tour, at 7,280 yards. Then architect Joe Lee came in and made some changes. The result is that this is surely the only course on the Tour that is shorter now than it was a quarter-century ago. Not surprisingly, the pros tend to tear it up, with an average winning score over the last decade of 269—19 under par.

But power alone will not get the job done here. With most of the par fours and fives bend-

15TH HOLE

ABOVE (TOP TO BOTTOM): 17TH AND 18TH HOLES **RIGHT:** 17TH HOLE

ing slightly left or right, accuracy from the tee is paramount, and although the big, sloping greens (averaging 7,000 square feet) are easy enough to hit, two-putting from one hundred feet or more is never an easy assignment.

Hole number one is a good indication of things to come, a reachable (567-yard) par five, especially when there's a tailwind. But four bunkers narrow the landing area, there's out of bounds on the left, and this green is multi-tiered and 150 feet long. Many players hit the green in two, only to three-putt for par.

Holes two and three are the toughest back-to-back holes on the course. Number two plays 431 yards through a tight corridor with overhanging trees on both sides and more OB to the left. The green, guarded on the left by a large bunker, slopes steeply from back to front, so those who overshoot will have their hands full saving par. The third hole, at 187 yards, is the shortest of the par threes but it is also the most difficult, partly because it plays into the prevailing wind and partly because of the three large bunkers that hug its green, another target with a steep back-to-front cant.

The fun—and the low scoring—truly begins on the back nine, specifically at holes 12 and 14, a pair of short par fours—340 and 322 yards, respectively. Under the assault of today's cannons, both of them are driveable, and in contrast to the modern version of the short four—fraught with peril—these holes offer little in the way of intimidation. Those who don't go for the large, forgiving greens in one will wedge close for birdie putts.

However, birdies will be scarce at 15, traditionally the most difficult hole at Warwick Hills.

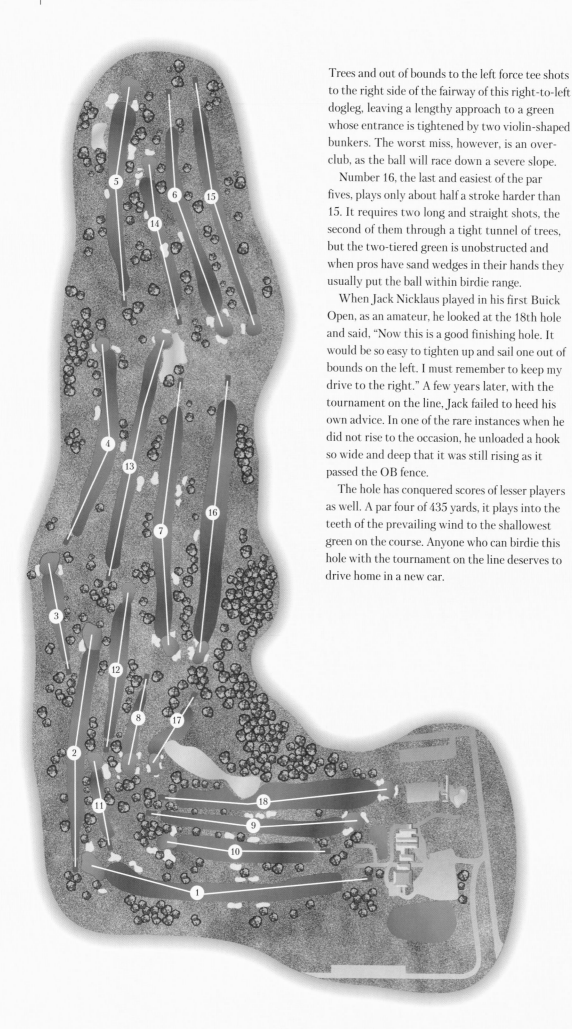

Trees and out of bounds to the left force tee shots to the right side of the fairway of this right-to-left dogleg, leaving a lengthy approach to a green whose entrance is tightened by two violin-shaped bunkers. The worst miss, however, is an over-club, as the ball will race down a severe slope.

Number 16, the last and easiest of the par fives, plays only about half a stroke harder than 15. It requires two long and straight shots, the second of them through a tight tunnel of trees, but the two-tiered green is unobstructed and when pros have sand wedges in their hands they usually put the ball within birdie range.

When Jack Nicklaus played in his first Buick Open, as an amateur, he looked at the 18th hole and said, "Now this is a good finishing hole. It would be so easy to tighten up and sail one out of bounds on the left. I must remember to keep my drive to the right." A few years later, with the tournament on the line, Jack failed to heed his own advice. In one of the rare instances when he did not rise to the occasion, he unloaded a hook so wide and deep that it was still rising as it passed the OB fence.

The hole has conquered scores of lesser players as well. A par four of 435 yards, it plays into the teeth of the prevailing wind to the shallowest green on the course. Anyone who can birdie this hole with the tournament on the line deserves to drive home in a new car.

SCORECARD

HOLE	PAR	YARDAGE
1	5	567
2	4	431
3	3	187
4	4	401
5	4	437
6	4	421
7	5	584
8	3	199
9	4	434
OUT	36	3661
10	4	401
11	3	190
12	4	340
13	5	544
14	4	322
15	4	457
16	5	580
17	3	197
18	4	435
IN	36	3466
TOTAL	72	7127

ONLY HERE

Tiger Watch: Since this is Buick's flagship event, and he's their main man, Tiger Woods often plays here even though it is played the week before a major, the PGA Championship.

Weak Defenses: The only player to win back-to-back titles here has been the late Tony Lema in 1964 and 1965.

Wire-to-wirelessness: The only player to take the lead outright in round one and hold it through all four rounds is Julius Boros in 1963, who kept his hot hand the following week for a victory in the U.S. Open.

PLAYING TIP

Two Ways to Beat a Hook
Out of bounds haunts the left side of several holes at Warwick Hills, including the tension-filled first and 18th, where even the best players can get a bit quick and hit a snap hook. If you're one of those people, here are a couple of quick set-up changes that will give you some anti-hook insurance.

Number one, tee your ball at the extreme left side of the tee box. This will put the out of bounds more at your back and will encourage you to direct your tee shot to the right side of the fairway, away from the trouble. That way, even if you do hook the ball, you'll have a cushion.

Second, tighten your grip pressure at address, especially in the last three fingers of your left hand, and maintain that firm pressure throughout your swing. With a firmer grip pressure, you'll be less likely to turn your right hand over your left as you swing through impact, a major cause of a hook.

TONY LEMA IS THE BUICK OPEN'S ONLY BACK-TO-BACK WINNER.

JIM FURYK, 2003 WINNER

It's the only event of the year where the highest score wins. The only event with a cut on Saturday. And the only event where par counts for nothing. Welcome to The International, the most distinctive tournament on the PGA Tour.

It started with millionaire businessman Jack Vickers and his desire to make his mark on professional golf. He began by purchasing a 5,000-acre tract near Castle Rock, Colorado, about half an hour and 1,000 feet above Denver. Step two was to hire Jack Nicklaus as his architect, with carte blanche instructions to produce a world-

class course. And the final ingredient—the element that has separated this event from all others on the Tour—was its format. The International is a 72-hole event based upon a variation of the Stableford scoring system, with points awarded in relation to par: A par is worth zero, but a birdie adds two points, an eagle adds five, and the rare double eagle is worth eight points. On the minus side, a bogey means one point off and a double bogey or worse brings a loss of three points.

For the first seven years of The International, each new round was a tournament in itself—the

previous day's points were erased and everyone began the next day from scratch. In 1993, however, the format was changed and now points are accumulated over the four days. After round two, the 144-man field is cut to the low 70 and ties and after the third round a second cut pares the field to the low 36 and ties. Originally, the field was cut to an exact number each day, with ties resolved by playoffs, but that was changed in 1998.

Nicklaus predicted the scoring system, with birdies more than canceling out bogeys, would breed aggressive golf. "In playing for points

ABOVE: 10TH HOLE **OPPOSITE:** 12TH HOLE **BELOW:** 14TH HOLE

OPPOSITE: 15TH HOLE **ABOVE:** 18TH HOLE

rather than protecting a score, a player is forced to attack the course more than usual." But Jack also helped to fulfill his prophesy by creating a course—and especially a series of closing holes— where players brave enough to take a risk, and talented enough to pull it off, will be rewarded.

At 7,559 yards, Castle Pines is the longest golf course on the Tour and it begins with a par five of 644 yards. But that number is deceiving. First of all, the hole plays steeply downhill for more than one hundred feet and secondly this is mile-high country—where the ball flies about 15 percent farther than at sea level—and thus the actual "playing" distance is about 550 yards. The truth is that the longer hitters get home in two here with middle irons.

That hole, in its contour as well as its length, sets the tone for this course where elevation change is a constant in the fairways, in the swooping collection areas near the greens, and in the putting surfaces, many of which have multiple tiers. Although no stats are kept on this course, the hardest hole is probably number five, uphill for all 477 of its yards, with bunkers menacing both the drive and the approach and a deep swale fronting the green.

The back nine begins similarly to the front, with a dramatically downhill hole, but this one is a par four that *Golf Digest* has called one of America's best 18 holes. Doglegging right through deep stands of pine and oak, it's reminiscent of the 10th hole at Augusta, except that it's even more difficult, with a pond protecting the right-front of the green. Nicklaus meant it to be a par five, but Vickers convinced him to convert it to a four. It's also a scenic hole, with Pike's Peak visible in the background.

It's downhill again at number 14, another reachable 600-yarder to a wide green. Coming down the stretch, this is where players expect to start putting some serious points on the board. Birdies will be a bit tougher to come by at the 15th, a tree-lined dogleg-right par four with a pond lapping at the right side of the green and three bunkers to the left. When the pin is cut near the water, it's just as easy for a player to lose three points with a double bogey as to add two with a birdie.

The most feared hole on the way in is number 16, a par three of 209 yards. The green is three-tiered, fast, and even some tee shots that find its surface will feed back into a deep, steep-faced collection bunker at the front. From there, saving par is just short of a miracle.

But the centerpiece of every International, the thriller hole on which the outcome invariably turns, is unquestionably number 17, a dogleg par five of just 492 yards. It plays uphill, but remember, this is Denver, so any pro who can find the narrow, canted fairway with his drive will be rewarded with a middle iron—maybe even a short iron—to the green. This is one hole where players step to the tee expecting a birdie and hoping for an eagle—but with a gauntlet of pines,

rock outcroppings, deep rough, and a trio of bunkers at the green, this hole also tags the players for its share of bogeys and worse.

Eighteen is 480 yards and uphill, but with the altitude long hitters can get home with a short iron if their drive avoids a series of bunkers on the left.

The unique format and tease-and-taunt aspects of the golf course have combined to produce consistently interesting, usually dramatic finishes at The International, but never has there been a more exhilarating stretch run than the one staged in 2002 by Steve Lowery. He was eight points behind with four holes to go when he sank a 127-yard wedge shot at 15 for an eagle and five points. A bogey and a one-point loss followed at

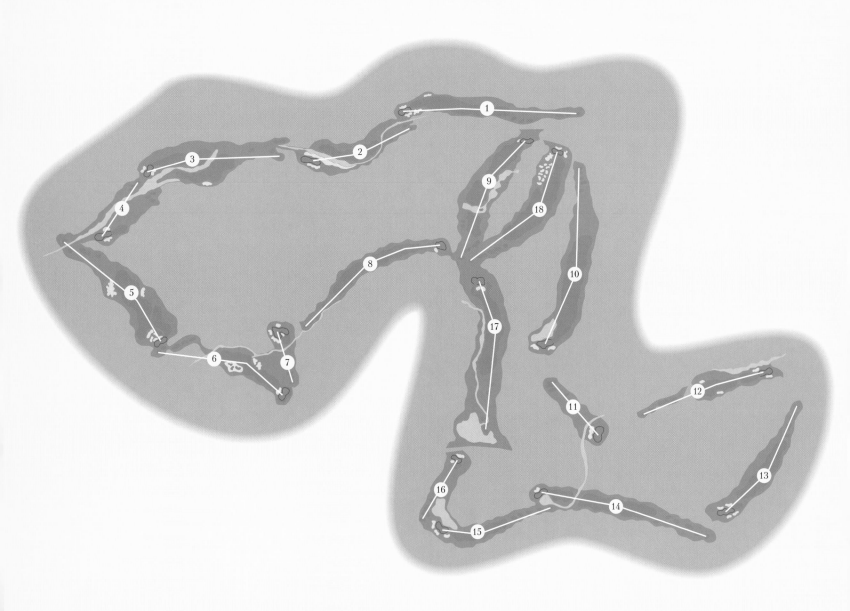

16, but then at the 17th, he holed his 6-iron second shot from 190 yards for a double eagle. Eight points, and suddenly, with one hole to go he was just one behind leader Rich Beem, who had eagled the 17th. At 18, Lowery stuck his approach shot within 12 feet of the hole, and made a good putt, but the ball stopped on the lip of the cup.

On the other hand, the format also occasionally backfires, as in 2003 when Davis Love made three eagles in round two and staked himself to a double-digit lead that made the last two days about as exciting as a one-horse race.

ONLY HERE

Ultimate Milkshakes: Any player will tell you, the best milkshakes on Tour are found in the clubhouse at the International. Thick, creamy, and made with Häagen-Dazs ice cream, they add several feet to the collective waistline of the Tour. Members of the press also get to indulge, but sadly, the shakes aren't available to spectators.

Shortness of Breath: Castle Pines sits at an elevation of 6,290 feet, where the air is thin and breathing can become labored, especially after climbing the hill at number five or 17.

Pristine Condition: Except for Augusta National, Castle Pines is probably the most exclusive club on the Tour, with 350 members, most of whom don't live within the immediate area. As such it gets very little play, which means these are some of the fairest fairways and greens the pros see all year.

Foreign Flags: True to its name, this event has a diverse field of players from around the world.

PLAYING TIP

Into Thin Air

There's one thing the pros deal with at Castle Pines and nowhere else on Tour—mile-high air. This adds some complication to their course management, because in the Rockies, the ball flies appreciably farther than at sea level.

How much farther? It's not a matter of yards, it's a percentage. The higher you are in elevation, the greater percentage you should add to your shots. Also, you should expect the percentage to be greater on your high-flying shots than on the clubs that produce a lower, more boring trajectory. At Castle Pines, the increase is generally agreed to be 10 to 15 percent. Thus, if you normally hit a 5-iron 160 yards, expect to hit up to 184. Your 250-yard drive probably won't go the full 15 percent, but don't be surprised if you pick up at least 25 yards.

It takes a bit of experience to determine how your shots will react, but you can be sure of one thing—everyone picks up power in Denver.

SCORECARD

HOLE	PAR	YARDAGE
1	5	644
2	4	408
3	4	462
4	3	205
5	4	477
6	4	417
7	3	185
8	5	535
9	4	458
OUT	36	3791
10	4	485
11	3	197
12	4	440
13	4	439
14	5	623
15	4	403
16	3	209
17	5	492
18	4	480
IN	36	3768
TOTAL	72	7559

RICH BEEM, 2002 WINNER

3RD HOLE

9TH HOLE

The WGC-NEC Invitational is among the youngest and least defined events on the PGA Tour, but it is contested on one of the oldest and most familiar courses.

Those six initials bear some explaining. WGC stands for World Golf Championships. This is one of four international events which debuted in 1999 under the joint auspices of six pro tours—the PGA Tour, Asian PGA, European Tour, Japan Golf Tour, PGA Tour of Australasia, and Southern Africa Tour. NEC is the computer company that sponsors this event.

As the more straightforward part of its title—invitational—implies, this is a limited-field event—but not that limited—with the criteria for eligibility as follows:

1) Playing members of the last named United States and International Presidents Cup teams.

2) Playing members of the last named United States and European Ryder Cup teams.

3) If not otherwise eligible, players ranked among the top 50, including any players tied for 50th place, on the Official World Golf Ranking as of Monday of tournament week.

4) If not otherwise eligible, tournament winners of worldwide events since the prior year's WGC-NEC Invitational with an Official World Golf Ranking Strength of Field Rating of 100 points or more.

5) If not otherwise eligible, the winner of one selected tournament from each of the following tours: Australasian Tour, Southern Africa Tour, Asian PGA, and Japan Golf Tour.

What needs no introduction for serious golfers is the venue for this event. The South Course at Firestone Country Club in Akron, Ohio, has been hosting professional tournaments for more than half a century. When Akron's Harvey Firestone opened the course in 1929, pro golf was the furthest thing from his mind. He simply wanted a recreational facility for the employees of his Firestone Tire and Rubber Company. But the course was strong enough that, in 1954, it played host to the first Rubber City Open, won by Tommy Bolt on a score of 265—23 under par.

Five years later, the course was selected to host the PGA Championship, and architect Robert Trent Jones was summoned to toughen it up a bit.

LEFT (TOP TO BOTTOM): 13TH, 14TH, 15TH, AND 18TH HOLES
ABOVE: 16TH HOLE

The result was major surgery: He built 50 new bunkers, added two ponds, doubled the size of the greens, and stretched the rubber man's course to nearly 7,200 yards while reducing the par from 72 to 70. That PGA was won by Jay Hebert with a score of 281—one over par.

During the '60s and '70s Firestone hosted an average of more than two professional events per year—two PGA Championships, 14 American Golf Classics, eight CBS Golf Classics, and 18 editions of the World Series of Golf. In 1966, the latter event launched what the press now refers to as the "silly season" by bringing together the winners of the year's four major championships for an unofficial event. In 1976, the World Series expanded its field and became an official event. Twenty-three years later the WGC tournament replaced it. The result of all this exposure is that Firestone South is among the most recognizable tournament venues in the world, not to mention one of the most difficult.

Critics say the course is monotonous and bereft of charm. Virtually all of its fairways run parallel to one another, and few of the par threes and fours call for an approach with anything shorter than a middle iron—at least they didn't until the driving distance explosion of the last decade. Subtlety is not the long suit at Firestone. However, the course has the near-unanimous admiration of the Tour players, who see it as a supremely honest, straightforward examination of their skills. Furthermore, if the object of a championship course is to identify the best players, Firestone has succeeded. Jack Nicklaus won seven events here, and in the first three stagings of the WGC-NEC Invitational, the victor was Tiger Woods.

The front nine features a string of holes that perhaps only Jack and Tiger could love. The stretch from holes three to nine includes five par fours averaging 464 yards and two "short holes" of 200 and 219 yards. The biggest brute comes at the end—number nine is a par four that runs 484 yards back toward the clubhouse, culminating at a green ringed by bunkers. The length of this par-35 front nine—3,633 yards—adds wonder to the accomplishment of Jose Maria Olazabal who in 1990 opened the tournament with five straight 3s—birdie, eagle, birdie, birdie, par—and went on to shoot a course-record 61. After that he strung together three 67s, setting records after each round and winning by a phenomenal 12 strokes.

Another gauntlet of bruisers forms the finishing stretch, starting with the 471-yard 13th, a rightward dogleg where the drive must find safe haven between sand on the left and a large, grasp-ing oak on the right. The approach is to an elevated green with more bunkers right and left and deep rough beyond.

A new tee at the 14th hole has lengthened this par four by 30 yards and brought the drive-zone bunkers back into play while adding length to the shot to one of the shallowest greens on the course. Then it's another of Firestone's long short holes, 221-yard number 15 where the narrow green is bunkered tightly on both sides.

But the signature hole on this course surely is 16, recently armed with a new championship tee that has stretched it to 667 yards, the longest hole on the PGA Tour. Granted it plays downwind from an elevated tee, but on most days for most members of the human race—Tour players included—this is a three-shot par five, and all three shots had better be good ones. Trees impinge on both the drive and second shot, and the right two-thirds of the green is fronted by a 50-yard pond. On Sunday, the pin is usually located up front, just beyond the water. Should a player's second shot stray into the rough, getting the ball close on that third shot over water becomes a very tall assignment.

In the 1975 PGA Championship, Jack Nicklaus made one of the best fives of his life here. After hitting his tee shot into trees on the left, he took a penalty drop, and then hit his third shot into trees on the right. From there he played a gargantuan 8-iron over the tops of the trees and over the water to within 20 feet of the pin. He sank the putt for par and went on to win.

Somewhat less heroic—but no less inventive—was the par made by Lon Hinkle in the final round of the 1979 World Series. After pushing his second shot into those same trees Nicklaus found, Hinkle did not have the option of lofting over them, and the pond prevented a low shot—or so it seemed. Hinkle closed the face of his iron, took the club back low, and punched the ball straight at the surface of the water. It skipped once, twice, and

hopped up the bank and onto the green. He made his par and went on to win the tournament.

One last behemoth of a par four is saved for the finish. Eighteen plays 464 tree-lined yards, slightly downhill, while turning softly to the left. The better side of the fairway is the right, but two bunkers there caution against too aggressive a drive. The green, which was once enormous, is now medium-large, surrounded by bunkers, and nestled into an amphitheater.

Hundred-foot putts are not uncommon here, and neither are three-putts, but the hole is probably best remembered for the "shot in the dark" played in 2000 by Tiger Woods. Due to a lengthy rain delay, the sun had set by the time the last two competitors—Woods and Hal Sutton—reached 18, but with Tiger holding an eight-stroke lead, they decided to finish. Woods put an exclamation point on his week by striking his final approach shot within two feet of the hole to ice the second of his three victories in this event.

ONLY HERE

Repairing: Since the field is limited, playing partners and tee times for round two are determined by first-round scores, as opposed to most events where the players tee off in the same threesomes on Thursday and Friday.

No Cut: The players have earned their way into this event, and they aren't about to be dismissed early—everyone stays at least four days, and even the last-place finisher goes home on Sunday with at least $20,000.

Utility Woods: Long par fours, thick rough, raised, well-protected greens—it all adds up to the need for high, soft-landing shots, which means several pros will drop their 2-irons in favor of high-lofted woods.

Foreign Conquerors: The international aspect of this event and the preceding World Series is well reflected in its list of champions, which includes Nick Price, Greg Norman, David Frost, Denis Watson, Fulton Allem, Jose Maria Olazabal, Craig Parry, and Darren Clarke.

PLAYING TIP

Fairway Metals Made Easy

On a brutally long course such as Firestone, even the pros sometimes have to haul out their fairway metal clubs. For amateurs, of course, these clubs see duty every day.

Modern technology has made these clubs easier to hit, as the graphite shaft and lower center of gravity eases the golfer's task of getting the ball airborne. At the same time, the high-lofted woods and trouble clubs have become popular for their ability to extricate the ball from thick rough and bunkers.

When playing from the fairway with the steeper-faced club you should use essentially the same swing as with your driver, a one-piece takeaway that keeps the club low to the ground going back, low coming into impact. However, for shots from the rough with the more lofted metal woods, a slightly different technique is required. This time you need an impact that is closer in nature to a middle iron, a more downward hit on the ball. To pre-program that kind of hit, position the ball a bit farther back in your stance, and if you're in thick rough, a bit closer to your body as well. These changes will set you up for a more vertical impact that will gouge the ball out of a difficult lie.

SCORECARD

HOLE	PAR	YARDAGE
1	4	399
2	5	497
3	4	442
4	4	471
5	3	200
6	4	469
7	3	219
8	4	452
9	4	484
OUT	35	3633
10	4	410
11	4	370
12	3	180
13	4	471
14	4	467
15	3	221
16	5	667
17	4	400
18	4	464
IN	35	3650
TOTAL	70	7283

TIGER WOODS, THREE-TIME WINNER

ABOVE (TOP TO BOTTOM): 7TH AND 8TH HOLES **OPPOSITE:** 16TH HOLE

During the same four days that the game's elite battle for a million-dollar first prize in Ohio (at the WGC-NEC Invitational) the rank-and-file ply their trade a bit less flamboyantly at the Reno-Tahoe Open. One of the Tour's most recent additions, this event has been on the calendar since 1999, but the folks in the Nevada foothills have embraced it enthusiastically—as well they should. After all, the only other premier sporting events hereabouts are the Reno Air Races and the Reno Rodeo.

The course is only one year older than the tournament, but its designer, Jack Nicklaus, says it will go down as one of the four or five best courses he has ever done. Not an idle claim when you consider that the Golden Bear is approaching his 200th design. When it opened in 1998, Montreux was named by *Golf Digest* as one of the "Best New Private Courses" of the year.

It sits in Nevada's Galena Forest, some of its narrow fairways framed by tall pines and others set in the high desert. As befits an area known for casino gambling, the layout offers plenty of opportunities for risk and reward, including two driveable par fours, the first of them coming at hole number five (number 14 as the members know it, since the nines are reversed for the tournament). Three hundred and sixty-seven yards from the pro tee, it plays slightly downhill and usually downwind to a long but narrow green that falls off on all sides. A gentle fade—powerfully struck—is the only way to hit and hold this surface.

No one will be driving the next hole, a par four of 439 yards that is one of the most demanding assignments on the course. The tight driving area is guarded on the right by pine trees and on the left by two large bunkers. The approach must favor the left side of the green or the ball will spin off into a chipping area from which an up-and-down will require some artistry.

Nicklaus's design at number eight brings to mind perhaps his most heralded hole, the 14th at Muirfield Village, except that this hole is roughly one hundred yards longer. The drive is played from a promontory 138 feet above the fairway and the ribbon of a green sits hard by Galena Creek with a deep bunker on each side.

The stretch run begins at the Bear Trap, a dramatic trio of holes 15, 16, and 17, featuring shimmering lakes, breathtaking mountain views, and

undulating greens. Fifteen is the most heavily treed on the course, a 477-yard right-to-left par four that calls for a tee shot down the right side to take advantage of the sloping fairway. The approach to this sloping green must avoid a left-side bunker that is extremely deep.

Sixteen is the shortest hole on the course, but with a carry over water to a narrow, shallow target bisected by a ridge, club selection is critical. There's room on the right half of the green, but the Sunday hole location is usually tucked in the left-hand corner, beneath a canopy of pines and just beyond a nasty pot bunker.

The longest and straightest hole at Montreux is 636-yard number 17, but accuracy is as important here as distance. The tee shot must avoid a lake to the left of the fairway. Despite its length, the hole is reachable, especially with the prevailing wind, but peril awaits greenside in the form of a cavernous right-hand bunker.

Strategy comes heavily into play at the home hole, a par four of 429 yards. A shorter club off the tee will avoid the large fairway bunker that lurks on the right, while long hitters who take the driver have a chance to carry that bunker—roughly 280 yards out. The second shot is to a hogbacked green with bunkers front-right and back-left. The green was designed in an amphitheater setting in the hope of someday attracting a major championship. In the minds of the Reno-Tahoe folks, that mission is already accomplished.

9TH HOLE

KIRK TRIPLETT, 2003 WINNER, ON THE 18TH HOLE

ONLY HERE

Big Game: Among the frequent visitors to this course are mountain lions and bears.

Big Names: Among the members of this club are PGA Tour pro Scott McCarron and LPGA stars Annika Sorenstam and Patty Sheehan. Sheehan also designed a 160-yard par three that is part of the practice facilities.

A Twin: Montreux is generally regarded as the finest course in Nevada. Six thousand miles to the East, in the town of Evian, is the course generally regarded as the best in Switzerland. Its name: Montreux.

PLAYING TIP

Escaping from a Pot

If you miss enough greens at Montreux, you'll eventually find yourself in a pot bunker. Although associated with the links courses of the British Isles, these insidious little sand-filled caves are becoming more and more common in the U.S., so it pays to know how to handle them.

The first advice is to take your medicine—don't try for a heroic shot of any appreciable distance. Just be sure to get your ball back in play. In the most severe cases, when you have a high lip in front of you, the best move may be to play out to the side, or even back toward the tee, rather than risking failure to clear the lip.

Assuming you have a reasonable lie, play the ball from a wide-open stance, and build some extra loft into your sand wedge (or ideally, lofted wedge) by opening the blade and laying it back so that the clubface at address is parallel to the surface of the sand. The swing should be an up-and-down chopping motion, beginning with an early cocking of the wrists. Hit down sharply about an inch behind the ball—give it plenty of force—and be sure to finish the swing. If you "quit" on this shot, you'll have to hit it again.

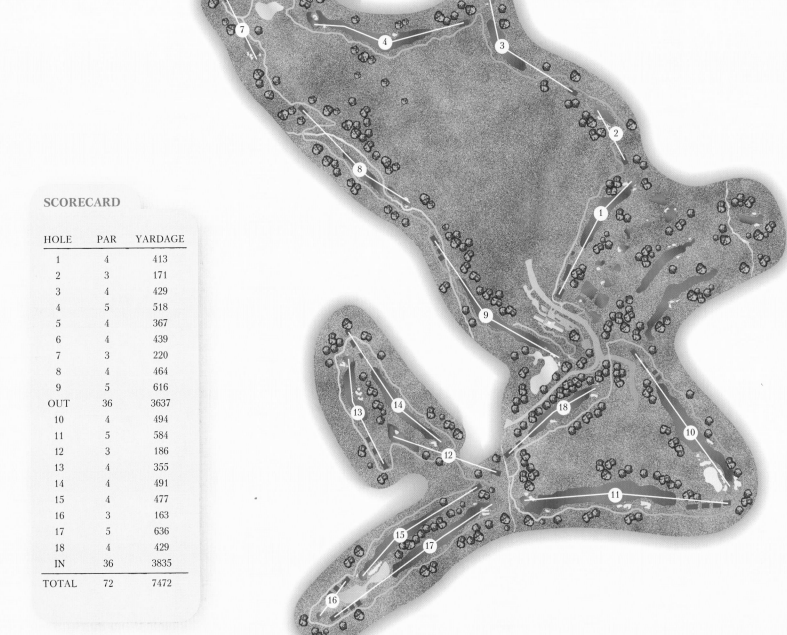

SCORECARD

HOLE	PAR	YARDAGE
1	4	413
2	3	171
3	4	429
4	5	518
5	4	367
6	4	439
7	3	220
8	4	464
9	5	616
OUT	36	3637
10	4	494
11	5	584
12	3	186
13	4	355
14	4	491
15	4	477
16	3	163
17	5	636
18	4	429
IN	36	3835
TOTAL	72	7472

1ST HOLE

4TH HOLE

Imagine a capacity crowd at a major league ball-park—say 50,000 or so fans. Now imagine them transported to a golf course. Now imagine them all on the same hole. That's what happens on Sunday at the Buick Championship.

This is New England's single biggest sporting event, and when the final pairing walks up the amphitheater 18th hole, it can seem as if the entire state of Connecticut has turned out to welcome them. Ask Peter Jacobsen, who won here in 1984—the first time the tournament was played at this course—and won again 19 years later in 2003. "The roar of the crowd on that hole," he says, "is unlike any other noise in golf."

The TPC at River Highlands is the third name and the third iteration for the golf course 15 miles south of the state capitol in Hartford. In the beginning there was Edgewood, a flat and relatively featureless course designed in 1928 by a cousin of famed golf course architect Donald Ross. Then came the original TPC of Connecticut, a half-revamp by Pete Dye, who created a modern target-style course on the back nine while making few major changes to the front. When it opened, critics called it Jekyll and Hyde Country Club. So six years later the PGA Tour stepped in, bought 52 acres of adjoining property, and changed virtually every hole. A Tour designer with the unlikely name Bobby Weed did the

15TH HOLE

transformation, fashioning seven new holes, adding two lakes and 80 bunkers, and lengthening the course while at the same time reducing its par from 71 to 70. Even the name changed—to the TPC at River Highlands—to reflect the dramatic tract of land on which the new holes are routed, a ridge that runs 70 feet above the Connecticut River. The result is a nouveau old-style layout, many of its rolling fairways lined with trees and many of its smallish greens raised and contoured in the mode of Donald Ross.

The 434-yard first hole plays downhill from the backyard of a New England-style white clap-

board clubhouse. The tee shot is to a swooping valley with the approach back uphill to an undulating green bisected by a ridge. Par here is a good start, even for the pros.

The toughest test on the front side is probably number four (which used to be the 15th hole on the Dye version of the course), a rightward-bending dogleg of 460 yards, with bunkers at both the drive zone and the green. When there's any kind of a wind, this severely sloped surface can be very difficult to hit and hold.

At number 10, the aiming point is just to the right of a lone tree on the left side of the fairway,

roughly 275 yards from the tee. Those who can thread their drives between the tree and two bunkers to the right will have a middle iron left to a crowned green that rejects shots not hit to the proper spot.

This event typically produces a dramatic finish, and the reason is holes 15, 16, and 17, which are plotted diabolically around a four-acre lake. Number 15 is a gem. Just 296 yards long, it tempts every player in the field to go for its green. But facing the lake on the left, bunkers to the right, and a raised putting surface with more humps than a herd of camels, all but the bravest

17TH HOLE

lay up, leaving a wedge to the green. In the final round in 1995, Greg Norman went for broke and missed the green, finding one of the bunkers instead. The shot he left himself was a tough one, with the lake staring him in the face, but Norman not only got his ball out and on, he holed it for eagle and went on to victory.

Sixteen is 171 yards, but most of them are over the lake, and for those who take plenty of club, bunkers await at the rear. When the pin is up front, as it invariably is on Sunday, this tee shot is the biggest test of the day.

The view from the elevated tee of number 17 is a daunting one, with a hillside of rough and bunkers to the left, water all the way down the right and what appears to be just a sliver of fairway between. Those who land safely will then face a short-iron shot across the water to a bulk-headed green. It's a tough shot from the fairway, a daring one from the rough or sand.

After those three water-bound holes, number 18 comes as something of an anticlimax, a straight, slightly uphill mid-length par four. Fairway bunkers right and left add some interest to the drive, and the approach must avoid a swale to the left of the green and more sand to the right.

During tournament week, however, the real pressure on this hole comes from those thousands of spectators assembled on the shouldering hills.

18TH HOLE

PETER JACOBSEN, 1984 AND 2003 WINNER

ONLY HERE

Tight Finishes: From 1983 to 2003, 14 of 21 tournaments were decided by one shot or a playoff, and only two by more than two shots.

TV Time: The headquarters of ESPN is in Bristol, Connecticut, not far away, and on Tuesday night of tournament week they throw a party, allowing the pros and their families to go into the studio and do interviews and promos with the on-air talent.

PLAYING TIP

Hitting it High

As with many stadium courses, a key to playing well at River Highlands is the ability to hit high, soft shots. For most players, however, this does not require a big adjustment. Simply take your address so that the ball is positioned a bit forward of its normal place in your stance. If you usually play it off your left heel, set up so it's off your left instep. This should insure that you make contact with the ball just as your club begins its ascent into the finish, so the clubface will have a few degrees of extra loft. If this doesn't do the trick, try distributing your weight more on your right foot at address, and keeping it there throughout the swing. Think of staying "behind the ball" through impact. Stay back and let your hands slip through the ball—that will give your shot plenty of loft.

SCORECARD

HOLE	PAR	YARDAGE
1	4	434
2	4	341
3	4	431
4	4	460
5	3	223
6	5	574
7	4	443
8	3	202
9	4	406
OUT	35	3514
10	4	462
11	3	158
12	4	411
13	5	523
14	4	421
15	4	296
16	3	171
17	4	420
18	4	444
IN	35	3306
TOTAL	70	6820

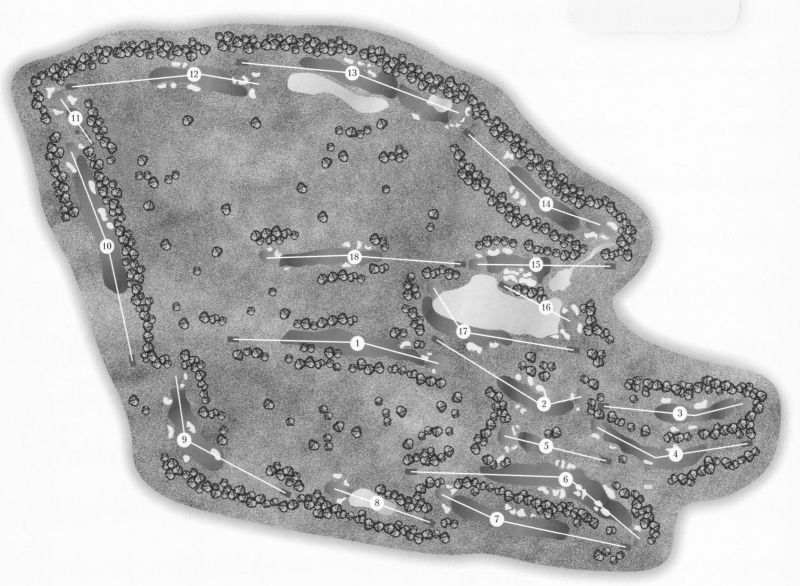

LEFT: 5TH HOLE **ABOVE:** 2ND HOLE

One of the Tour's youngest tournaments, the Deutsche Bank Championship was first played in 2003, and its venue, the TPC of Boston, is nearly as new, having opened in June of 2002. Despite its youth, however, this event has a few things going for it. Number one, it's played over the extended Labor Day weekend, making it the only event on the Tour that begins on Friday and concludes on Monday. Number two, the chief charitable beneficiary is the Tiger Woods Foundation, meaning this is one event that can be assured of Tiger's perfect attendance. Number three, this is the only game in town for the golf-hungry Boston market. For more than 30 years, the Tour came to the Pleasant Valley Country Club in Sutton, Massachusetts, about 45 miles from Boston, but that ended in 1998 for lack of a sponsor. With Deutsche Bank now firmly in place, Bostonians have an event to embrace. In its first year, the tournament was a sellout.

And finally, there is the golf course. Designed by Arnold Palmer on densely forested property with numerous wetland areas, the TPC of Boston looks more like the Carolinas than New England. Strength and shotmaking skill are rewarded equally on this par 71 of 7,415 yards.

ABOVE: 7TH HOLE **BELOW:** 6TH HOLE

ABOVE: 13TH HOLE BELOW: 18TH HOLE

A prime example is the second hole, a dogleg par five of 554 yards where the pros have a choice of trying to hit two mammoth shots—with the second of them having to carry a rock-bound lake—or laying up for a wedge attack at the three-tiered green. Local boy Brad Faxon calls this his favorite hole on the course.

The toughest stretch of the course begins at number four with a sharply rightward-doglegging par four of 425 yards. Cutting the corner is not an option as trees and bunkers line both sides of the fairway. The fifth was a relatively benign hole when the course opened but was quickly lengthened a whopping 63 yards and is now a par four of 475 yards. A rocky stream crosses the fairway at the 300-yard mark, assuring that the approach to this green—another three-level surface—will be a lengthy one.

The 464-yard sixth is essentially a straight hole but is best negotiated as a sort of double dogleg, the drive steering clear of fairway bunkers to the right side and the approach giving a wide berth to the lake that guards the green on the left. After those three holes, the par-five seventh—at 600 yards—is actually a breather for the pros, but the par three that follows it is not. A tee shot of 213 yards must carry water and vegetation to a deep, rolling, and well bunkered green.

The first par three on the back nine, the 11th, is even more formidable. Indeed, the first-time player who steps to the back tee of this hole and looks uphill at the target, 231 yards away and fronted by a trio of bunkers, may justifiably mistake it for a par four.

Another hole that saw a dramatic redo in its first year was number 13, where a chute was cut in the trees to create a new tee, lengthening the hole from 369 to 443 yards. The drive must now carry a rock ledge to a plateau fairway that leads to one of the smallest targets on the course, the only hazard on the hole being a tiny thumbprint bunker at the right-front of the green.

A trio of dramatic finishing holes begins with another hefty par three, 211 yards over water to a green that falls away steeply from front to back. When the flagstick is located at the front of this green, just over the far edge of the pond, only a brave—or underclubbed—shot will leave a viable putt for two. However, birdie will be in the minds of the pros as they tee up at the 420-yard 17th, a dogleg left where a big looping hook will leave just a wedge to the bunkerless green.

The 18th hole assembles all the salient elements of the course—tall cordoning trees, wetlands, and rock outcroppings—in a twisting par five. Those who can carry a bunker complex in the right of the drive zone will have a good chance of getting home in two, but the second shot will have to carry a wetland area that extends to the edge of the green. In the tradition of TPC courses, it makes for a dramatic finish.

ADAM SCOTT, 2003 WINNER

PLAYING TIP

The "Tweener" Shots
On courses such as the TPC of Boston, with large multi-tiered greens, it pays to know how to handle "tweener" shots, an iron shot where the distance falls smack between your capabilities with two clubs—a bit too short for one, a bit too long for the other.

How do you handle these? The key is to know yourself. If you're a Type A personality who likes to play hard-charging, aggressive golf, take the shorter club and give it all you've got. If, on the other hand, you're laid back by nature, you probably have an evenly paced, controlled swing. Your strategy should be to take the longer club, grip down a hair, and make your usual smooth pass at the ball, letting the club do the work.

ONLY HERE

Golf Central: On the same site as the TPC of Boston are the headquarters of the Massachusetts Golf Association, the Francis Ouimet Scholarship Fund, and the Ouimet Golf Museum.
Free Concerts: Adjacent to the course is the Tweeter Center, where outdoor concerts are held in the summer; music may sometimes be heard on some of the back nine holes.
Lots of Lumber: The numerous wetland areas are spanned by over 2,800 feet of wooden bridges.

SCORECARD

HOLE	PAR	YARDAGE
1	4	365
2	5	554
3	3	184
4	4	425
5	4	475
6	4	464
7	5	600
8	3	213
9	4	480
OUT	36	3760
10	4	425
11	3	231
12	4	461
13	4	443
14	4	495
15	4	426
16	3	211
17	4	420
18	5	543
IN	35	3655
TOTAL	70	7415

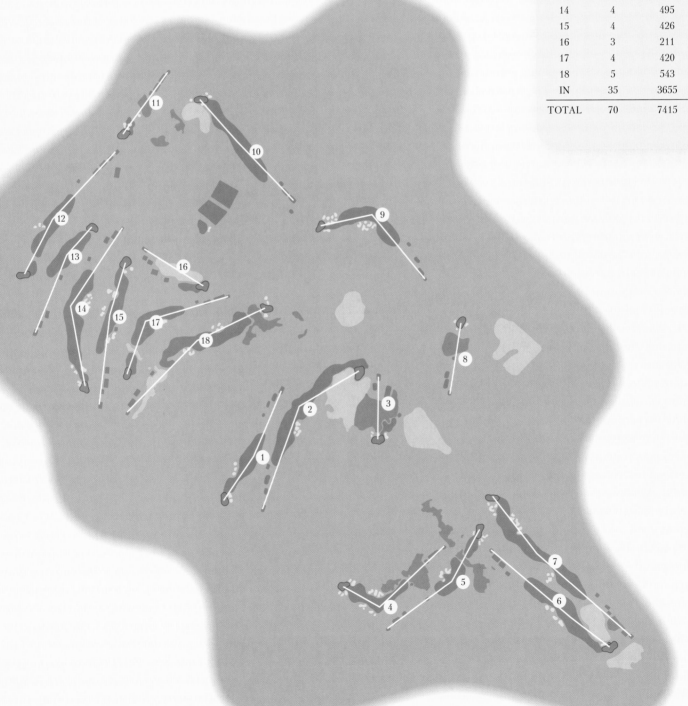

LEFT: 1ST HOLE **ABOVE:** 8TH HOLE

The Canadian Open was first played in 1904.
Among national championships, only the British
and U.S. Opens are older. In contrast to the
other two, however, the Canadian has had an
uneven history. During its first seven decades,
the tournament moved around the country,
rarely visiting the same club more than once.
Some of these venues were decidedly stronger
than others, but by rotating the event in this
way, the Royal Canadian Golf Association
enabled Canadians of all longitudes to see the
championship.

Then, in 1977, it settled in for a long run at
one site—the Glen Abbey Golf Club in Ontario—
which was not coincidentally the headquarters
of the RCGA. In 1994, yielding to financial pres-
sures, the tournament added a corporate sponsor—Bell Canada. Then, in 2000, the RCGA sold
the Glen Abbey property and began once again
to rotate the championship to other courses
throughout the country.

In 2005, for the first time in almost 40 years,
the Canadian Open will return to Western
Canada, to the Shaughnessy Golf & Country
Club. Located in the tony west side of Vancou-
ver, British Columbia, on the banks of the Fraser
River, Shaughnessy was designed in 1912 by A.

11TH HOLE

10TH HOLE

12TH HOLE

Vernon Macan, an Irish-born lawyer and Pacific Amateur champion who produced numerous courses in the U.S. and Canadian West, perhaps most notably the California Club, near San Francisco.

Shaughnessy has hosted the national championship once before, in 1966, when its 6,700 yards were considered longish for a par 71. Today, a course of that length would be almost laughably short for the Tour pros. The irony, according to Bob Weeks, editor of Canada's *Score Golf* magazine, is that "at one time, Shaughnessy played to more than 7,200 yards, but the members complained it was too long, so the back tees were abandoned." Many of those tees are now unusable due to trees that have grown in or land that has been built upon. For the Open, however, they've restored three hundred yards, while narrowing the fairways, growing the rough, and firming up the greens. And then there are the trees—giant redwoods, sequoias, and pines—

that add both beauty and difficulty. Twice the height, breadth, and thickness that they were forty years ago, they impose a straight and narrow path on anyone who hopes to conquer this course.

This time the Open will be played to a par of 70, but for the Shaughnessy members, par is 73. One of the three holes where par will be reduced is number one, a docile five that becomes a fearsome four at 475 yards. The hole plays uphill while doglegging slightly right through an aisle of sequoias. Bunkers flank the front of the green for the lengthy approach, so anyone who can write four on the card will be off to a very good start.

Generally, the greens at Shaughnessy putt at about 10 on the Stimpmeter, but in the cool Canadian climate, speeds of 13 and more are attainable. That would surely increase the challenge at the par-three eighth, which plays 210 uphill yards to a narrow two-tiered putting surface.

Accuracy will be paramount off the tee of number 10. The opening shot on this 453-yard par four is blind, as the fairway swoops downhill at about the 250-yard mark. What the player does see as he looks down this fairway, however, is a row of trees on the right and a row of out-of-bounds stakes on the left.

Number 14, a par four of just 315 yards, is the thrill-a-minute hole. Some of the pros may not even need drivers to reach this one, but they will need precision, as greenside bunkers, swales, hillocks, and ankle deep rough will complicate the second shot for those who are errant on the first.

Number 18 plays a scenic and tree-shaded 472 yards to a narrow, closely bunkered two-level green. Any player who can find that green safely in two shots and find the cup in two more will stride to the clubhouse beyond with a smile on his face.

18TH HOLE

ONLY HERE

Advantage Arnie: This is one event where Arnold Palmer has an edge on Jack Nicklaus. Arnie claimed his first career victory at the 1955 Canadian Open, while this is the only significant event Jack failed to win, finishing second an incredible seven times.

The Gap: In 1919, J. Douglas Edgar won the Canadian Open by 16 strokes, a record that still stands. One of the three players who tied for second was a 17-year-old amateur named Bobby Jones.

Weir Number 1: A Canadian has not won the championship in half a century, but Mike Weir has the game to do it. He also has the support. Each year thousands of people come to this event just to cheer on their 2003 Masters champion and national hero.

PLAYING TIP

Cold Weather Strategy
By September, the air in Canada can become pretty brisk, especially for those facing early-morning tee times. The locals know how to deal with a short season, but if you normally play in southern climes, you should prepare for the challenge of cold weather.

The first rule is to stay warm but limber. Several thin layers of clothing will serve you better than one bulky sweater or jacket. But most important, keep your hands warm—keep them in your pockets, wear gloves, use hand warmers—do anything necessary to keep the feel in your fingers.

As on rainy days, you can expect to lose some distance in the cold, so remember two things: Take a long club and a short swing. Use at least one club more than you would from the same distance in warm weather and keep your swing compact because on cold days your body tends to stiffen up and there is no percentage in swinging all out. Besides, if the ground is cold and hard, you'll get plenty of distance—the ball will bounce and roll a long way.

SCORECARD

HOLE	PAR	YARDAGE
1	4	475
2	4	389
3	3	200
4	4	418
5	4	471
6	4	428
7	5	551
8	3	210
9	4	421
OUT	35	3433
10	4	453
11	4	471
12	3	173
13	4	442
14	4	315
15	5	577
16	4	372
17	3	158
18	4	472
IN	35	3563
TOTAL	70	6996

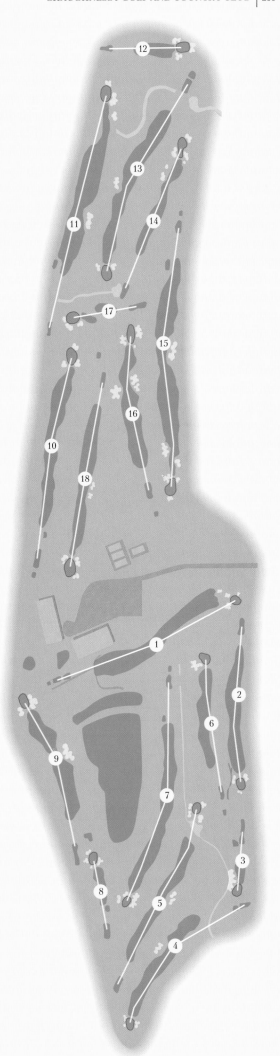

**MIKE WEIR IS CANADA'S
FAVORITE SON.**

7TH HOLE

When you step to the seventh tee of the Resort Course at La Cantera, the first thing that catches your eye is not the hole you're about to play. What commands your attention instead is a roller coaster. In the distance, just beyond the boundaries of this course on the outskirts of San Antonio, is the Six Flags Fiesta Amusement Park, complete with "The Rattler," an enormous thrill ride that is the park's centerpiece. Every half a minute or so, the serenity of golf is interrupted by the frenzied shrieks of Rattler riders as they cascade into the ride's initial drop.

If, on the other hand, you were to stand atop that roller coaster, and look back across the fence, you would be looking at some real estate with a fair number of thrills of its own. The course that hosts the Valero Texas Open packs plenty of excitement into its 6,881 yards.

Carved from a limestone quarry (Cantera means "quarry stone" in Spanish), La Cantera opened for play in 1995 and almost immediately was named by *GOLF* Magazine as one of the "Top 100 Courses You Can Play." It is one of the last courses designed jointly by Tom Weiskopf and Jay Morrish, and the two architects took full advantage of the hill country terrain they were given. Dramatic elevation changes and carries over ravines abound, as do panoramic views of the San Antonio area.

Play begins on a hilltop, with a Texas-sized par five of 631 yards. The San Antonio skyline is visible 15 miles to the south as this slight dogleg left drops 125 feet in elevation on its way to a skull-shaped green with bunkers right and left. Despite being the number-one handicap hole for resort guests, this is generally a birdie start for the pros.

A much tougher assignment is the hole that follows, a 448-yard par four that doglegs viciously right. The fairway is nearly a 250-yard carry over rough from the back tees, and a drive of at least that length is needed to see around the trees for the next shot. There are no bunkers at the green, but a false front and a deep swale on the left will swallow less than crisply struck shots.

A Weiskopf/Morrish trademark is the driveable par four, and at La Cantera it's number seven. It begins on a cliff 80 feet above the fairway. From there, the carry to the green plays less than its 316 yards, but in full view from that tee is all the trouble en route. A large bunker sits in the middle of the fairway, several others hovering around it like satellites. Beyond the sand and to the right side of this dogleg right sits a lake—one of 10 natural hazards on this course—ready to penalize anyone who gets ambitious from the tee. At greenside three more bunkers lie in wait.

Playing in his first Valero Texas Open, Hank Kuehne, a Texan and one of the longest hitters on the Tour, drove this hole and made birdie. Then on the next hole, a par four of 361 yards,

ABOVE (TOP TO BOTTOM): 1ST, 12TH, AND 16TH HOLES

18TH HOLE

ABOVE: JUSTIN LEONARD, 2000 AND 2001 WINNER
RIGHT: TOMMY ARMOUR III, 2003 WINNER

SCORECARD

HOLE	PAR	YARDAGE
1	5	631
2	4	448
3	3	202
4	4	444
5	4	494
6	3	162
7	4	316
8	4	361
9	4	380
OUT	35	3438
10	4	460
11	4	427
12	4	415
13	3	142
14	5	527
15	4	446
16	4	380
17	3	186
18	4	426
IN	35	3443
TOTAL	70	6881

he actually drove over the green and recorded a nine. This is one course that does not favor long hitters, as the list of winners attests. Medium-length Justin Leonard has won twice here and in 2002 the winner was 47-year-old Loren Roberts, who was not a power player even at half that age.

The signature hole on this course is probably number 12, a 415-yard par four. An immense limestone wall lines the left side of the fairway, where a series of church-pew bunkers also lurks, while the approach is all carry to an elevated green protected in front by a rocky ravine and a running creek. Anything short of the putting surface definitely will not bounce forward.

The toughest hurdle on the way in is surely number 15, uphill all the way at 446 yards. A huge bunker lines the entire left side of the angled green. Sixteen is another one of those short par fours that give pause on the tee. It's only 380 yards but that length is dotted with a minefield of nine bunkers, and the one to the left of the green is larger than the green itself.

The last and most difficult of the par threes comes at number 17, which plays 186 yards to a lightbulb-shaped green, wider in back than front. Three bunkers hug the putting surface, and they are safe havens compared to the ravine that awaits more errant shots.

Compared to the holes that precede it, the finisher is routine, a mid-length straightaway par four with a pair of bunkers in the landing area and a creek to the right of the fairway. The green is long and narrow and a miss to the right will likely find either a tiny pot bunker or its much larger cousin.

ONLY HERE

Champions' Ridge: Each winner here gets his name engraved on a rock near the elevated ninth tee.

Identity Crisis: Although this is one of the longest-running events on the Tour, dating back to 1922, in recent years it has struggled to gain sponsorship. As a result, since 1986 the tournament has had no fewer than eight different names.

PLAYING TIP

Handling Sidehillers

On a course with as many ups and downs as La Cantera, you're bound to run into a few hilly lies. The most vexing are the sidehillers, where the ball is either well above or well below your feet.

When the ball is above your feet, your tendency will be to pull the shot left. You should allow for this by aiming a bit right of your target. (In the case of a severe slope, open the face of your club slightly to counteract the closing of the clubface that occurs with a pull.) The ball also will be closer to your hands than with a level lie, so you should adjust by gripping down a bit on the club—this may also mean that you'll have to take one club more than for a shot from a level lie.

When the ball is below your feet, everything is reversed. Expect a push shot to the right and compensate by aiming a bit left of your target. (On a severe lie, address the ball with a slightly closed clubface.) Be aware that the ball is farther from your hands than usual, and adjust by putting some extra flex into your knees to lower your hands.

No matter which type of lie you have, keep your swing "quiet" and compact. With an awkward stance, you must stay centered over the ball to insure solid contact.

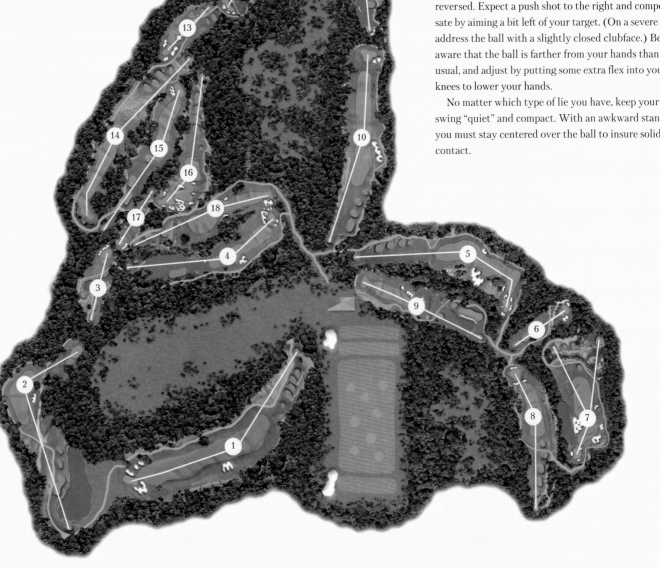

For many years, the slogan printed on license plates in the Keystone State was "You Have a Friend in Pennsylvania." These days, it's the PGA Tour that has friend in Pennsylvania and his name is Joe Hardy.

Hardy is the octogenarian founder of 84 Lumber, the largest privately held supplier of building materials in the United States, with 400 stores coast to coast and headquarters in the town of Eighty-Four, 20 miles south of Pittsburgh. Among his company's holdings is the Nemacolin Woodlands Resort & Spa, in Pennsylvania's western mountains. In 2002, Joe Hardy got a bee in his bonnet.

"He said he wanted to have the hardest golf course in the world," says Pete Dye, designer of the Mystic Rock course at Nemacolin. "And then he said he wanted it to host a Tour event. I told him he was crazy."

Dye had designed Mystic Rock seven years earlier as a bucolically pleasing and moderately challenging resort course. Hardy told him to go back and put some teeth in it—enough teeth to take a bite out of Tiger Woods and company. Today, Mystic Rock is not the toughest in the world—or even the toughest in its neighborhood (which encompasses Oakmont)—but it is nonetheless a full test for the pros and has become the host of the 84 Lumber Classic of Pennsylvania.

No expense was spared by Hardy, and Dye, notorious for the joy he derives from tormenting the game's best players, did not hold back. Nine new tees were constructed, lengthening the course by 500 yards. All the fairways were reworked, and all the bunkers were excavated and refilled with PGA Tour spec sand. In addition, a 10-acre practice facility was constructed exclusively for the pros, along with a $50-million clubhouse, modeled after the opulent Lodge at Sea Island.

Bear in mind, this was a challenging place to stick a golf course. Dye's original design of Mystic Rock took three years to build because in the process he had to bury 200,000 boulders. "I used more dynamite than they did at Normandy," he said. There was also no useable soil on the property, so all the fill dirt had to be trucked in from off site. The new course weaves through that daunting terrain while also encompassing five water hazards, dozens of yawning Saharan bunkers, and some of the largest and most severely contoured greens the Tour players see all year.

The fun starts right at the first hole, a par four of 371 yards that is within reach of the Tour's longer hitters. But a steep slope down the entire right side of this hole cautions against overzealousness.

A statue of Gene Sarazen watches over the tee of the second hole, but the Squire, with his hicko-

ABOVE: 5TH HOLE RIGHT: 12TH HOLE

ABOVE (TOP TO BOTTOM): 14TH, 17TH, AND 18TH HOLES (WITH J.L. LEWIS, 2003 WINNER)

ry-shafted clubs, would never have been able to handle the bold route from the new championship tee, an all-carry poke of nearly 275 yards over rocks, water, and sand. Those who land safely will face a sloping green with a deep bunker to the left.

Dye's most dramatic change came at number five, where more than 80 yards were added, bringing this par five to 592 yards. The stronger pros will still reach this long, slender green, because the hole plays slightly downhill, but many will also find the large bunker to the left.

Between the fifth green and sixth tee is a $600,000 waterfall worthy of Donald Trump, but it's the natural water hazard on the left and the woods on the right of this par four that will get the pros' attention.

Dye was in charge of nearly all the course changes, but a change at number 11 was the suggestion of John Daly, who has an endorsement deal with 84 Lumber and serves as the unofficial tournament host. The new tee at this par five sits well below the old one and lengthened the hole by more than 90 yards, to 633 yards. It also created a blind tee shot and a much longer approach over a lake to a green guarded on the right side by rocks and water.

The signature hole at Mystic Rock is number 12, a beautifully landscaped 171-yard par three that plays to a green with water at its left side. The target here is more than ample—11,000 square feet, or nearly twice the size of a normal green—but it has four tiers, not to mention a lake to the left side and a deep bunker beyond.

Another arresting view awaits at the tee of the 461-yard 14th, where an immense bunker—120 yards long and 40 yards wide—stares assailants in the face. Then it's on to another risk-reward par five, the 526-yard 16th, where those in quest of the green will have to thread a line between water at the left and back and sand front and right. Those who miss this fairway will tend to lay up and trust their wedges to bring them birdies.

Water runs down the entire left side of the 17th hole, a par three of 193 yards. There's a large, elevated bail-out area to the right, but with this green sloping steeply downhill from front to back, saving par will be a challenge, especially when the tournament is on the line.

A small forest of trees was removed from the right side of the 18th fairway to make room for a village of hospitality tents. But a new tee has increased the dogleg on this short uphill par four and brought in full view another gigantic fairway bunker. Any approach that misses this severely sloped green to the left will find either a steep hill or a bunker that sits fully 20 feet below the putting surface. From there, making bogey will be an achievement.

SCORECARD

HOLE	PAR	YARDAGE
1	4	371
2	4	457
3	3	231
4	4	383
5	5	592
6	4	412
7	3	173
8	5	565
9	4	455
OUT	36	3639
10	4	438
11	5	633
12	3	171
13	4	363
14	4	461
15	4	461
16	5	526
17	3	193
18	4	391
IN	36	3637
TOTAL	72	7276

ONLY HERE

Fine Decor: The Nemacolin Woodlands Resort houses a multi-million-dollar art collection.

Easy In/Easy Out: As an attraction to the airplane-owning marquee players, the resort also has its own 3,900-foot airstrip.

PLAYING TIP

The Hardest Putt

Like many resort courses, Mystic Rock has large greens, to allow for several pin positions and thereby spread out the traffic and wear and tear on the surfaces. The result is that one often faces the most difficult of all putts—a long one that must be hit straight. Why is it so hard? There's no room to fiddle with speed and break—you *must* hit the ball on line and with the proper pace.

If you have trouble with such putts, it's probably because you tend to pull or push the ball off line, or allow your wrists to become too active in the stroke. Take a tip from the Tour pros, most of whom use a pure arm-and-shoulder stroke, with no wrist action. By letting the bigger muscles determine the length and pace of your stroke, you have better control over the distance than you do by involving the more sudden and volatile movements of the wrists. (This is the same reason so many players now use the long putter.) Besides, by keeping your wrists stiff you also improve your accuracy: Set the back of your left hand straight at your target, keep it facing that way throughout the stroke, and you'll insure that the ball starts straight on line.

JOHN DALY IS THE UNOFFICIAL HOST.

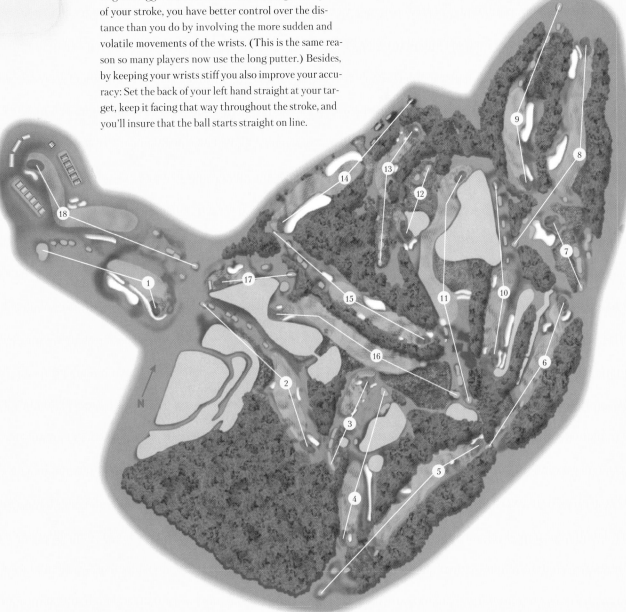

In 1996 a summit conference was held among the leaders of the world's professional golf tours, and the result was the creation of the World Golf Championships, four events with the goal of enhancing the level and activity of worldwide competition. Implicit in that goal was the notion of playing these championships not just in the U.S., but in all the countries represented by the "International Federation of PGA Tours"—in Europe, Asia, Australia, and South Africa.

The performance has been mixed. The World Cup, which existed for half a century before becoming a WGC event, and which involves just two players from each representative country, has continued to move around the globe. But two of the three fuller-field events have been more or less domesticated. The WGC-Accenture Match Play Championship has remained in the U.S. all but one year and the WGC-NEC Championship has never left the states.

Only the fourth of them—the WGC-American Express Championship—has gone somewhat global. Two of the first five stagings of this limited-field event have been in continental Europe (at Spain's Valderrama Golf Club), two more have gone to Ireland (to the Mount Juliet estate), and just one has been in the U.S. (at the Capital City Club in Atlanta).

In 2005 the tournament will once again be played in the U.S., and if this smacks of a return

4TH HOLE

to parochialism, it can be forgiven if for no other reason than the specific venue itself: Harding Park Golf Course in San Francisco.

Designed in 1925 by little-known Scottish architect Willie Watson, this elegant municipal course on the shores of Lake Merced was once regarded just as highly as its posh next door neighbor clubs, the Olympic Club and San Francisco Golf Club. The Tour actually played there during the 1960s, with Gary Player, Billy Casper, and Chi Chi Rodriguez among the winners of the old Lucky International. San Francisco boy Ken Venturi played his very first round of golf there (his parents used to run the pro shop), and Johnny Miller, George Archer, and Bob Rosburg all learned the game at Harding Park.

But time, politics, and poor management combined to leave the course in a state just above deplorable. The fairways had become bald, the once majestic cypress trees lining the holes became twisted and overgrown, gasping for air, and Harding's greens became so marked and bumpy, they were all but unputtable.

Enter the savior, San Francisco lawyer and former USGA President Sandy Tatum. During the late 1990s, Tatum spearheaded an effort to raise $16 million in city funding to restore Harding to its former glory. The carrot for the city fathers was the promise of a major tournament—and its attendant revenue.

7TH HOLE

ABOVE (TOP TO BOTTOM): 13TH, 15TH, AND 17TH HOLES **RIGHT:** 18TH HOLE

The course was closed for over a year and architect Chris Gray of PGA Tour Design Services was brought in to do the work. Few changes were made in the routing of the course, but every fairway was reshaped and re-grassed, every green was enlarged, re-contoured, and seeded with bentgrass, and more than 150 trees were removed, with many others being pruned substantially.

Each hole was fitted with five sets of tees, and the tournament markers of this par 70 now stretch to 7,141 yards, nearly 500 yards longer than before. (Incidentally, the tournament course can't be played on a normal day. Some of the tournament tees are located on an adjacent nine-hole course.) The larger greens help the conditioning on a course that receives heavy play, but with the added contours there are plenty of difficult hole locations that can be used when the pros come to town. Likewise, the fairways will be narrowed considerably for tournaments compared to everyday play.

Even the clubhouse was shifted and rebuilt. The move allowed for a new tee at number one, lengthening that hole by 30 yards. In the only alteration to the path of the course, holes two and seven were exchanged. Otherwise, the front nine remains as it was, a prelude to the more dramatic and testing inward half.

The 13th green was moved 60 yards to the left, but that affords what is now the best second shot in the city—the view to the green goes clear across Lake Merced to the Olympic Club, where you can see the red-tiled roof of the Spanish-styled clubhouse jutting through the trees.

But the biggest change occurred at the par-four 18th where a parking lot was eliminated to make room for the tee and the practice green was moved to allow for the contoured, 6,150-square-foot green. The result is 477 yards of breathtaking challenge, every inch of the assignment clearly visible from the tee, beginning with a tee shot that calls for a powerful draw across the lake.

KEN VENTURI AND JOHNNY MILLER (FAR RIGHT) GREW UP PLAYING HARDING PARK.

ONLY HERE

A Reminder: In 2001 this event was scheduled to be played at Bellerive Country Club in St. Louis. However, the dates were September 13-16. It was cancelled because of the September 11 terrorist attacks on New York City and Washington, D.C.

Tiger's Den: The press wags can be forgiven for suggesting that WGC actually stands for Woods Gets Cash. Tiger won this event three of the first four times it was played, banking a million dollars each time. On top of that, he represents American Express.

The Rich Get Richer: Like the Tour Championship, this is an end-of-season bonus for the players who have already played well. The field is limited to about 70 players, including the top 50 on the Official World Ranking and the leaders of the six Tours' Official Money Lists/Orders of Merit. There is no cut, and even the last-place finisher goes home with at least $25,000.

PLAYING TIP

The #1 Shot Saver
Modern golf courses generally call for high-flying approaches to greens, over hazards and bunkers, but at classic old designs such as Harding Park, a low-to-the-ground, running approach—a pitch and run—will save you many shots.

You can play the shot with a range of clubs, from the 5-iron through the wedges, but the 7- or 8-iron might be the best overall choice. The key to the technique is minimalism. Minimize the length of the club by gripping down on the shaft a couple of inches. Minimize the backspin (and therefore the loft) of the shot by keeping both your backswing and follow-through short. And, as a final key, minimize the speed of your swing. It's better to hit a soft shot with a 6-iron, letting the clubface produce the bounce and forward roll, than to try to manufacture a shot by hitting more vigorously with a 9-iron.

SCORECARD

HOLE	PAR	YARDAGE
1	4	412
2	4	451
3	3	186
4	5	607
5	4	429
6	4	479
7	4	335
8	3	236
9	4	494
OUT	35	3629
10	5	554
11	3	191
12	4	483
13	4	428
14	4	472
15	4	405
16	4	332
17	3	175
18	4	477
IN	35	3512
TOTAL	70	7141

Welcome to the Consolation Prize Open, the best golf tournament you've never heard of. For nearly 40 years, the Southern Farm Bureau Classic—formerly known as the Magnolia State Classic and then the Deposit Guaranty Classic—has been fighting the good fight for recognition and respectability.

Unfortunately, timing is everything, and this tournament has always been the Tour calendar's whipping boy. It debuted in 1968, during the second week in April—ideal golf weather for this part of the world, but unfortunately the same week as The Masters. So when Mac McLendon and Pete Fleming battled for a dramatic nine holes of sudden death before McLendon won, no one noticed.

The event remained opposite The Masters for another quarter century before switching to late July, making it the most hazy, hot, and humid stop on the Tour. But none of the game's prominent players protested. That week, they were all enjoying sweater weather, across the pond at the British Open. That lasted a few years, and then there was another jump down the schedule—to the very last week of the year. In early November, the playing conditions were lovely, but once again attention was focused elsewhere as the Tour's top 30 money winners competed in the Tour Championship. Then, a couple of years ago, it switched again—to late September. Free at last? Hardly. Now it plays opposite the WGC-American Express Championship, one of the four high-profile events run by the International Federation of PGA Tours—a tournament with

BELOW (TOP TO BOTTOM): 2ND AND 16TH HOLES   17TH HOLE

twice the prestige, twice the exposure, twice the prize money, and even two more initials in its name than the SFBC.

Tiger Woods has never played the Southern Farm Bureau Classic, and likely never will. Jack Nicklaus never played here either. However, he did work here. The host course since 1994, Annandale Golf Club, is one of the first produced by the Nicklaus design firm. When it opened in 1981, it was also the first course in Mississippi with bentgrass greens. Bent is generally the pre-

ferred surface among knowledgeable golfers, but it is a rarity in the Deep South because it does-n't tolerate intense heat. But Jack's experiment at Annandale worked. The course has consis-tently been ranked among the best in Dixie, and has even hosted a National Championship, the 1986 U.S. Mid-Amateur.

Like many of Nicklaus's early efforts, this one reflects his game at its prime. A par 72 of nearly 7,200 yards from the tips, it rewards distance off the tee and high, soft-landing approaches to its

small, often elevated and always well-protected greens—not to mention a smooth, fearless stroke on those slick bent surfaces. Eight water hazards dot the course along with 70 sand bunkers and numerous grass bunkers reminiscent of the Scottish links courses Nicklaus admires.

The par-three holes are particularly strong, beginning with number two, 213 yards over water to a slender green guarded by a tree and a bunker to the left and two bunkers and a creek to the right. The green is 43 yards from

18TH HOLE

front to back, so club selection can vary widely, depending upon where the flag is positioned. Some years, this plays as the hardest hole in the tournament.

Its sibling on the front nine, number eight, is a beautiful hole, particularly if you like a water view. The green is a near-island, with water at its front, back, and right. This is the largest target on the course, but its sloping surface also produces the largest number of three-putts.

The longest par four on the course is number 14 at 473 yards. It's dead straight, but out of bounds looms on the left and a creek runs behind and to the left of the green with a large bunker at the front right.

Speaking of large bunkers, there are few in the world to compare with the one at number 16. On this par four of just over 400 yards, some players actually lay up off the tee in order to avoid the start of this Saharan behemoth that stretches

150 yards diagonally across the right side of the fairway and all the way to the green.

A Nicklaus signature appears at 17, a double fairway. A water hazard bisects the landing area, creating a longer, doglegging path to the left and a direct route—via a small peninsula—on the right. For those who want to gamble, a long iron can be landed on the peninsula, leaving a wedge to the small and slender green. The left fairway, however, is not exactly a bail-out, with out of bounds to the left, water to the right. The Annandale members will tell you this is their signature hole.

Eighteen is your basic PGA Tour finishing hole, a mid-length par five with a lake down the entire left side and a stream curling in front of the green. It's a classic risk-reward hole, and when everything is on the line in the final round of the Southern Farm Bureau Classic, look for the players to give it a go. Just not the big-name players.

PAYNE STEWART, 1982 WINNER

SCORECARD

HOLE	PAR	YARDAGE
1	4	385
2	3	213
3	4	406
4	4	465
5	5	522
6	4	424
7	5	556
8	3	209
9	4	450
OUT	36	3630
10	4	407
11	5	579
12	3	171
13	4	414
14	4	473
15	3	176
16	4	408
17	4	409
18	5	532
IN	36	3569
TOTAL	72	7199

PLAYING TIP

Bent vs. Bermuda

The majority of courses in the Deep South feature greens sown with bermudagrass, but Annandale is an oasis of bentgrass, the predominant strain on northern greens. Locals who visit here will have to make some adjustments.

Bent greens are smoother surfaces. The difference is that the ball rolls across the bending backs of the blades of grass, whereas with bermudagrass it rolls across the tips. As such, putts on bent are less susceptible to the grain—or direction of growth—of the grass. Whereas the bristles of bermuda tend to push the ball in one direction, the bowed leaves of bent have comparatively little effect.

Each grass presents a different putting challenge. On bermuda the assignment is to read the grain and allow for it both in the pace and break of your putt: Play extra break when the slope and grain move in the same way, less break when they're opposite; hit down-grain putts more softly, upgrain putts harder. With bent—especially on well-conditioned courses—the main challenge is to control the speed, which can be very fast. For this reason, most good players raised on bent greens tend to have smooth arm-and-shoulder strokes that glide through the ball, whereas players brought up on bermuda are more likely to use a rapping-type hit. The prevailing wisdom is that if you can putt bermuda, you can adapt easily to bent, but it's tougher to go the other way.

ONLY HERE

Famous Debuts: As you might expect, this event produces lesser-light winners, many of them scoring their first victories. But among those to win here were Craig Stadler (1978) and Payne Stewart (1982).

Part-Time Jobs: Rain has occasionally deluged this event, with the result that this is the only tournament on the Tour whose list of past winners includes players with victories after 54 holes, 36 holes, and yes, 18 holes—Roger Maltbie in 1980. That year, everyone went home and watched The Masters on TV.

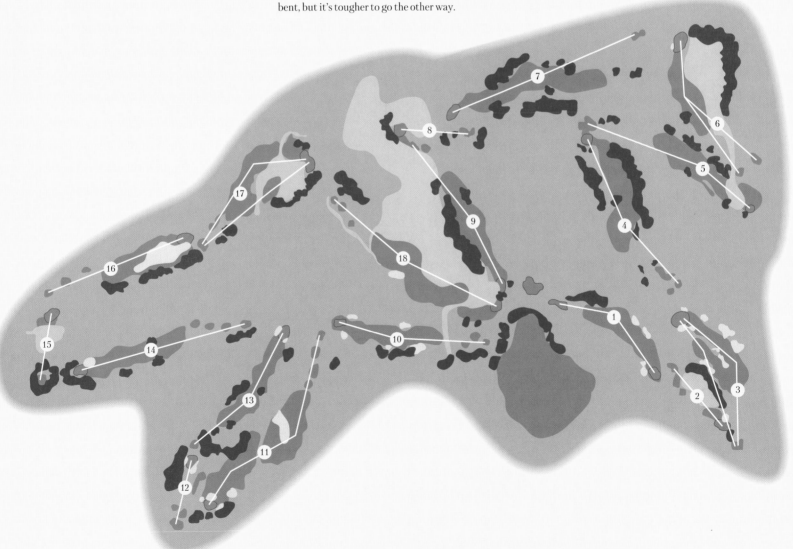

TPC AT SUMMERLIN
TPC AT THE CANYONS

Las Vegas Invitational, Nevada

Here's a trivia question you should be able to handle: Where did Jack Nicklaus win his first tournament as a professional? The answer: Oakmont Country Club. It was, of course, the 1962 U.S. Open, and Nicklaus won in a dramatic 18-hole playoff over Arnold Palmer, an auspicious beginning to be sure.

Now for bonus points, try the same question with regard to Tiger Woods. A bit tougher, isn't it, despite being 34 years more recent. Answer: The 1996 Las Vegas Invitational. Four strokes back after four rounds of the 90-hole event, the

20-year-old Stanford dropout closed with a 64 to catch Davis Love III and then won on the first hole of sudden-death. It was his fifth start as a pro, and he has been the game's best player ever since.

It's perhaps appropriate that Tiger—now the richest athlete in the world—began his reign at the TPC at Summerlin, a course named after the mother of billionaires, Howard Hughes. Summerlin is in fact much more than a golf course—it's a 22,500-acre tract developed by Hughes's heirs to become the largest master-planned community

in America. Ultimately, it will be the home to 160,000 citizens in 30 distinct villages.

The TPC, designed by Bobby Weed with consultation from Fuzzy Zoeller, opened in 1991 to strong reviews and has hosted the Invitational since 1992. Zoeller, who likes to build courses that are fun, said his goals at Summerlin were simple: to give players clear targets from the tees, to allow them a chance to roll their approach shots onto the greens, and to keep the green undulations subtle.

SUMMERLIN, 5TH HOLE

SUMMERLIN, 3RD HOLE

Those elements keep the course playable for members, but when the pros come to town, they find birdies in abundance in the desert. In 2003, for example, Summerlin was the fifth easiest course on the Tour, yielding an average score of 69.248 against a par of 72.

The third hole, a 492-yard par five, was the second easiest hole on the Tour that year, its 4.215 average lower than some of the par fours at other venues. It is one of several holes where a desert wash comes into play, but, in this case, it's not in play very often.

SUMMERLIN, 8TH HOLE

OPPOSITE (TOP TO BOTTOM): SUMMERLIN, 15TH HOLE; SUMMERLIN, 16TH HOLE; CANYONS, 2ND HOLE **ABOVE:** SUMMERLIN, 18TH HOLE

The three hardest holes at Summerlin are the par threes, including both on the front nine. The fifth plays 197 yards to a diagonal green, while the eighth is a formidable 239 yards to a green guarded by six bunkers.

The closing four holes are designed for thrills down the stretch, offering birdie possibilities, but with enough danger lurking that high numbers are also possible.

The 15th and 16th are holes where players expect birdies, or even eagles, but to fully take advantage of them, long and accurate drives are required. The 15th is a par four of 341 yards where many players take out the driver and go for the green. If they do, they need to avoid the desert to the left. The safe route, a layup off the tee and a wedge to the green, also can yield birdies. The 16th is a 560-yard par five, where, even with a lake in front, many players can get home in two. Still, there's the occasional disaster—there are more triple bogeys here than any other hole on the course.

The 196-yard 17th is the hardest hole on the course. The green is long and narrow, sloping towards a lake on the left. While there's no recovery from a pulled tee shot, bunker shots from the right are no bargain, either.

On the 18th, a 444-yard par four that doglegs to the left, players can bite off as much of the desert as they dare. A big tee shot can leave a

wedge to the green, but the approach to a putting surface guarded by water on the left is dangerous with a longer club.

The tournament's secondary course is another TPC, this one part of the Resort at Summerlin, where two hotels offer tourists an alternative to the Las Vegas Strip. The public-access TPC at The Canyons offers the pros the same chance for subpar scoring that they find at the tournament's host layout.

Like the TPC at Summerlin, The Canyons was created out of the desert by architect Weed and a player consultant, this time Raymond Floyd. The TPC at The Canyons, which opened in 1996, retains more of a natural, rugged look than its sister course, though it plays about the same.

Two more similarities: The Canyons has one of the easiest par fives on the PGA Tour (the 544-yard, downhill fourth) and its toughest holes are the par threes. That's especially true of the par threes on the front nine. The 196-yard second hole plays downhill to a green that is essentially an island in the desert. The 209-yard seventh has plenty of trouble on the left, with a dry wash and bunkers.

The two most natural and striking holes on the back nine are the 13th and 14th, each hole featuring a deep arroyo. On the 423-yard 13th, the arroyo runs up the right side, tempting the player to cut off as much distance as he can. He needs to be careful, though, because the fairway slopes to the right so that a slightly pushed drive could roll into trouble if the player gets too greedy. The 14th is shorter at 365 yards, with a green sitting precariously on a ledge, fronted by a cavernous arroyo.

The Las Vegas tournament made a big splash when it debuted in 1983 with the largest purse on the Tour. Since then, as purses have escalated elsewhere, Vegas has been overtaken in prize money and moved to less favorable fall dates. In 2004, it was in danger of dropping off the schedule until it received a three-year financial boost from an individual benefactor. Pros who like shooting low numbers rejoiced at the reprieve.

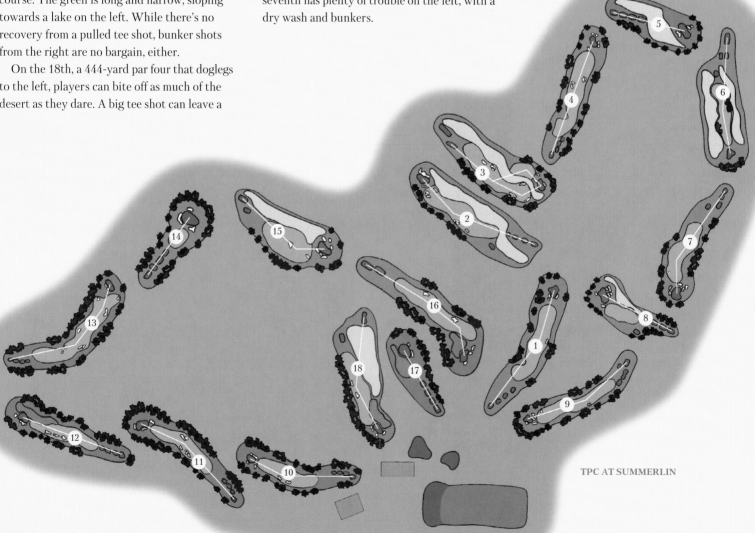

TPC AT SUMMERLIN

SCORECARD

TPC AT SUMMERLIN

HOLE	PAR	YARDAGE
1	4	408
2	4	469
3	5	492
4	4	450
5	3	197
6	4	430
7	4	382
8	3	239
9	5	563
OUT	36	3630
10	4	420
11	4	448
12	4	442
13	5	606
14	3	156
15	4	341
16	5	560
17	3	196
18	4	444
IN	36	3613
TOTAL	72	7243

ONLY HERE

Legalized Gambling: The PGA Tour prohibits its players from betting on themselves, but that doesn't stop you—this is the only Tour site where you can play golf all week long and walk home with more money than Tiger Woods. But don't bet on it.

A Grateful Widow: Thomas A. Morton loved playing in the pro-am for this event—loved it so much that, in appreciation, his widow, Helen, decided to contribute $5 million over a three-year period, starting in 2004, to help keep the tournament going when its future was in doubt due to the lack of a corporate sponsor.

Outrageous Scoring: In 1991, Chip Beck shot a 59 in this tournament at Sunrise Golf Club, the only year that course was used for the event. He didn't win. In 2003, Jerry Kelly reeled off eight straight birdies on holes seven through 14 at the TPC at Summerlin in the third round, matching the PGA Tour record, then, following a par on 15, recorded an eagle on the 16th to go 10-under in a 10-hole stretch. He didn't win either.

A Warm Welcome: Traditionally, the winner is embraced by a pair of scantily clad showgirls.

BELOW: TIGER WOODS, 1996 WINNER, IS CONGRAT-ULATED BY HIS MOTHER.
RIGHT: FUZZY ZOELLER DESIGNED SUMMERLIN WITH AMATEURS IN MIND.

PLAYING TIP

Battling a Breeze

Las Vegas is arid and warm for much of the year, but it can also be one of the windiest cities in the country. So when you play the TPC at Summerlin, prepare to battle a stiff breeze. One of the best weapons you can have is a calm attitude. Look at the wind as your friend. When it's at your back, clearly it helps you, not only by lengthening your shots but by straightening them, as a following wind reduces the sidespin on your ball. Less obvious is the fact that a wind in your face can help. In fact, the pros prefer a bit of headwind, as it enables them to play aggressively toward the flag, to hit shots that will come down straight and with little roll.

The other important thing is to think control. Even when you're hitting downwind, keep your swing compact and smooth—don't overswing. By swinging smoothly, you'll improve your chance of making the solid contact that enables you to ride the following breeze. Into the wind, add some control by widening your stance an inch or two—this will do two things: 1) restrict your backswing turn and thereby keep you stable, and 2) lower your center of gravity a bit, creating a shallower angle of attack to the ball which will help produce the lower-trajectory, boring shot that is vital when playing into a wind.

SCORECARD

TPC AT THE CANYONS

HOLE	PAR	YARDAGE
1	4	359
2	3	196
3	4	466
4	5	544
5	4	378
6	5	604
7	3	209
8	4	458
9	4	349
OUT	36	3563
10	4	419
11	4	444
12	3	145
13	4	423
14	4	365
15	5	612
16	3	202
17	4	443
18	4	447
IN	35	3500
TOTAL	71	7063

Just as the players compete on the PGA Tour, the tournaments compete against each other, vying to attract the game's stars and thereby boost their gate receipts, concession sales, and television ratings. Tiger Woods plays only 20 or so events each year, but every tournament wants him in its field, along with Phil Mickelson, Ernie Els, Sergio Garcia, and the other marquee players.

Players decide to play an event—or skip it—based on several factors, but the three main ones are the date of the event, the size of the purse, and the attractiveness of the course. On all three counts, the Greater Greensboro Open was wag-

ing a losing battle. Then, in 2002, its organizers addressed all three issues.

Number one, they jumped to a much later date on the calendar, from April (when wind, rain, and dates too close to The Masters plagued them) to mid-October (one of the prettiest times in North Carolina). Number two, they attracted the Tour's biggest sponsor, Chrysler, with the result that the purse increased 20 percent, making it one of the richest events of the fall stretch. And number three—and most important—they commissioned an overhaul of their golf course.

Forest Oaks, designed in 1964 by Ellis Maples,

had become in the eyes of many players a boring layout, and despite a 1992 renovation by Clyde Johnston and Fuzzy Zoeller, it was repelling more players than it was attracting. Moreover, like many Tour courses during the 1990s, it had begun to yield too many birdies as today's players, armed with their high-tech clubs and balls, turned 450-yard par fours into drive-and-wedge holes.

The course record—a ten-under-par 62—belonged to Davis Love III, and so it was perhaps appropriate that his design firm was selected to restore the charm and challenge of Forest Oaks. Besides adding about 200 yards to the course,

ABOVE: 7TH HOLE OPPOSITE (TOP TO BOTTOM): 8TH, 13TH, AND 17TH HOLES

bringing it to 7,311 yards from the back markers, Love and his crew changed every green, repositioned several tees and bunkers, and added rough as deep as eight inches around most of the fairway bunkers. When the players arrived in the fall of 2003, they saw a course with a strikingly different look.

Traditionally one of the toughest holes on the course was number three, a lengthy par four with a small pond on the right side of the drive zone. Love added another 50 yards to the back tees and also positioned them to add some rightward bend to the hole.

Little yardage was added to number seven, and now, depending on the tee being used, this green can be driven—but so can the pond just to the left of it.

The old version of the eighth hole had three bunkers hugging the green. Now this par three has no sand at all—but the contoured green, with Augusta-like fall-offs to the front and sides, needs no added protection. Number nine used to be a very reachable par five. Now, with a repositioned back tee, a drive of 290 yards will be needed to carry a bunker on the inside of the dogleg, and the green—located several yards to the right of its former location—makes this almost a double dogleg hole.

The most dramatic tree surgery came at the 13th, where several trees were removed on the left side of this par five with the result that it now tempts the Tour's power hitters to go for a big drive across a pond—an all-carry shot of 280 yards—that will leave just 170 yards to the green, which has been recontoured with two plateaus and an internal swale.

Number 16, formerly one of the easier holes on the course, has become one of the hardest with a new tee that has added a whopping 53 yards to its length. A drive must now carry 280 yards to reach the top of the fairway, with another long shot—into the prevailing wind—to follow.

The uphill par-three 17th, which used to play longer than its 188 yards, now plays longer than its 222 yards, and like the approach to 16, this shot is dead into the prevailing wind. Finally at 18, where the Tour pros once pummeled their drives over a hill, getting a 50-yard bounce and roll forward, a new tee insures that they will now be driving into the face of that hill. The ball will stop quickly, leaving a much longer shot into the home green.

And so, with a new time, a new sponsor, and a new course, all the pieces of the puzzle are in place. Will the revamped Forest Oaks, played amid fall foliage for a five-million-dollar purse, attract Tiger *et al.* to Greensboro? Only time will tell.

18TH HOLE

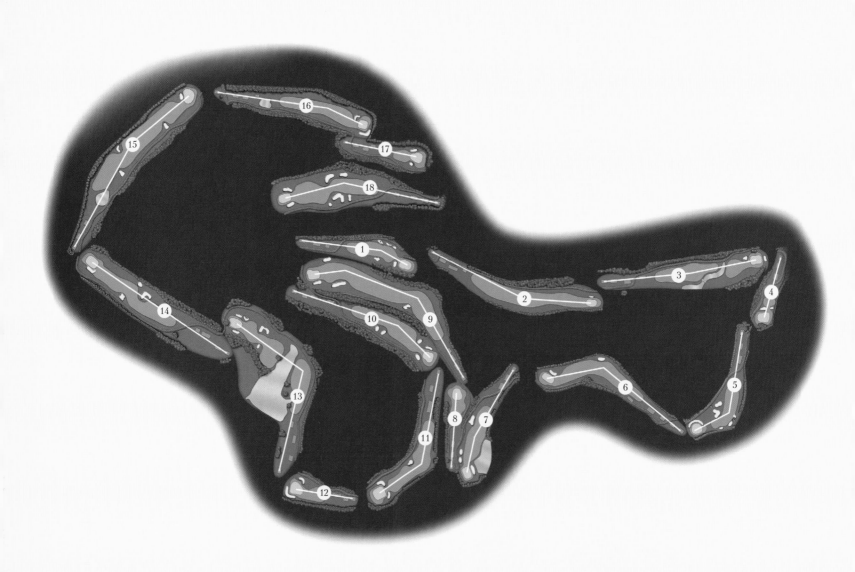

ONLY HERE

Veteran Victors: The average age of the last eight winners at Forest Oaks through 2003 is 38.

The Shadow of the Slammer: Sam Snead won this event eight times, a PGA Tour record for the most victories in a single event. His first win came in 1938 and his last was in 1965 (at age 52), and that 27-year span is also an all-time record. Had Snead competed for the current prize money, he would have banked $7.5 million from his play in this event alone.

A Rare Double: In 1942 this event was won by Sam Byrd, making him the only person to have won a Tour event and a World Series. Byrd was an outfielder for the New York Yankees championship team in 1932.

PLAYING TIP

Megaputts

Any time you play a course with greens as big as those at Forest Oaks, you're bound to encounter one of golf's most unnatural shots—the mammoth putt—a shot that's too long to be stroked and too short to be swung at.

The first rule, especially if you have a pro-type arm-and-shoulder stroke, is to allow for some wrist action. This is one time to loosen it up a bit—allow a little natural hinging and unhinging of the wrists at the end of your backswing.

Rule number two: Concentrate on distance rather than direction. Most three-putts begin when the approach putt is left several feet too long or short of the hole. If you can get your distance right, you'll rarely have more than a couple of feet for your second putt.

Finally, to simplify things, divide the putt in half. If you have a 60-footer, walk to a point about 30 feet from the hole and read the putt from there. Since the ball rolls more slowly as it nears the hole, it will be most susceptible to the slope and grain of the green during the second half of its journey. Once you have a feel for the last 30 feet, go back to the ball and focus your mind and muscles on striking a 60-foot putt that rolls over that halfway point.

SCORECARD

HOLE	PAR	YARDAGE
1	4	375
2	5	557
3	4	443
4	3	203
5	4	360
6	4	455
7	4	354
8	3	226
9	5	584
OUT	36	3557
10	4	437
11	4	442
12	3	189
13	5	529
14	4	462
15	5	555
16	4	467
17	3	222
18	4	451
IN	36	3754
TOTAL	72	7311

SHIGEKI MARUYAMA, 2003 WINNER

SAM SNEAD, EIGHT-TIME WINNER

For the Tour pros, golf tends to rank a distant second to family fun during the week of the Funai Classic, as 1994 champion Rick Fehr can attest. Fehr nearly missed his tee time for the final round because on that afternoon his car was with his wife and kids at Disney World and his ride to the course was late.

But while the moms and kids eat lunch with sea lions, shake hands with Goofy and Cinderella, and hurl themselves deliriously down Space Mountain, the dads get to have some fun, too. When the weather is right, the Palm and Magnolia Courses that host this event yield birdies faster than a chicken hatchery. Indeed, in 2002 a record was set here for the lowest cut in PGA Tour history, six under par—and over the course of the week, the field routinely tallies in excess of 1,800 holes in red numbers.

Both the Palm and Magnolia were built in the early 1970s by Joe Lee, a prolific architect whose work includes a collaboration with Ben Hogan on The Trophy Club in Fort Worth. Although the two courses sit on similar terrain and within a few thousand yards of each other, they have distinct personalities. The Magnolia is medium length and relatively expansive off the tees. When the wind blows, some of those birdies can turn into bogeys as ten water hazards and 100 bunkers come quickly into play. At the shorter, tighter Palm, water comes into play even on a calm day, as do the trees that line most of the fairways. Rounds one and two are played over both courses, while the Magnolia plays host alone on the weekend.

The number-one handicap hole at the Palm is number six, a 412-yard par four where the nerve-rattling assignment is to find a safe haven of fairway between a lake on the left and a thick stand of trees down the right. The approach is all-carry over water to a two-tiered green with an enormous bunker in back. Arnold Palmer once took an 11 on this hole.

OPPOSITE: PALM, 6TH HOLE **ABOVE:** PALM, 14TH HOLE **BELOW:** PALM, 18TH HOLE

The finisher at the Palm is a par four of 454 yards that has ranked as high as fourth among the Tour's most difficult holes. It calls for a rock-solid tee shot between two stands of woodlands, but it is the approach that is truly daunting, as the last third of this hole is an island, with the water close to the right side of the green and bunkers front, left, and rear. After playing this hole on Thursday or Friday, the pros are happy not to have to face it in the stretch on Saturday and Sunday.

The Magnolia was named for the more than 1,500 magnolia trees that surround it. But it might easily have been named the mangrove, as its holes snake through 175 acres of thick Florida wetlands, with water coming into play on 11 holes.

Number six is literally a signature hole, or at least a silhouette hole, as the bunker fronting this par three is the shape of Mickey Mouse's head. But the best hole on the front nine may be the last, a 431-yard straightaway par four with a green flanked by water on the left and bunkers on all sides.

The best par three on either course is number 15, which plays 203 yards to an elevated undulating green that tosses off missed shots and makes up-and-down pars elusive. In a sudden-death playoff for the 1986 title, Ray Floyd won here by making a par.

Relative unknown Bob Burns won this event in 2002, his first victory on Tour, and he had to beat Tiger Woods to do it. Woods roared home with a 63 and then took a seat near the putting green to watch Burns, two strokes ahead, hit his tee shot on the 17th hole.

"This is the tournament, right here," said Tiger. With water staring him in the face from both sides of the fairway, Burns, to his credit, striped it down the middle. The approach to this 427-yard hole is equally perilous, with more water on the right along with bunkers on both sides. This is no Mickey Mouse hole.

Nor is the finisher, the longest par four on the course at 455 yards. But accuracy is more important than length on this tee shot. Two bunkers in the drive zone snag minor mishits, trees await bigger errors, and water parallels the entire right side, most perilously at the green, where a trio of bunkers lurks on the left. Two strong and straight shots are a must. Then dad can go play with the family.

MAGNOLIA, 12TH HOLE

OPPOSITE (TOP TO BOTTOM): MAGNOLIA, 6TH AND 18TH HOLES **ABOVE:** MAGNOLIA, 17TH HOLE

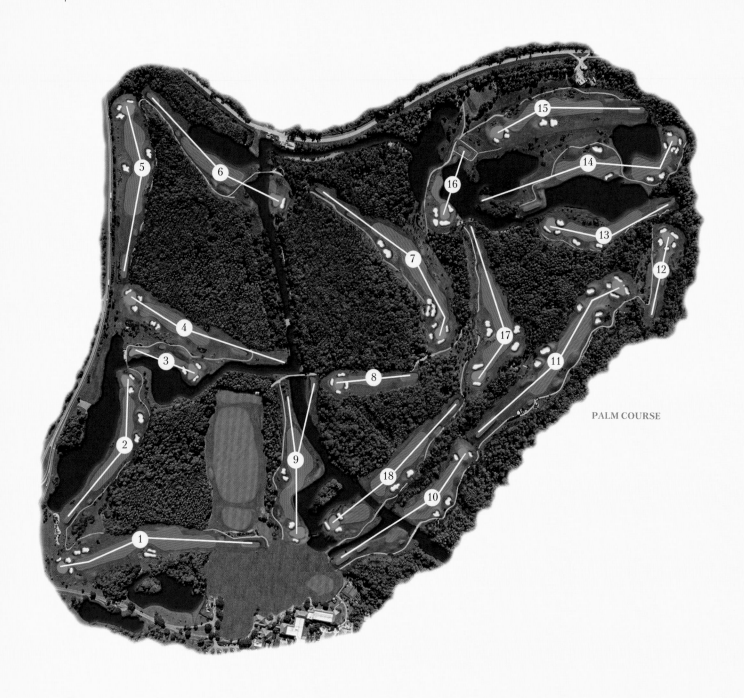

PALM COURSE

ONLY HERE

Child's Play: Part of the family atmosphere is a parent-child golf tournament—six holes of alternate-shot competition. Mike Hulbert and his son won it in 2002, and that year Hulbert, an Orlando resident, wasn't even entered in the main event.

Finishing Sprints: The season-ending Tour Championship is played just after this event (sometimes one week later, sometimes two), and its field is limited to the top 30 money winners. For that reason, the field at Disney usually attracts all the players ranked between 25 and 35.

PLAYING TIP

The Splash

Roughly 200 bunkers must be navigated over the Palm and Magnolia courses. If you've watched closely when a Tour pro plays from sand, you've undoubtedly noticed that he makes less an explosion than a splash, with the ball riding out on a thin, wispy cushion of sand. This allows him to apply some spin to the ball, thereby enhancing control, particularly when he has relatively little green between bunker and pin.

This splash technique is a bit more demanding than the thumping-down into the sand that characterizes most amateurs' bunker play. Essentially, the idea is to take a shallower divot of sand behind and under the ball.

If you'd like to develop this method, try two things: 1) Open the blade of your sand wedge as wide as you can—it should be so open and laid back that you could place a full glass of water on it without losing a drop; and 2) Instead of taking the club straight back and abruptly upward on the backswing, make a flatter swing, taking the club a bit to the inside. This will encourage a flatter, less steep angle of attack, and, combined with the open face at impact, will produce a softer, wispier cloud of sand, and a shot that will stop quickly after it hits the green. Just be warned: This shot takes some serious practice.

MAGNOLIA COURSE

SCORECARD

PALM COURSE

HOLE	PAR	YARDAGE
1	5	495
2	4	389
3	3	165
4	4	422
5	4	403
6	4	412
7	5	532
8	3	205
9	4	373
OUT	36	3396
10	4	450
11	5	552
12	3	199
13	4	364
14	5	567
15	4	426
16	3	172
17	4	397
18	4	454
IN	36	3561
TOTAL	72	6957

SCORECARD

MAGNOLIA COURSE

HOLE	PAR	YARDAGE
1	4	428
2	4	417
3	3	170
4	5	552
5	4	448
6	3	195
7	4	410
8	5	614
9	4	431
OUT	36	3665
10	5	526
11	4	385
12	3	169
13	4	375
14	5	595
15	3	203
16	4	400
17	4	427
18	4	455
IN	36	3535
TOTAL	72	7200

VIJAY SINGH, 2003 WINNER

The Westin Innisbrook, near the fishing village of Tarpon Springs on Florida's west central coast, has long been regarded as one of the finest resorts in America, with numerous awards from the major golf publications. Five courses sprawl across its rolling acreage, and the clear standout among them is the Copperhead, a par-71 layout that stretches to 7,315 yards from the back tees.

Over the past decade or so, the Copperhead has also been a heavy host of the pro tours, in the 1980s and '90s as the site of the J.C. Penney Classic, a now-defunct team event that paired players from the LPGA and PGA Tours, and then as the venue for the PGA Tour's Tampa Bay Classic. When, in 2003, the Chrysler Corporation increased its commitment to pro golf with the creation of the Chrysler Championship, the Copperhead Course was once again called into service.

With its tree-lined fairways and dramatic changes in elevation, this natural setting is more reminiscent of a Carolina layout than Florida's west coast. The narrow fairways snake through tall pines dripping with moss, but also sliver through murky swamp waters of the kind found only in Florida. Eight hazards dot the course, but water doesn't really come into play on the front nine except at the third, a par four that doglegs hard to the right around the edge of a lake. The toughest hole on the outward half is surely number six, a downhill dogleg par four of 465 yards, where even a long and straight drive will leave a testing approach from a sloping lie to an elevated and severely contoured green.

The Copperhead begins to show its fangs at 14, a double-dogleg par five that plays uphill 590 yards through towering pines. This is a true three-

1ST HOLE

1ST HOLE

3RD HOLE

ABOVE: 9TH HOLE RIGHT: 12TH HOLE

shot hole, and the last one had better be accurate because the green is protected by the largest bunker on the Innisbrook property. Fifteen is a picturesque 215-yard par three over a pond to a narrow, sloping green. The water will not come into play for the pros, but two deep bunkers will.

Copperhead's most visually intimidating hole may be the 16th, arching gently right for 460 yards with a lake step-for-step down its right side. Then it's another 215-yard par three, where three greenside bunkers and trees encroaching from both sides make the slender, elevated green seem even more slender. The 445-yard home hole, while not one of the toughest, requires precision, with two groups of bunkers in the tee shot landing area and two bunkers at an elevated, semi-hidden green that is ridged and slopes sharply from back to front.

18TH HOLE

RETIEF GOOSEN, 2003 WINNER

SCORECARD

HOLE	PAR	YARDAGE
1	5	560
2	4	435
3	4	455
4	3	195
5	5	605
6	4	465
7	4	420
8	3	235
9	4	425
OUT	36	3800
10	4	445
11	5	575
12	4	380
13	3	175
14	5	590
15	3	215
16	4	460
17	3	215
18	4	445
IN	35	3515
TOTAL	71	7315

ONLY HERE

Subplots: As the final full-field event of the season, this is more than just a tournament. For marginal players, it's the last chance to earn enough money to finish among the top 125 on the list and thus retain their exempt status for the following year. For the next group, making the top 70 means they're in the field for the next year's invitational events (Bay Hill, Heritage, Memorial, Colonial). For the leading players, it's the last opportunity to break into the top 30 on the money list and earn a spot in the Tour Championship, played the following week, and a chance to earn dollars toward the money title. Finally, there's the Fall Finish, where the player who earns the most points over the final 11 events of the year takes home a $500,000 bonus.

Flipper and More: In the past, tournament organizers have made good use of their local attractions to induce players to commit to this event. Fishing tournaments, dinner cruises on Tampa Bay, and tickets to nearby Busch Gardens and the Dolphin Encounter are among the goodies proffered.

PLAYING TIP

Up and Downhill Lies

When you take on the Copperhead course, you have to be prepared for some ups and downs.

Uphill lies are generally a bit easier to play. The key, as for downhills, is to set yourself to the ball in the correct way. This begins with your alignment, where you should attempt to set your hips parallel to the flow of the land. In other words, be sure your left hip is higher than your right. Usually, that means putting a bit of extra weight on your right foot, or adding some flex in that knee. One way to check that you've done this correctly is to hold a club across your beltline—if it isn't parallel to the ground, make the necessary adjustment in your stance. The other key is to position the ball a bit forward of its usual point in your stance. This is because, with an uphill lie, the bottom point of your swing will occur a bit later. The tendencies from this lie are to pull the ball to the left a bit and to hit a high shot that flies shorter than from a level lie, so in severely uphill situations, take at least one club more and aim a bit to the right.

From a downhill lie, the reverse applies. As you take your stance, be sure your right hip is higher than your left. Play the ball back in your stance to allow for the earlier meeting of clubface and turf, and on severe slopes take one club less (because the ball will fly low and hot) and allow for a bit of rightward push by aiming slightly to the left of your target.

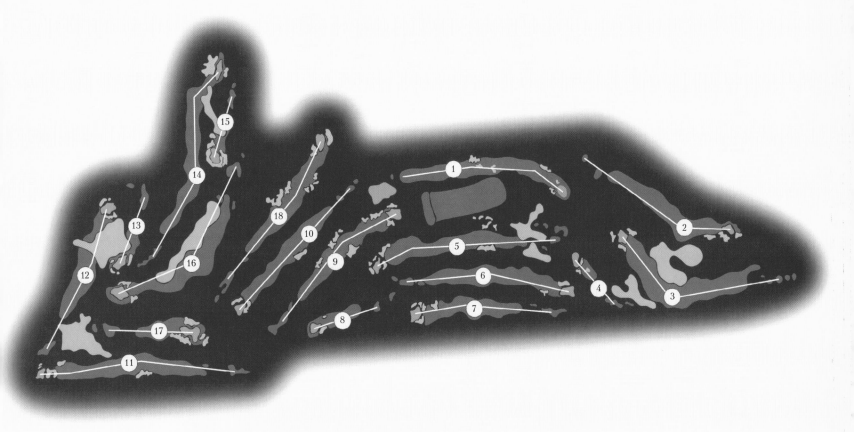

LEFT: 2ND HOLE **ABOVE:** 3RD HOLE

During the 1980s the PGA Tour decided it needed its own Super Bowl or World Series—a definitive season-ending event. First it was thought that a match play event would do the trick—enter the ill-fated Seiko Tucson Match Play Championship, a limited-field affair which alienated the rank-and-file players and did nothing to capture fan interest. After two years, it was abandoned. In its place in 1987 came the Nabisco Championship. It had been introduced a year earlier as a full-field event called the Vantage Championship the week before the match play. When it became the marquee event at the end of the schedule, it was renamed and major changes were made—the field was cut to 30 players and the purse was doubled, from one to two million dollars, the largest on the Tour. Appropriately, first prize that year went to the man who had dominated the Tour for the previous decade, Tom Watson, who sank a six-foot birdie putt on the 72nd hole. It turned out to be the start of

something big—an event that would come to be called, simply, The Tour Championship.

The elite field and huge purse (now $6 million with more than a million to the winner) have helped, but a major key to the success of this event has been the succession of courses on which it has been played over the last decade and a half: Pebble Beach, Pinehurst, Olympic, Harbour Town, Champions, and on four occasions, with the fifth coming in 2005, the East Lake Golf Club in Atlanta.

If the Tour Championship has come a long way since its beginnings, then East Lake may be its ideal venue. Surely, no course has ever made a bigger comeback than this one. In the 1890s, East Lake was the site of an amusement park and penny arcade, where for the price of one cent people could take a peek at photos of Pike's Peak or the 1889 World's Fair in Paris or at bathing beauties in revealing bloomers. When, in 1908, a private golf course was added nearby, the mem-

ABOVE: 8TH HOLE RIGHT (TOP TO BOTTOM): 6TH, 13TH, AND 17TH HOLES

bership roster included Colonel Robert P. Jones, whose six-year-old son Bobby had just taken up the game. East Lake would be the place where Bobby Jones would learn his Grand Slam winning swing.

Course renovations, fifty years apart, by Donald Ross and George Cobb, kept East Lake's challenge and reputation high, and by 1963 it was chosen to host the 15th biennial Ryder Cup Matches. Not long after those matches, however, East Lake began to slide. The surrounding neighborhood—a low-income housing development with 650 units crammed into 50 acres—became a center of poverty, drugs, and violence. Locals

referred to it as "Little Vietnam." East Lake's members started a new club, Atlanta Athletic Club, far north of the city. By the 1980s, once-proud East Lake was tired and all but forgotten, seemingly as hopeless as the area around it.

Enter its savior, Tom Cousins. A prosperous real estate developer who had developed the Omni Complex and NationsBank Plaza in downtown Atlanta, Cousins had fond memories of East Lake from when he had played it as a youngster in the 1940s. Employing the resources of his own charitable foundation, he revamped the golf club and used it as a tool to revitalize the surrounding area. The housing project was razed

and replaced with 500 mixed-income apartments and townhouses surrounding the golf course, which was given a dramatic makeover by Rees Jones. At the same time, Cousins sold 100 corporate memberships at $75,000 each (asking each corporation to contribute an additional $200,000 to the revival of the area). "It was golf with a purpose," he said. "Our plan was to make the golf club the economic engine to drive the revitalization of the neighborhood."

That plan succeeded brilliantly and today East Lake is a paragon of modern urban renewal. Moreover, the East Lake Golf Club has returned to its original stature, standing proudly among

the Top 100 Courses in the World. Its coming-out party was the 1998 Tour Championship, won in dramatic fashion by Hal Sutton with a birdie in a sudden-death playoff, and the success of that event has brought the Tour back four times in the ensuing seven years.

East Lake is a mid-length par 70 of 7,132 yards, with two of its par fives for members converted to fours for the pros. On the front side, the marquee hole is number six, a 209-yard par three that plays from an elevated tee to an angled green (part of the original Tom Bendelow course, designed a century ago) with water left, right, and in front of the green as well as behind part of the back. *Golf Digest* called this the oldest continuously used island green in the U.S. It seems Bobby Jones had particular difficulty with number six. Asked once by Jimmy Demaret, "What do you use off the tee of that hole?" Jones said, "A water ball."

East Lake's back nine boasts one superior hole after another, but the finish is unforgettable, beginning with the uphill, yet very reachable 495-yard par-five 15th. Number 16 plays downhill but into the wind, and enjoys sensational views of not only East Lake itself, its waters glistening in the late afternoon sun, but also of the Atlanta skyline.

The par-four 17th is simply a marvelous hole. Rees Jones repositioned the fairway so that it hugs the lake for its entire 453-yard journey. With bunkers to the right and a wind from the left, it requires a brave and accurate tee shot. The unusual green is sloped back-to-front on the first half, then right-to-left on the back portion, causing havoc with both approach shots and putts.

It's unorthodox for a course to end with a par three, but here it works, with a bruising uphill beauty of 232 yards. When a pro tournament is on the line at East Lake, the last full swing under pressure will be a full-blooded long iron, maybe even a fairway wood.

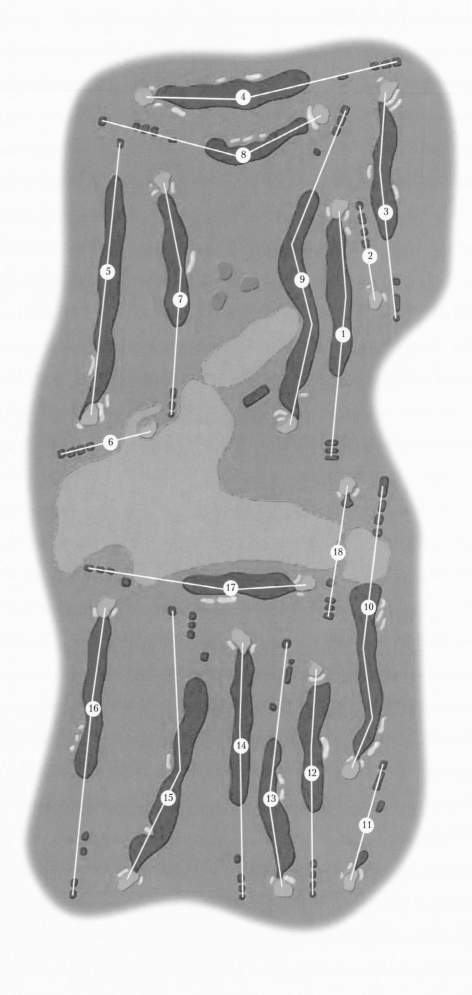

SCORECARD

HOLE	PAR	YARDAGE
1	4	424
2	3	214
3	4	387
4	4	440
5	4	480
6	3	209
7	4	394
8	4	405
9	5	584
OUT	35	3537
10	4	469
11	3	193
12	4	391
13	4	439
14	4	442
15	5	495
16	4	481
17	4	453
18	3	232
IN	35	3595
TOTAL	70	7132

ONLY HERE

The Only Defense is a Good Offense: This is one of
the few events where the defending champion is not
automatically exempt for the following year. Like
everyone else, he has to play himself into the top 30.

Southern Exposure: Since it's the last official event
of the year—and played in November—one guarantee
is that this tournament will also be played at a course
south of the Mason-Dixon line.

Pair Pressure: In round one, the pairings are done
according to rank on the money list. The two players
ranked 30th and 29th tee off first, the guys ranked second and first go last.

Smiling Faces: You'll find nothing but happy campers
among the pros at this event, and why not? They've all
had great years, they're about to get a two-month vaca-
tion (or make tons of money abroad or in the unofficial
off-season events) and no matter how poorly they play
this week, they'll leave with at least $90,000.

Grinding: By Sunday, things get serious. Besides the
hefty first prize, there are often other things at stake,
including the season's Player of the Year honors,
Vardon Trophy, and leading money winner—ample
reasons to put on one's game face.

18TH HOLE

PLAYING TIP

Performing Under Pressure

In an event such as the Tour Championship, where
much prestige and money hinge on a single stroke, the
level of pressure ratchets up a notch. But at one time or
another pressure affects golfers at all levels. When it
does, shots that seemed simple suddenly become difficult, and the mind races in a million unproductive
directions.

The best way to counteract pressure is to keep your
mind focused positively, and that focus begins before
you even arrive at the course. Prepare yourself with a
game plan for your course—chart your "personal par"
for each hole and then play each hole mentally. Determine where you want to place each of your drives and
approach shots.

Once you're on the course, stick with your game
plan and then narrow your focus to each shot. Visualize
that ideal shot in your mind—try to see the desired
path and trajectory of the ball—and keep that picture
firmly in focus as you move through your setup and
swing.

By focusing on the positives you'll leave less room
for negative thoughts, less room for pressure.

HAL SUTTON, 1998 WINNER

MERCEDES CHAMPIONSHIPS

RECORD	PLAYER(S)	SCORE	YEAR
Low 18	K.J. Choi	62	2003
Low first 36	Ernie Els	129 (64-65)	2003
Low 36	Rocco Mediate	128 (65-63)	2003
Low first 54	Ernie Els	194 (64-65-65)	2003
Low 54	Ernie Els	194 (64-65-65)	2003
Low 72	Ernie Els	261 (64-65-65-67)	2003
Highest winning score	Gene Littler	285	1957
Largest winning margin	David Duval (266)	9 strokes	1999
Largest 18-hole lead	Tom Kite (64)	4 strokes	1985
Largest 36-hole lead	David Duval (130)	5 strokes	1999
Largest 54-hole lead	David Duval (198)	7 strokes	1999
Lowest start by winner	Tom Kite	64	1985
	Ernie Els		2003
Highest start by winner	Johnny Miller	74	1974
Lowest finish by winner	Sergio Garcia	64	2002
Highest finish by winner	Al Geiberger	73	1975
	Tom Watson		1980
	Lanny Wadkins		1982
Best final-round comeback	Gary Player	7 back	1978
Lowest 36-hole cut score	No cut		

SONY OPEN IN HAWAII

RECORD	PLAYER(S)	SCORE	YEAR
Low 18	Davis Love III	60	1994
Low first 36	Davis Love III	128 (68-60)	1994
	John Huston	(63-65)	1998
	Paul Azinger	(63-65)	2000
	Brad Faxon	(64-64)	2001
	John Cook	(66-62)	2002
Low 36	Frank Lickliter	127 (62-65) (rounds 2-3)	2004
Low first 54	John Huston	194 (63-65-66)	1998
Low 54	John Huston	194 (63-65-66)	1998
Low 72	John Huston	260 (63-65-66-66)	1998
Highest winning score	Dudley Wysong	284	1967
Largest winning margin	John Huston (260)	7 strokes	1998
	Paul Azinger (261)		2000
Largest 18-hole lead	Jack Nicklaus (69)	4 strokes	1969
Largest 36-hole lead	Paul Azinger (128)	5 strokes	2000
	Brad Faxon (128)		2001
Largest 54-hole lead	Jack Nicklaus (201)	6 strokes	1974

Lowest start by winner	Howard Twitty	63	1990
	John Huston		1998
	Paul Azinger		2000
Highest start by winner	Gay Brewer	74	1965
Lowest finish by winner	Grier Jones	64	1972
	Corey Pavin		1987
Highest finish by winner	Dudley Wysong	73	1967
Best final-round comeback	Corey Pavin	6 back	1987
	Lanny Wadkins		1991
Lowest 36-hole cut score		139	1998
			2001
			2004
Highest 36-hole cut score		152	1965

BOB HOPE CHRYSLER CLASSIC

RECORD	PLAYER(S)	SCORE	YEAR
Low 18	David Duval	59	1999
Low first 36	Joe Durant	126 (65-61)	2001
Low 36	John Cook	125 (62-63) (rounds 4-5)	1997
	Tim Herron	125 (64-61) (rounds 2-3)	2003
Low first 54	Joe Durant	193 (65-61-67)	2001
Low 54	Tim Herron	190 (64-61-65) (rounds 2-4)	2003
Low first 72	Joe Durant	259 (65-61-67-66)	2001
Low 72	Tom Kite	258 (67-64-65-62)(rounds 2-5)	1993
Low 90	Joe Durant	324 (65-61-67-66-65)	2001
Highest winning score	Doug Sanders	349	1966
	Tom Nieporte		1967
Largest winning margin	Rik Massengale (337)	6 strokes	1977
	Tom Kite (325)		1993
Largest 18-hole lead	Rik Massengale (64)	3 strokes	1977
	Craig Stadler (63)		1983
Largest 36-hole lead	Craig Stadler (129)	6 strokes	1983
Largest 54-hole lead	Jack Nicklaus (207)	5 strokes	1963
	Bruce Lietzke (196)		1981
Largest 72-hole lead	Rik Massengale (270)	6 strokes	1977
Lowest start by winner	Jay Haas	63	1988
Highest start by winner	Tom Nieporte	76	1967
	Steve Jones		1989
Lowest finish by winner	David Duval	59	1999
Highest finish by winner	Jack Nicklaus	72	1963
	Billy Casper		1965
Lowest 72-hole cut score		275	2002
			2003
Highest 72-hole cut score		295	1976

FBR OPEN

RECORD	PLAYER(S)	SCORE	YEAR
Low 18	Grant Waite	60	1996
	Mark Calcavecchia		2001
Low first 36	Mark Calcavecchia	125	2001
		(65-60)	
Low 36	Mark Calcavecchia	124	2001
		(60-64)	(rounds 2-3)
Low first 54	Mark Calcavecchia	189	2001
		(65-60-64)	
Low 54	Mark Calcavecchia	189	2001
		(65-60-64)	
Low 72	Mark Calcavecchia	256	2001
		(65-60-64-67)	
Highest winning score	Ky Laffoon	281	1935
Largest winning margin	Johnny Miller	14 strokes	1975
	(260)		
Largest 18-hole lead	Arnold Palmer	3 strokes	1962
	(64)		
	Davis Love III		1988
	(63)		
Largest 36-hole lead	Byron Nelson	6 strokes	1939
	(133)		
	Johnny Miller		1975
	(128)		
Largest 54-hole lead	Byron Nelson	12 strokes	1939
	(198)		
Lowest start by winner	Steve Jones	62	1997
Highest start by winner	Dudley Wysong	73	1966
Lowest finish by winner	Mark Calcavecchia	63	1992
	Vijay Singh		2003
Highest finish by winner	Jimmy Demaret	73	1949
	Jerry Pate		1977
Best final-round comeback	Sandy Lyle	7 back	1977
Lowest 36-hole cut score		138	2003
Highest 36-hole cut score		153	1953

AT&T PEBBLE BEACH NATIONAL PRO-AM

RECORD	PLAYER(S)	SCORE	YEAR
Low 18	Tom Kite	62	1983
	David Duval		1997
	Matt Gogel		2001
Low first 36	Matt Gogel	131	2001
		(69-62)	
Low 36	Tiger Woods	127	1997
		(63-64)	(rounds 3-4)
Low first 54	David Duval	198	1997
		(65-71-62)	
Low 54	David Duval	198	1997
		(65-71-62)	
Low 72	Mark O'Meara	268	1997
		(67-67-67-67)	
Highest winning score	Ken Venturi	286	1960
	Doug Ford		1962
Largest winning margin	Lloyd Mangrum	5 strokes	1948
	(205)		
	Cary Middlecoff		1956
	(202)		
	Jack Nicklaus		1967
	(286)		
	Fuzzy Zoeller		1986
	(205)		
Largest 18-hole lead	Jack Nicklaus	3 strokes	1972
	(66)		
	Billy Casper		1973
	(66)		
	Tom Watson		1978
	(66)		
Largest 36-hole lead	Bob Rosburg	5 strokes	1958
	(132)		

	Billy Casper		1973
	(133)		
	Pat Perez		2002
	(131)		
Largest 54-hole lead	Ted Kroll	5 strokes	1961
	(203)		
	Lon Hinkle		1979
	(207)		
	Fuzzy Zoeller		1986
	(205)		
Lowest start by winner	Phil Mickelson	65	1998
Highest start by winner	Jack Burke Jr.	75	1950
	Bruce Crampton		1965
	Ben Crenshaw		1976
Lowest finish by winner	Davis Love III	63	2001
Highest finish by winner	Ken Venturi	77	1960
	Lon Hinkle		1979
Best final-round comeback	Bob Rosburg	7 back	1971
Lowest 54-hole cut score		213	1997
Highest 54-hole cut score		227	1967

BUICK INVITATIONAL

RECORD	PLAYER(S)	SCORE	YEAR
Low 18	Mark Brooks	61	1990
Low first 36	Lennie Clements	129	1996
		(64-65)	
Low 36	Tiger Woods	127	1999
		(62-65)	(rounds 3-4)
Low first 54	Woody Blackburn	198	1985
		(66-66-66)	
Low 54	Gil Morgan	197	1988
		(62-67-68)	(rounds 2-4)
Low 72	George Burns	266	1987
		(63-68-70-65)	
Highest winning score	Jack Nicklaus	284	1969
Largest winning margin	Tom Watson	5 strokes	1977
	(269)		
	Fuzzy Zoeller		1979
	(282)		
Largest 18-hole lead	Jimmy Powell	2 strokes	1968
	(64)		
	Gene Littler		1972
	(66)		
	Tommy Aaron		1973
	(69)		
	Jay Haas		1993
	(70)		
Largest 36-hole lead	Jay Haas	3 strokes	1978
	(136)		
	Johnny Miller		1982
	(132)		
	Tom Kite		1983
	(133)		
	Payne Stewart		1993
	(138)		
	David Toms		1994
	(130)		
Largest 54-hole lead	J.C. Snead	5 strokes	1976
	(200)		
Lowest start by winner	George Burns	63	1987
Highest start by winner	Pete Brown	76	1970
	Fuzzy Zoeller		1979
Lowest finish by winner	Billy Casper	64	1966
	Davis Love III		1996
	Scott Simpson		1998
Highest finish by winner	John Daly	75	2004
Best final-round comeback	Pete Brown	7 back	1970
Lowest 36-hole cut score		139	1985
Highest 36-hole cut score		151	1993

NISSAN OPEN

RECORD	PLAYER(S)	SCORE	YEAR
Low 18	George Archer	61	1983
	Ted Tryba		1999
Low first 36	Davis Love III	130	1992
		(67-63)	
	Shigeki Maruyama	(64-66)	2004
	Mike Weir	(66-64)	2004
Low 36	Arnold Palmer	128	1966
		(66-62)	(rounds 2-3)
Low first 54	Mike Weir	196	2004
		(66-64-66)	
Low 54	Mike Weir	196	2004
		(66-64-66)	
Low 72	Lanny Wadkins	264	1985
		(63-70-67-64)	
Highest winning score	Denny Shute	296	1930
Largest winning margin	Phil Rodgers	9 strokes	1962
	(268)		
Largest 18-hole lead	Terry Mauney	4 strokes	1982
	(63)		
Largest 36-hole lead	Henry Ransom	4 strokes	1951
	(136)		
	Davis Love III		1992
	(130)		
Largest 54-hole lead	Pat Fitzsimons	6 strokes	1975
	(205)		
Lowest start by winner	Charles Sifford	63	1969
	Lanny Wadkins		1985
Highest start by winner	Jimmy Thomson	75	1938
Lowest finish by winner	Phil Rodgers	62	1962
Highest finish by winner	Fred Wampler	75	1954
Best final-round comeback	Ken Venturi	7 back	1959
	Mike Weir		2003
Lowest 36-hole cut score		140	1991
Highest 36-hole cut score		156	

WGC-ACCENTURE MATCH PLAY CHAMPIONSHIP

No tournament records because of match-play format.

CHRYSLER CLASSIC OF TUCSON

RECORD	PLAYER(S)	SCORE	YEAR
Low 18	David Frost	60	1990
Low first 36	David Duval	128	1998
		(66-62)	
Low 36	Johnny Palmer	126	1948
		(62-64)	(rounds 3-4)
	Mark Wiebe	126	1988
		(65-61)	(rounds 2-3)
Low first 54	Joe Campbell	194	1959
		(65-64-65)	
Low 54	Joe Campbell	194	1959
		(65-64-65)	
Low 72	Lloyd Mangrum	263	1949
		(64-66-68-65)	
	Phil Rodgers	(64-68-65-66)	1962
	Johnny Miller	(66-69-67-61)	1975
Highest winning score	Joe Campbell	278	1966
Largest winning margin	Don January	11 strokes	1963
	(266)		
Lowest start by winner	Johnny Miller	62	1974
Highest start by winner	Jeff Sluman	75	1997
Lowest finish by winner	Johnny Miller	61	1975
Highest finish by winner	Arnold Palmer	73	1967
	Miller Barber		1972
	Tom Watson		1978
Lowest 36-hole cut score		139	1959
Highest 36-hole cut score		148	1964

FORD CHAMPIONSHIP AT DORAL

RECORD	PLAYER(S)	SCORE	YEAR
Low 18	Stephen Ames	61	2000
Low first 36	Franklin Langham	129	2000
		(66-63)	
Low 36	Franklin Langham	129	2000
		(66-63)	
Low first 54	Greg Norman	195	1993
		(65-68-62)	
Low 54	Greg Norman	195	1993
		(65-68-62)	
Low 72	Greg Norman	265	1993
		(65-68-72-70)	
	Jim Furyk	(65-67-68-65)	2000
Highest winning score	Mark McCumber	284	1985
Largest winning margin	Hubert Green	6 strokes	1976
	(276)		
Largest 18-hole lead	Lee Trevino	4 strokes	1973
	(64)		
Largest 36-hole lead	Lee Trevino	4 strokes	1973
	(134)		
Largest 54-hole lead	Ernie Els	8 strokes	2002
	(199)		
Lowest start by winner	Lee Trevino	64	1973
Highest start by winner	Dan Sikes	76	1973
Lowest finish by winner	Greg Norman	62	1990
Highest finish by winner	Gardner Dickinson	72	1968
	Andy Bean		1977
	Mark McCumber		1979
	Bill Glasson		1989
	Rocco Mediate		1991
	Ernie Els		2002
Best final-round comeback	Greg Norman	7 back	1990
Lowest 36-hole cut score		141	2000
			2001
Highest 36-hole cut score		153	1962

THE HONDA CLASSIC

RECORD	PLAYER(S)	SCORE	YEAR
Low 18	Hale Irwin	62	1979
	Dan Pohl		1989
	Tim Herron		1996
	Jerry Kelly		2003
	Adam Scott		2003
Low first 36	Dan Pohl	128	1989
		(66-62)	
Low 36	Dan Pohl	128	1989
		(66-62)	
Low first 54	Davis Love III	196	2003
		(66-65-65)	
Low 54	Blaine McCallister	196	1989
		(67-65-64)	(rounds 2-4)
	Davis Love III	(66-65-65)	2003
Low 72	Justin Leonard	264	2003
		(63-70-64-67)	
Highest winning score	Kenny Knox	287	1986
Largest winning margin	Jack Nicklaus	5 strokes	1977
	(275)		
Largest 18-hole lead	Mike Sullivan	4 strokes	1987
	(65)		
Largest 36-hole lead	Tim Herron	6 strokes	1996
	(130)		
Largest 54-hole lead	Steve Pate	5 strokes	1991
	(204)		
Lowest start by winner	Tim Herron	62	1996
Highest start by winner	Bruce Lietzke	72	1984
Lowest finish by winner	Blaine McCallister	64	1989
Highest finish by winner	Steve Pate	75	1991
Best final-round comeback	Vijay Singh	5 back	1999
Lowest 36-hole cut score		138	2003
Highest 36-hole cut score		151	1987
			1990

BAY HILL INVITATIONAL PRESENTED BY MASTERCARD

RECORD	PLAYER(S)	SCORE	YEAR
Low 18	Andy Bean	62	1981
	Greg Norman		1984
	Fred Couples		1992
	Stuart Appleby		1997
Low first 36	Andy Bean	130 (68-62)	1981
	Tom Watson	(64-66)	1981
Low 36	Payne Stewart	128 (63-65)	1987 (rounds 3-4)
Low first 54	Andy Bean	197 (68-62-67)	1981
Low 54	Payne Stewart	195 (67-63-65)	1987 (rounds 2-4)
Low 72	Payne Stewart	264 (69-67-63-65)	1987
Highest winning score	Mike Nicolette	283	1983
Largest winning margin	Tiger Woods (269)	11 strokes	2003
Largest 18-hole lead	Tom Byrum (64)	3 strokes	1990
Largest 36-hole lead	Paul Azinger (132)	4 strokes	1988
	Tiger Woods (132)		2002
Largest 54-hole lead	Mike Nicolette (204)	6 strokes	1983
	Fred Couples (199)		1993
Lowest start by winner	Mike Nicolette	66	1983
	Paul Azinger		1988
	Tim Herron		1999
	Chad Campbell		2004
Highest start by winner	Phil Mickelson	72	1997
Lowest finish by winner	Gary Koch	63	1984
Highest finish by winner	Dave Eichelberger	74	1980
	Mike Nicolette		1983
Best final-round comeback	Tom Kite	6 back	1982
	Gary Koch		1984
Lowest 36-hole cut score		144	1982
			1997
			2000
			2004
Highest 36-hole cut score		152	1983

THE PLAYERS CHAMPIONSHIP

RECORD	PLAYER(S)	SCORE	YEAR
Low 18	Fred Couples	63	1992
	Greg Norman		1994
Low first 36	Greg Norman	130 (63-67)	1994
Low 36	Greg Norman	130 (63-67)	1994
Low first 54	Greg Norman	197 (63-67-67)	1994
Low 54	Greg Norman	197 (63-67-67)	1994
Low 72	Greg Norman	264 (63-67-67-67)	1994
Highest winning score	Mark Hayes	289	1977
	Jack Nicklaus		1978
Largest winning margin	Steve Elkington (272)	7 strokes	1997
Largest 18-hole lead	Billy Ray Brown (64)	3 strokes	1992
Largest 36-hole lead	Lanny Wadkins (135)	3 strokes	1979
	Greg Norman (130)		1994
Largest 54-hole lead	Larry Mize (200)	4 strokes	1986
Lowest start by winner	Greg Norman	63	1994
Highest start by winner	Hal Sutton	73	1983
Lowest finish by winner	Fred Couples	64	1996
	Davis Love III		2003
Highest finish by winner	Jack Nicklaus	75	1978
Best final-round comeback	Ray Floyd	6 back	1981
Lowest 36-hole cut score		142	1993
Highest 36-hole cut score		155	1977

BELLSOUTH CLASSIC

RECORD	PLAYER(S)	SCORE	YEAR
Low 18	Andy Bean	61	1979
Low first 36	Larry Nelson	129 (63-66)	1988
Low 36	Ben Crane	127 (64-63)	2003 (rounds 3-4)
Low first 54	Larry Nelson	195 (63-66-66)	1988
Low 54	Andy Bean	195 (67-61-67)	1979 (rounds 2-4)
	Larry Nelson	(63-66-66)	1988
Low 72	Andy Bean	265 (70-67-61-67)	1979
	Dave Barr	(66-68-66-65)	1987
Highest winning score	Bob Charles	282	1967
Largest winning margin	Andy Bean (265)	8 strokes	1979
Largest 18-hole lead	Mark Lye (63)	4 strokes	1979
Largest 36-hole lead	Jack Nicklaus (133)	4 strokes	1973
	Larry Nelson (129)		1988
	Rory Sabbatini (130)		1999
Largest 54-hole lead	Jack Nicklaus (199)	6 strokes	1973
Lowest start by winner	Larry Nelson	63	1988
Highest start by winner	Ben Crane	73	2003
Lowest finish by winner	Calvin Peete	63	1983
	Ben Crane		2003
Highest finish by winner	Jack Nicklaus	73	1973
	Larry Nelson		1988
	Scott McCarron		2001
Best final-round comeback	Calvin Peete	7 back	1983
Lowest 36-hole cut score		141	1987
Highest 36-hole cut score		151	1967

THE MASTERS

RECORD	PLAYER(S)	SCORE	YEAR
Low 18	Nick Price	63	1986
	Greg Norman		1996
Low first 36	Ray Floyd	131 (65-66)	1976
Low 36	Johnny Miller	131 (65-66)	1975 (rounds 3-4)
	Ray Floyd	(65-66)	1976
	Tiger Woods	131 (66-65)	1997 (rounds 2-3)
Low first 54	Ray Floyd	201 (65-66-70)	1976
	Tiger Woods	201 (70-66-65)	1997
Low 54	Tiger Woods	200 (66-65-69)	1997 (rounds 2-4)
Low 72	Tiger Woods	270	1997

Record	Player(s)	Score	Year
Highest winning score	Sam Snead	(70-66-65-69) 289	1954
	Jack Burke Jr.		1956
Largest winning margin	Tiger Woods (270)	12 strokes	1997
Largest 18-hole lead	Craig Wood (66)	5 strokes	1941
Largest 36-hole lead	Herman Keiser (137)	5 strokes	1946
	Jack Nicklaus (135)		1975
	Ray Floyd (131)		1976
Largest 54-hole lead	Tiger Woods (201)	9 strokes	1997
Lowest start by winner	Ray Floyd	65	1976
Highest start by winner	Craig Stadler	75	1982
Lowest finish by winner	Gary Player	64	1978
Highest finish by winner	Arnold Palmer	75	1962
Best final-round comeback	Jack Burke Jr.	8 back	1956
Lowest 36-hole cut score		145	1979 1992 1995 2001
Highest 36-hole cut score		154	1982

MCI HERITAGE

Record	Player(s)	Score	Year
Low 18	David Frost	61	1994
Low first 36	Jack Nicklaus	129 (66-63)	1975
	Phil Mickelson	129 (65-64)	2002
Low 36	Jack Nicklaus	129 (66-63)	1975
	Ian Baker-Finch	129 (64-65)	1991 (rounds 2-3)
	David Edwards	129 (65-64)	1994 (rounds 3-4)
	Phil Mickelson	129 (65-64)	2002
Low first 54	Justin Leonard	197 (67-64-66)	2002
Low 54	Justin Leonard	197 (67-64-66)	2002
Low 72	Loren Roberts	265 (66-69-63-67)	1996
Highest winning score	Arnold Palmer	283	1969
Largest winning margin	Davis Love III (266)	7 strokes	1998
Largest 18-hole lead	Jack Nicklaus (66)	3 strokes	1975
Largest 36-hole lead	Jack Nicklaus (129)	6 strokes	1975
Largest 54-hole lead	Tom Watson (199)	8 strokes	1979
Lowest start by winner	Graham Marsh	65	1977
	Tom Watson		1979
	Greg Norman		1988
	Payne Stewart		1989
	Davis Love III		1991
	Nick Price		1997
Highest start by winner	Bob Goalby	74	1970
Lowest finish by winner	Stewart Cink	64	2004
Highest finish by winner	Arnold Palmer	74	1969
Best final-round comeback	Stewart Cink	9 strokes	2004
Lowest 36-hole cut score		142	1996 2001 2002 2003
Highest 36-hole cut score		152	1971

SHELL HOUSTON OPEN

Record	Player(s)	Score	Year
Low 18	Ron Streck	62	1981
	Fred Funk		1992
Low first 36	Curtis Strange	129 (66-63)	1980
	Blaine McCallister	129 (64-65)	1993
Low 36	Wayne Levi	128 (65-63)	1979 (rounds 2-3)
Low first 54	Curtis Strange	195 (66-63-66)	1980
Low 54	Curtis Strange	195 (66-63-66)	1980
Low 72	Curtis Strange	266 (66-63-66-71)	1980
	Lee Trevino	(67-66-68-65)	
	Vijay Singh	(67-65-66-68)	2002
Highest winning score	Cary Middlecoff	283	1953
Largest winning margin	Jack Burke Jr. (277)	6 strokes	1952
	Vijay Singh (266)		2002
Largest 18-hole lead	David Duval (65)	3 strokes	1997
Largest 36-hole lead	Curtis Strange (129)	4 strokes	1980
	Mike Donald (134)		1989
	Jeff Maggert (130)		1991
Largest 54-hole lead	Curtis Strange (195)	6 strokes	1980
Lowest start by winner	Gary Player	64	1978
	Ed Sneed		1982
Highest start by winner	Mike Sullivan	76	1989
Lowest finish by winner	Ron Streck	62	1981
Highest finish by winner	Bill Collins	75	1960
Best final-round comeback	Mike Sullivan	7 back	1989
	Fulton Allem		1991
	Payne Stewart		1995
Lowest 36-hole cut score		140	1993
Highest 36-hole cut score		159	1947

HP CLASSIC OF NEW ORLEANS

Record	Player(s)	Score	Year
Low 18	Paul Stankowski	61	2001
Low first 36	Scott Verplank	128 (65-63)	2003
Low 36	David Toms	127 (63-64)	2001 (rounds 3-4)
Low first 54	Scott Verplank	195 (65-63-67)	2003
Low 54	Chip Beck	193 (64-65-64)	1988
Low 72	Chip Beck	262 (69-64-65-64)	1988
Highest winning score	Jimmy Demaret	286	1940
Largest winning margin	Lee Trevino (267)	8 strokes	1974
Largest 18-hole lead	Mike Reasor (65)	4 strokes	1976
	Skip Dunaway (64)		1981
	John Mahaffey (63)		1985
	Jose Maria Olazabal (63)		1994
Largest 36-hole lead	Chip Beck	4 strokes	1992

	(132)		
Largest 54-hole lead	Billy Casper	5 strokes	1975
	(201)		
	Calvin Peete		1986
	(201)		
Lowest start by winner	Tom Watson	66	1980
	Bob Eastwood		1984
	Ben Crenshaw		1987
	Carlos Franco		1999
Highest start by winner	Lon Hinkle	74	1978
Lowest finish by winner	Vijay Singh	63	2004
Highest finish by winner	Mason Rudolph	75	1964
Best final-round comeback	Larry Hinson	5 back	1969
Lowest 36-hole cut score		139	2003
Highest 36-hole cut score		152	1993

WACHOVIA CHAMPIONSHIP

RECORD	PLAYER(S)	SCORE	YEAR
Low 18	Kirk Triplett	64	2004
Low first 36	Tiger Woods	135	2004
		(69-66)	
Low 36	David Toms	135	2003
		(69-66)	(rounds 2-3)
	Steve Flesch	135	2004
		(66-69)	(rounds 3-4)
	Tiger Woods	(69-66)	2004
Low first 54	David Toms	205	2003
		(70-69-66)	
	Arron Oberholser	(69-68-68)	2004
Low 54	David Toms	205	2003
		(70-69-66)	
	Arron Oberholser	(69-68-68)	2004
Low 72	Joey Sindelar	277	2004
		(69-69-70-69)	
	Arron Oberholser	(69-68-68-72)	2004
Highest winning score	David Toms	278	2003
Largest winning margin	David Toms	2 strokes	2003
	(278)		
Largest 18-hole lead	Kirk Triplett	2 strokes	2004
	(64)		
Largest 36-hole lead	Tiger Woods	2 strokes	2004
	(135)		
Largest 54-hole lead	David Toms	5 strokes	2003
	(205)		
Lowest start by winner	Joey Sindelar	69	2004
Highest start by winner	David Toms	70	2003
Lowest finish by winner	Joey Sindelar	69	2004
Highest finish by winner	David Toms	73	2003
Best final-round comeback	Joey Sindelar	3 back	2004
Lowest 36-hole cut score		144	2004
Highest 36-hole cut score		145	2003

EDS BYRON NELSON CLASSIC

RECORD	PLAYER(S)	SCORE	YEAR
Low 18	Sam Snead	60	1957
Low first 36	Lee Rinker	128	1997
		(65-63)	
Low 36	Sam Snead	126	1957
		(60-66)	(rounds 2-3)
	Ernie Els	126	1995
		(61-65)	(rounds 2-3)
Low first 54	Loren Roberts	194	1999
		(66-66-62)	
Low 54	Mark Calcavecchia	193	1987
		(66-63-64)	
Low 72	Loren Roberts	262	1999
		(66-66-62-68)	
Highest winning score	Ben Hogan	284	1946
Largest winning margin	Byron Nelson	10 strokes	1944

BANK OF AMERICA COLONIAL

RECORD	PLAYER(S)	SCORE	YEAR
	(276)		
	Sam Snead		1957
	(264)		
Lowest start by winner	Don January	64	1956
	Tom Watson		1979
	Tom Watson		1980
	Tiger Woods		1997
Highest start by winner	Tom Watson	72	1975
Lowest finish by winner	Peter Thomson	63	1956
Highest finish by winner	Ben Hogan	73	1946
Best final-round comeback	Peter Thomson	7 back	1956
Lowest 36-hole cut score		137	1989
Highest 36-hole cut score		149	1970
			1984

RECORD	PLAYER(S)	SCORE	YEAR
Low 18	Keith Clearwater	61	1993
	Lee Janzen		1993
	Greg Kraft		1999
	Kenny Perry		2003
	Justin Leonard		2003
	Chad Campbell		2004
Low first 36	Fulton Allem	129	1993
		(66-63)	
	David Frost	(66-63)	1997
	Brad Faxon	(63-66)	1997
	Paul Goydos	(64-65)	1997
Low 36	Kenny Perry	125	2003
		(64-61)	(rounds 2-3)
Low first 54	Kenny Perry	193	2003
		(68-64-61)	
Low 54	Kenny Perry	193	2003
		(68-64-61)	
	Kenny Perry	193	2003
		(64-61-68)	(rounds 2-4)
Low 72	Kenny Perry	261	2003
		(68-64-61-68)	
Highest winning score	Ben Hogan	285	1959
Largest winning margin	Chandler Harper	8 strokes	1955
	(276)		
Largest 18-hole lead	George Schneiter	4 strokes	1946
	(67)		
	Tommy Bolt		1953
	(67)		
Largest 36-hole lead	Chandler Harper	7 strokes	1955
	(134)		
Largest 54-hole lead	Chandler Harper	6 strokes	1955
	(204)		
	Kenny Perry		2003
	(193)		
Lowest start by winner	Bruce Lietzke	63	1980
Highest start by winner	Ben Hogan	74	1952
	Mike Souchak		1956
Lowest finish by winner	Phil Mickelson	63	2000
	Sergio Garcia		2001
Highest finish by winner	Arnold Palmer	76	1962
Best final-round comeback	Nick Price	7 back	1994
Lowest 36-hole cut score		140	1987
			1997
Highest 36-hole cut score		148	1971

FEDEX ST. JUDE CLASSIC

RECORD	PLAYER(S)	SCORE	YEAR
Low 18	Al Geiberger	59	1977
Low first 36	John Cook	126	1996
		(64-62)	
Low 36	John Cook	125	1996
		(62-63)	(rounds 2-3)

Low first 54	John Cook	189 (64-62-63)	1996
Low 54	John Cook	189 (64-62-63)	1996
Low 72	John Cook	258 (64-62-63-69)	1996
Highest winning score	Dave Hill	283	1973
Largest winning margin	John Cook (258)	7 strokes	1996
Largest 18-hole lead	Bert Yancey (63)	3 strokes	1966
	Larry Silveira (62)		1990
	Bob Estes (61)		2001
Largest 36-hole lead	Gardner Dickinson (128)	7 strokes	1961
Largest 54-hole lead	David Toms (195)	7 strokes	2004
Lowest start by winner	Bob Estes	61	2001
Highest start by winner	Tommy Bolt	72	1960
	Al Geiberger		1977
	Gil Morgan		1979
	Tom Kite		1990
Lowest finish by winner	Jay Haas	64	1992
	Len Mattiace		2002
	David Toms		2003
Highest finish by winner	Dave Hill	73	1967
	David Toms		2004
Best final-round comeback	Hal Sutton	8 back	1985
Lowest 36-hole cut score		138	1999
Highest 36-hole cut score		150	1972 1973 1986

THE MEMORIAL TOURNAMENT

RECORD	PLAYER(S)	SCORE	YEAR
Low 18	John Huston	61	1996
Low first 36	Scott Hoch	131 (67-64)	1987
Low 36	Tiger Woods	128 (63-65) (rounds 2-3)	2000
Low first 54	Scott Hoch	198 (67-64-67)	1987
Low 54	Scott Hoch	198 (67-64-67)	1987
	Tiger Woods	198 (63-65-70) (rounds 2-4)	2000
Low 72	Tom Lehman	268 (67-67-67-67)	1994
Highest winning score	Roger Maltbie	288	1976
Largest winning margin	Tiger Woods (271)	7 strokes	2001
Largest 18-hole lead	Fred Couples (69)	4 strokes	1990
Largest 36-hole lead	Roger Maltbie (134)	6 strokes	1982
Largest 54-hole lead	Tiger Woods (199)	6 strokes	2000
Lowest start by winner	Kenny Perry	65	2003
Highest start by winner	Ray Floyd	74	1982
Lowest finish by winner	Jim Furyk	65	2002
Highest finish by winner	Roger Maltbie	76	1976
Best final-round comeback	David Edwards	5 back	1992
Lowest 36-hole cut score		145	1992 1993 1995 1998
Highest 36-hole cut score		157	1976 1979 1990

BUICK CLASSIC

RECORD	PLAYER(S)	SCORE	YEAR
Low 18	Dan Sikes	62	1967
	Jimmy Wright		1976
	Peter Jacobsen		1982
Low first 36	Bob Gilder	127 (64-63)	1982
Low 36	Bob Gilder	127 (64-63)	1982
Low first 54	Bob Gilder	192 (64-63-65)	1982
Low 54	Bob Gilder	192 (64-63-65)	1982
Low 72	Bob Gilder	261 (64-63-65-69)	1982
Highest winning score	Vijay Singh	280	1993
Largest winning margin	David Frost (268)	8 strokes	1992
	Ernie Els (271)		1996
Largest 18-hole lead	Tom Weiskopf (64)	3 strokes	1973
	David Graham (65)		1979
Largest 36-hole lead	Tom Weiskopf (129)	7 strokes	1975
Largest 54-hole lead	Bob Gilder (192)	6 strokes	1982
	Ernie Els (200)		1996
Lowest start by winner	David Graham	63	1976
Highest start by winner	Bob Tway	73	1986
Lowest finish by winner	Bobby Nichols	65	1973
	Scott Simpson		1984
Highest finish by winner	Wayne Grady	72	1989
	Vijay Singh		1995
Best final-round comeback	Bobby Nichols	5 back	1973
	Vijay Singh		1993
Lowest 36-hole cut score		141	1982
Highest 36-hole cut score		147	1983 1993

BOOZ ALLEN CLASSIC

RECORD	PLAYER(S)	SCORE	YEAR
Low 18	Jerry McGee	61	1979
Low first 36	Fred Funk	130 (64-66)	1998
Low 36	Billy Andrade	128 (64-64) (rounds 2-3)	1991
	Jeff Sluman	128 (64-64) (rounds 2-3)	1991
Low first 54	Hal Sutton	195 (66-65-64)	1991
Low 54	Jeff Sluman	193 (64-64-65) (rounds 2-4)	1991
Low 72	Billy Andrade	263 (68-64-64-67)	1991
	Jeff Sluman	(70-64-64-65)	
Highest winning score	Fred Couples	287	1983
Largest winning margin	Craig Stadler (275)	7 strokes	1982
	Tom Kite (270)		1987
Largest 18-hole lead	George Burns (64)	4 strokes	1983
Largest 36-hole lead	Greg Norman (136)	4 strokes	1984
Largest 54-hole lead	Greg Norman (207)	7 strokes	1984

Lowest start by winner	Jerry McGee	61	1979
Highest start by winner	Dick Lotz	72	1970
	Andy Bean		1978
	Craig Stadler		1982
	Bill Glasson		1985
	Greg Norman		1986
Lowest finish by winner	Andy Bean	66	1978
	Bill Glasson		1985
	Greg Norman		1986
Highest finish by winner	Fred Couples	77	1983
Best final-round comeback	Bill Glasson	6 back	1985
Lowest 36-hole cut score		140	1991
Highest 36-hole cut score		150	1983
			1984

CIALIS WESTERN OPEN

RECORD	PLAYER(S)	SCORE	YEAR
Low 18	Cary Middlecoff	63	1955
	Jeff Sluman		1992
	John Adams		1993
	Dudley Hart		1998
	Stephen Ames		2000
	Brian Henninger		2000
	Nick Price		2000
	Tiger Woods		2003
Low first 36	Hugh Royer	132	1970
		(67-65)	
Low 36	Scott Hoch	130	2001
		(66-64)	(rounds 3-4)
Low first 54	Tiger Woods	198	2003
		(63-70-65)	
Low 54	Scott Hoch	198	2001
		(68-66-64)	(rounds 2-4)
	Tiger Woods	(63-70-65)	2003
Low 72	Scott Hoch	267	2001
		(69-68-66-64)	
	Tiger Woods	(63-70-65-69)	2003
Highest winning score	Alex Smith	318	1903
Largest winning margin	Walter Hagen	9 strokes	1926
	(279)		
Largest 18-hole lead	David Graham	3 strokes	1975
	(65)		
	Nick Price		2000
	(63)		
Largest 36-hole lead	Bob Dickson	6 strokes	1976
	(136)		
Largest 54-hole lead	Tiger Woods	6 strokes	2003
	(198)		
Lowest start by winner	Tiger Woods	63	2003
Highest start by winner	Robert Simpson	84	1907
Lowest finish by winner	Cary Middlecoff	63	1955
Highest finish by winner	Jock Hutchison	80	1920
Best final-round comeback	Tom Kite	7 back	1986
Lowest 36-hole cut score		143	1996
			1999
			2000
			2001
			2002
			2003
Highest 36-hole cut score		153	1974

JOHN DEERE CLASSIC

RECORD	PLAYER(S)	SCORE	YEAR
Low 18	Mike Smith	61	1987
	J.P. Hayes		2002
Low first 36	David Frost	127	2000
		(65-62)	
Low 36	Blaine McCallister	125	1988

		(62-63)	(rounds 2-3)
Low first 54	Blaine McCallister	193	1988
		(68-62-63)	
	Brian Henninger	193	1999
		(66-63-64)	
Low 54	David Frost	191	1993
		(63-64-64)	(rounds 2-4)
Low 72	David Frost	259	1993
		(68-63-64-64)	
Highest winning score	Roger Maltbie	275	1975
Largest winning margin	David Frost	7 strokes	1993
	(259)		
Largest 18-hole lead	Several players	2 strokes	
Largest 36-hole lead	Dave Eichelberger	5 strokes	1975
	(132)		
Largest 54-hole lead	David Frost	5 strokes	1992
	(194)		
Lowest start by winner	David Frost	62	1992
Highest start by winner	Roger Maltbie	74	1975
Lowest finish by winner	Payne Stewart	63	1982
Highest finish by winner	David Frost	72	1992
Best final-round comeback	Roger Maltbie	7 back	1975
Lowest 36-hole cut score		138	1991
			1993
			1998
			1999
Highest 36-hole cut score		146	1975

B.C. OPEN

RECORD	PLAYER(S)	SCORE	YEAR
Low 18	Hal Sutton	61	1995
	Fred Funk		1999
Low first 36	Joey Sindelar	128	1987
		(65-63)	
	Steve Lowery	(64-64)	2003
Low 36	Calvin Peete	127	1982
		(63-64)	(rounds 2-3)
Low first 54	Calvin Peete	196	1982
		(69-63-64)	
	Steve Lowery	(64-64-68)	2003
Low 54	Calvin Peete	196	1982
		(69-63-64)	
	Calvin Peete	196	1982
		(63-64-69)	(rounds 2-4)
	Steve Lowery	(64-64-68)	2003
Low 72	Calvin Peete	265	1982
		(69-63-64-69)	
Highest winning score	Wayne Levi	275	1984
	Gabriel Hjertstedt		1997
Largest winning margin	Calvin Peete	7 strokes	1982
	(265)		
Largest 18-hole lead	Andy North	3 strokes	1975
	(63)		
	Calvin Peete		1981
	(64)		
	Mark O'Meara		1983
	(63)		
	Esteban Toledo		2000
	(64)		
Largest 36-hole lead	Joey Sindelar	7 strokes	1987
	(128)		
Largest 54-hole lead	Joey Sindelar	8 strokes	1987
	(197)		
Lowest start by winner	Bob Wynn	65	1976
	Rick Fehr		1986
	Joey Sindelar		1987
	Mike Sullivan		1994
Highest start by winner	Pat Lindsey	71	1983
	Hal Sutton		1995
Lowest finish by winner	Hal Sutton	61	1995

Highest finish by winner	Gabriel Hjertstedt	70	1997
Best final-round comeback	Craig Stadler	8 back	2003
Lowest 36-hole cut score		140	1994
Highest 36-hole cut score		147	1984

U.S. BANK CHAMPIONSHIP IN MILWAUKEE

RECORD	PLAYER(S)	SCORE	YEAR
Low 18	Ken Green	61	1988
	Robert Gamez		1991
	Steve Lowery		1999
Low first 36	Robert Gamez	127 (66-61)	1991
Low 36	Robert Gamez	127 (66-61)	1991
Low first 54	Jeff Sluman	193 (64-66-63)	2002
Low 54	Jeff Sluman	193 (64-66-63)	2002
Low 72	Loren Roberts	260 (65-66-63-66)	2000
Highest winning score	Dave Eichelberger	278	1977
Largest winning margin	Loren Roberts (260)	8 strokes	2000
Largest 18-hole lead	Loren Roberts (62)	3 strokes	1998
Largest 36-hole lead	Dave Stockton (132)	3 strokes	1973
	Kenny Perry (129)		2001
Largest 54-hole lead	Jay Haas (201)	5 strokes	1981
Lowest start by winner	Mark Brooks	63	1991
Highest start by winner	Ken Still	74	1969
Lowest finish by winner	Calvin Peete	65	1979
	Scott Hoch		1995
Highest finish by winner	Dave Stockton	73	1973
	Jay Haas		1981
Best final-round comeback	Jim Gallagher Jr.	5 back	1990
Lowest 36-hole cut score		139	1996 1998 2002
Highest 36-hole cut score		149	1969

BUICK OPEN

RECORD	PLAYER(S)	SCORE	YEAR
Low 18	Billy Mayfair	61	2001
Low first 36	Robert Wrenn	128 (65-63)	1987
Low 36	Robert Wrenn	128 (65-63)	1987
	Kenny Perry	128 (64-64)	2001 (rounds 2-3)
Low first 54	Kenny Perry	194 (66-64-64)	2001
Low 54	Kenny Perry	194 (66-64-64)	2001
Low 72	Robert Wrenn	262 (65-63-67-67)	1987
Highest winning score	Billy Casper	285	1958
Largest winning margin	Robert Wrenn (262)	7 strokes	1987
Largest 18-hole lead	Scott Hoch (63)	3 strokes	1991
Largest 36-hole lead	Rex Caldwell (132)	5 strokes	1980
Largest 54-hole lead	Julius Boros (205)	6 strokes	1963

	Robert Wrenn (195)		1987
Lowest start by winner	Woody Austin	63	1995
Highest start by winner	Tom Weiskopf	73	1968
Lowest finish by winner	Lanny Wadkins	65	1982
	Wayne Levi		1983
	Chip Beck		1990
	Tom Pernice		1999
Highest finish by winner	Art Wall	72	1959
	Bill Collins		1962
	Hale Irwin		1981
Best final-round comeback	Chip Beck	8 back	1990
Lowest 36-hole cut score		140	1995 2001
Highest 36-hole cut score		155	1958

THE INTERNATIONAL*

RECORD	PLAYER(S)	SCORE	YEAR
High 18	Greg Whisman	20	1992
	Tom Purtzer		1997
High first 36	Davis Love III	36 (19-17)	2003
High 36	Davis Love III	36 (19-17)	2003
High first 54	Davis Love III	41 (19-17-5)	2003
High 54	Davis Love III	41 (19-17-5)	2003
High 72	Phil Mickelson	48 (14-13-12-9)	1997
	Ernie Els	(15-19-6-8)	2000
Lowest winning score	Clarence Rose	31	1996
Largest winning margin	Davis Love III (46)	12 points	2003
Largest 18-hole lead	Davis Love III (19)	5 points	2003
Largest 36-hole lead	Davis Love III (36)	10 points	2003
Largest 54-hole lead	Davis Love III (41)	10 points	2003
Highest start by winner	Davis Love III	19	2003
Lowest start by winner	Clarence Rose	6	1996
Highest finish by winner	Rich Beem	19	2002
Lowest finish by winner	Tom Pernice Jr.	1	2001
Best final-round comeback	Steve Lowery	4 back	1994

*Scoring is by Stableford system, with points awarded for a player's score on each hole.

WGC-NEC INVITATIONAL

RECORD	PLAYER(S)	SCORE	YEAR
Low 18	Jose Maria Olazabal	61	1990
	Tiger Woods		2000
Low first 36	Tiger Woods	125 (64-61)	2000
Low 36	Tiger Woods	125 (64-61)	2000
Low first 54	Tiger Woods	192 (64-61-67)	2000
Low 54	Tiger Woods	192 (64-61-67)	2000
Low 72	Tiger Woods	259 (64-61-67-67)	2000
Highest winning score	Tom Purtzer	279	1991
Largest winning margin	Jose Maria Olazabal (262)	12 strokes	1990
Largest 18-hole lead	Jose Maria Olazabal (61)	4 strokes	1990
Largest 36-hole lead	Jose Maria Olazabal	9 strokes	1990

		(128)	
Largest 54-hole lead	Tiger Woods	9 strokes	2000
		(192)	
Lowest start by winner	Jose Maria Olazabal	61	1990
Highest start by winner	Greg Norman	73	1995
Lowest finish by winner	Fulton Allem	62	1993
Highest finish by winner	Dan Pohl	71	1986
	Curtis Strange		1987
	Tom Purtzer		1991
Best final-round comeback	Greg Norman	6 back	1995
Lowest 36-hole cut score	No cut		

RENO-TAHOE OPEN

RECORD	PLAYER(S)	SCORE	YEAR
Low 18	Notah Begay III	63	1999
	Brian Henninger		2000
	Kirk Triplett		2003
Low first 36	John Cook	133	2001
		(69-64)	
Low 36	Notah Begay III	132	1999
		(69-63) (rounds 2-3)	
	Doug Dunakey	132	2000
		(68-64) (rounds 2-3)	
	Bryce Molder	132	2001
		(65-67) (rounds 2-3)	
Low first 54	Jerry Kelly	201	2001
		(66-68-67)	
Low 54	Chris Riley	200	2002
		(66-67-67) (rounds 2-4)	
Low 72	John Cook	271	2001
		(69-64-74-64)	
	Chris Riley	(71-66-67-67)	2002
	Jonathan Kaye	(67-68-69-67)	2002
	Kirk Triplett	(67-68-73-63)	2003
Highest winning score	Scott Verplank	275	2000
Largest winning margin	Notah Begay III	3 strokes	1999
	(274)		
	Kirk Triplett		2003
	(271)		
Largest 18-hole lead	Franklin Langham	1 stroke	1999
	(65)		
	Brian Watts		2001
	(64)		
	Charles Howell III		2002
	(65)		
Largest 36-hole lead	Brian Henninger	1 stroke	2000
	(134)		
	John Cook		2001
	(133)		
Largest 54-hole lead	Notah Begay III	4 strokes	1999
	(202)		
Lowest start by winner	Kirk Triplett	67	2003
Highest start by winner	Chris Riley	71	2002
Lowest finish by winner	Kirk Triplett	63	2003
Highest finish by winner	Notah Begay III	72	1999
Best final-round comeback	John Cook	6 back	2001
Lowest 36-hole cut score		142	2001
Highest 36-hole cut score		145	1999
			2000
			2003

BUICK CHAMPIONSHIP

RECORD	PLAYER(S)	SCORE	YEAR
Low 18	Tommy Bolt	60	1965
Low first 36	Tim Norris	127	1982
		(63-64)	
Low 36	Ted Tryba	126	1999

		(64-62) (rounds 2-3)	
Low first 54	Tim Norris	193	1982
		(63-64-66)	
	Mark Calcavecchia	(65-64-64)	2000
Low 54	Tim Norris	193	1982
		(63-64-66)	
	Mark Calcavecchia	(65-64-64)	2000
Low 72	Tim Norris	259	1982
		(63-64-66-66)	
Highest winning score	Arnold Palmer	274	1956
	Billy Casper		1965
Largest winning margin	Sam Snead	7 strokes	1955
	(269)		
Largest 18-hole lead	Many players	2 strokes	
Largest 36-hole lead	Skee Riegel	4 strokes	1952
	(133)		
	Jack Burke Jr.		1958
	(130)		
	Wayne Levi		1997
	(129)		
Largest 54-hole lead	Sam Snead	5 strokes	1955
	(199)		
Lowest start by winner	Jack Burke Jr.	63	1958
	Tim Norris		1982
Highest start by winner	Phil Blackmar	72	1985
Lowest finish by winner	Mac O'Grady	62	1986
Highest finish by winner	Paul Azinger	72	1987
Best final-round comeback	Billy Casper	5 back	1963
	Mac O'Grady		1986
	Lanny Wadkins		1992
	Phil Mickelson		2002
Lowest 36-hole cut score		139	1998
			1999
			2000
Highest 36-hole cut score		152	1958

DEUTSCHE BANK CHAMPIONSHIP

RECORD	PLAYER(S)	SCORE	YEAR
Low 18	Adam Scott	62	2003
Low first 36	Adam Scott	131	2003
		(69-62)	
Low 36	Adam Scott	129	2003
		(62-67) (rounds 2-3)	
Low first 54	Adam Scott	198	2003
		(69-62-67)	
Low 54	Adam Scott	195	2003
		(62-67-66) (rounds 2-4)	
Low 72	Adam Scott	264	2003
		(69-62-67-66)	
Highest winning score	Adam Scott	264	2003
Largest winning margin	Adam Scott	4 strokes	2003
	(264)		
Largest 18-hole lead	Justin Rose	2 strokes	2003
	(63)		
Largest 36-hole lead	Adam Scott	2 strokes	2003
	(131)		
Largest 54-hole lead	Adam Scott	3 strokes	2003
	(198)		
Lowest start by winner	Adam Scott	69	2003
Highest start by winner	Adam Scott	69	2003
Lowest finish by winner	Adam Scott	66	2003
Highest finish by winner	Adam Scott	66	2003
Best final-round comeback	N/A		
Lowest 36-hole cut score		142	2003
Highest 36-hole cut score		142	2003

BELL CANADIAN OPEN

RECORD	PLAYER(S)	SCORE	YEAR
Low 18	Leonard Thompson	61	1981
	Andy Bean		1983
	Greg Norman		1986
Low first 36	Scott Dunlap	129	1996
		(64-65)	
Low 36	Scott Dunlap	129	1996
		(64-65)	
	Tiger Woods	129	2000
		(65-64)	(rounds 2-3)
	Tiger Woods	129	2000
		(64-65)	(rounds 3-4)
	Scott Verplank	129	2001
		(63-66)	(rounds 2-3)
Low first 54	Arnold Palmer	195	1955
		(64-67-64)	
Low 54	Tiger Woods	194	2000
		(65-64-65)	(rounds 2-4)
Low 72	Johnny Palmer	263	1952
		(66-65-66-66)	
Highest winning score	Charles Murray	314	1911
Largest winning margin	J. Douglas Edgar	16 strokes	1919
	(278)		
Largest 18-hole lead	Many players	2 strokes	
Largest 36-hole lead	Nick Price	6 strokes	1984
	(134)		
Largest 54-hole lead	Johnny Palmer	8 strokes	1952
	(197)		
Lowest start by winner	Arnold Palmer	64	1955
Lowest finish by winner	Tiger Woods	65	2000
	John Rollins		2002
Best final-round comeback	John Rollins	7 back	2002
Lowest 36-hole		141	2001
Highest 36-hole cut score		175	1922
			1923

VALERO TEXAS OPEN

RECORD	PLAYER(S)	SCORE	YEAR
Low 18	Al Brosch	60	1951
	Ted Kroll		1954
	Mike Souchak		1955
Low first 36	Paul Azinger	126	1988
		(64-62)	
	Tommy Armour III	(64-62)	2003
Low 36	Ron Streck	125	1978
		(63-62)	(rounds 3-4)
	Tommy Armour III	125	2003
		(62-63)	(rounds 2-3)
Low first 54	Tommy Armour III	189	2003
		(64-62-63)	
Low 54	Tommy Armour III	189	2003
		(64-62-63)	
Low 72	Tommy Armour III	254	2003
		(64-62-63-65)	
Highest winning score	Bill Mehlhorn	297	1928
Largest winning margin	Corey Pavin	8 strokes	1988
	(259)		
Largest 18-hole lead	Many players	2 strokes	
Largest 36-hole lead	Jodie Mudd	4 strokes	1985
	(129)		
	Blaine McCallister		1991
	(131)		
Largest 54-hole lead	Tommy Armour	6 strokes	2003
	(189)		
Lowest start by winner	Mike Souchak	60	1955
Highest start by winner	Ron Streck	73	1978
Lowest finish by winner	Ron Streck	62	1978
Highest finish by winner	Bill Mehlhorn	79	1928

	Best final-round comeback	Bruce Crampton	6 back	1964
	Lowest 36-hole cut score		137	1989
				2003
	Highest 36-hole cut score		146	1962

84 LUMBER CLASSIC

RECORD	PLAYER(S)	SCORE	YEAR
Low 18	J.L. Lewis	62	2003
Low first 36	Robert Damron	133	2003
		(67-66)	
	Cameron Beckman	(67-66)	2003
Low 36	Dan Forsman	129	2002
		(64-65)	(rounds 3-4)
Low first 54	Cameron Beckman	197	2003
		(67-66-64)	
Low 54	Kevin Sutherland	197	2001
		(65-64-68)	(rounds 2-4)
	Dan Forsman	197	2002
		(68-64-65)	(rounds 2-4)
	J.L. Lewis	197	2003
		(67-68-62)	(rounds 2-4)
	Cameron Beckman	(67-66-64)	2003
Low 72	J.L. Lewis	266	2003
		(69-67-68-62)	
Highest winning score	Chris DiMarco	270	2000
	Dan Forsman		2002
Largest winning margin	Chris DiMarco	6 strokes	2000
	(270)		
Largest 18-hole lead	Emlyn Aubrey	1 stroke	2000
	(65)		
Largest 36-hole lead	Robert Allenby	1 stroke	2001
	(135)		
	Billy Andrade		2002
	(134)		
Largest 54-hole lead	Chris DiMarco	3 strokes	2000
	(201)		
	Robert Allenby		2001
	(201)		
Lowest start by winner	Chris DiMarco	68	2000
Highest start by winner	Dan Forsman	73	2002
Lowest finish by winner	J.L. Lewis	62	2003
Highest finish by winner	Chris DiMarco	69	2000
Best final-round comeback	J.L. Lewis	7 back	2003
Lowest 36-hole cut score		141	2003
Highest 36-hole cut score		144	2001
			2002

WGC-AMERICAN EXPRESS CHAMPIONSHIP

RECORD	PLAYER(S)	SCORE	YEAR
Low 18	Retief Goosen	62	2002
	Sergio Garcia		2002
Low first 36	Tiger Woods	130	2002
		(65-65)	
Low 36	Tiger Woods	130	2002
		(65-65)	
	Retief Goosen	130	2002
		(68-62)	(rounds 3-4)
Low first 54	Tiger Woods	197	2002
		(65-65-67)	
Low 54	Tiger Woods	197	2002
		(65-65-67)	
	Retief Goosen	197	2002
		(67-68-62)	(rounds 2-4)
Low 72	Tiger Woods	263	2002
		(65-65-67-66)	
Highest winning score	Tiger Woods	278	1999
Largest winning margin	Mike Weir	2 strokes	2000
	(277)		
	Tiger Woods		2003
	(274)		

Record	Player(s)	Score	Year
Largest 18-hole lead	Nick Price (63)	3 strokes	2000
Largest 36-hole lead	Tiger Woods (133)	5 strokes	2003
Largest 54-hole lead	Tiger Woods (197)	5 strokes	2002
Lowest start by winner	Tiger Woods	65	2002
Highest start by winner	Tiger Woods	71	1999
Lowest finish by winner	Tiger Woods	66	2002
Highest finish by winner	Tiger Woods	72	2003
Best final-round comeback	Tiger Woods	1 back	1999
	Mike Weir		2000
Lowest 36-hole cut score	No cut		

SOUTHERN FARM BUREAU CLASSIC

RECORD	PLAYER(S)	SCORE	YEAR
Low 18	Keith Clearwater	61	1996
Low first 36	Allan Strange	129 (66-63)	1981
Low 36	Mike Nicolette	128 (64-64)	1992
Low first 54	Steve Lowery	196 (64-67-65)	2000
Low 54	Steve Lowery	196 (64-67-65)	2000
Low 72	Dan Halldorson	263 (64-67-66-66)	1986
Highest winning score	Larry Mowry	272	1969
	Bobby Walzel		1979
Largest winning margin	Frank Conner (267)	5 strokes	1988
Largest 18-hole lead	Many players	2 strokes	
Largest 36-hole lead	Dwight Nevil (131)	4 strokes	1973
	Allan Strange (129)		1981
Largest 54-hole lead	Mike Morley (200)	4 strokes	1972
Lowest start by winner	Dwight Nevil	64	1973
	Dan Halldorson		1986
	Jim Booros		1989
	Steve Lowery		2000
Highest start by winner	Bobby Walzel	72	1979
Lowest finish by winner	Craig Stadler	63	1978
	Russ Cochran		1983
	Frank Conner		1988
	Larry Silveira		1991
Highest finish by winner	Bob Wynn	71	1975
Best final-round comeback	Russ Cochran	7 back	1983
Lowest 36-hole cut score		140	1981
			1991
			1992
			2000
Highest 36-hole cut score		145	1973
			1975
			1983
			1989
			1999

LAS VEGAS INVITATIONAL

RECORD	PLAYER(S)	SCORE	YEAR
Low 18	Chip Beck	59	1991
Low first 36	Tom Lehman	125 (63-62)	2001
Low 36	Tom Lehman	125 (63-62)	2001
Low first 54	Scott Verplank	192 (64-62-66)	2003
	Steve Flesch	(62-64-66)	2003
Low 54	Scott Verplank	192 (64-62-66)	2003
	Steve Flesch	(62-64-66)	2003
Low first 72	Stuart Appleby	259 (62-68-63-66)	2003
Low 72	D.A. Weibring	259 (64-65-64-66)(rounds 2-5)	1991
	Stuart Appleby	(62-68-63-66)	2003
Low 90	Stuart Appleby	328 (62-68-63-66-69)	2003
	Scott McCarron	(69-62-64-67-66)	2003
Highest winning score	Denis Watson	341	1984
Largest winning margin	Davis Love III (331)	8 strokes	1993
Largest 18-hole lead	Bill Glasson (62)	3 strokes	1985
Largest 36-hole lead	Lon Hinkle (130)	3 strokes	1984
	Rick Fehr (126)		1996
Largest 54-hole lead	John Cook (196)	5 strokes	1992
Largest 72-hole lead	Fuzzy Zoeller (267)	6 strokes	1983
	Davis Love III (265)		1993
Lowest start by winner	Stuart Appleby	62	2003
Highest start by winner	Greg Norman	73	1986
Lowest finish by winner	Phil Tataurangi	62	2002
Highest finish by winner	Fuzzy Zoeller	73	1983
Best final-round comeback	Bob Estes	5 back	2001
	Phil Tataurangi		2002
Lowest 54-hole cut score		205	1999
Highest 54-hole cut score		215	1988

CHRYSLER CLASSIC OF GREENSBORO

RECORD	PLAYER(S)	SCORE	YEAR
Low 18	Davis Love III	62	1992
	Mark O'Meara		1996
	Jeff Maggert		1999
Low first 36	Jesper Parnevik	128 (65-63)	1999
Low 36	Jesper Parnevik	128 (65-63)	1999
Low first 54	Jesper Parnevik	195 (65-63-67)	1999
Low 54	Jesper Parnevik	195 (65-63-67)	1999
Low 72	Jesper Parnevik	265 (65-63-67-70)	1999
Highest winning score	Vic Ghezzi	286	1947
Largest winning margin	Ben Hogan (270)	9 strokes	1940
Largest 18-hole lead	Sam Snead (64)	3 strokes	1964
	Tom Weiskopf (64)		1975
Largest 36-hole lead	Sam Snead (135)	5 strokes	1956
	Tom Weiskopf (135)		1975
	Sandy Lyle (132)		1986
	Hal Sutton (131)		2000
	Shigeki Maruyama (129)		2003
Largest 54-hole lead	Ben Hogan (203)	7 strokes	1940

Lowest start by winner	Gary Player	63	1970
Highest start by winner	Buddy Allin	75	1971
Lowest finish by winner	Davis Love III	62	1992
Highest finish by winner	Dow Finsterwald	77	1959
Best final-round comeback	Steve Elkington	7 back	1990
	Mark Brooks		1991
	Jim Gallagher Jr.		1995

FUNAI CLASSIC AT THE WALT DISNEY WORLD RESORT

RECORD	PLAYER(S)	SCORE	YEAR
Low 18	Mark Lye	61	1984
	Bob Tway		1989
	Payne Stewart		1990
Low first 36	Chris DiMarco	127 (64-63)	2002
Low 36	Chris DiMarco	127 (64-63)	2002
Low first 54	Tim Simpson	193 (64-64-65)	1990
Low 54	Tim Simpson	193 (64-64-65)	1990
Low 72	John Huston	262 (66-68-66-62)	1992
	Duffy Waldorf	(65-66-69-62)	2000
Highest winning score	Jack Nicklaus	275	1973
	Ray Floyd		1986
Largest winning margin	Jack Nicklaus (267)	9 strokes	1972
Largest 18-hole lead	Bob Tway (61)	4 strokes	1989
Largest 36-hole lead	Tim Simpson (128)	4 strokes	1990
Largest 54-hole lead	Tim Simpson (193)	6 strokes	1990
Lowest start by winner	Bob Lohr	62	1988
Highest start by winner	Hal Sutton	71	1982
Lowest finish by winner	John Huston	62	1992
	Duffy Waldorf		2000
Highest finish by winner	Tiger Woods	73	1999
Best final-round comeback	Larry Nelson	6 back	1987
	Duffy Waldorf		2000
Lowest 36-hole cut score		138	2002
Highest 36-hole cut score		147	1973

CHRYSLER CHAMPIONSHIP

RECORD	PLAYER(S)	SCORE	YEAR
Low 18	K.J. Choi	63	2002
Low first 36	K.J. Choi	131 (63-68)	2002
Low 36	K.J. Choi	131 (63-68)	2002
Low first 54	K.J. Choi	199 (63-68-68)	2002
Low 54	K.J. Choi	199 (63-68-68)	2002
Low 72	K.J. Choi	267 (63-68-68-68)	2002
Highest winning score	Retief Goosen	272	2003
Largest winning margin	K.J. Choi (267)	7 strokes	2002
Largest 18-hole lead	Mike Hulbert (64)	2 strokes	2000
	K.J. Choi (63)		2002
Largest 36-hole lead	Carl Paulson (132)	2 strokes	2000
	K.J. Choi (131)		2002
Largest 54-hole lead	K.J. Choi (199)	5 strokes	2002
Lowest start by winner	K.J. Choi	63	2002
Highest start by winner	Retief Goosen	69	2003
Lowest finish by winner	John Huston	65	2000

Highest finish by winner	Retief Goosen	70	2003
Best final-round comeback	John Huston	4 strokes	2000
Lowest 36-hole cut score		143	2000 2002
Highest 36-hole cut score		145	2003

TOUR CHAMPIONSHIP PRESENTED BY COCA-COLA

RECORD	PLAYER(S)	SCORE	YEAR
Low 18	Chad Campbell	61	2003
Low first 36	Tom Watson	131 (65-66)	1987
Low 36	Chad Campbell	129 (61-68)	2003 (rounds 3-4)
Low first 54	Tom Lehman	197 (66-67-64)	1996
Low 54	Tom Lehman	197 (66-67-64)	1996
	David Toms	197 (66-64-67)	2001 (rounds 2-4)
Low 72	Phil Mickelson	267 (67-69-65-66)	2000
Highest winning score	Curtis Strange	279	1988
	Craig Stadler		1991
Largest winning margin	Tom Lehman (268)	6 strokes	1996
Largest 18-hole lead	Jim Gallagher Jr. (63)	5 strokes	1993
Largest 36-hole lead	Tom Watson (131)	4 strokes	1987
	Tom Kite (134)		1989
	Tom Lehman (133)		1996
Largest 54-hole lead	Tom Lehman (197)	9 strokes	1996
Lowest start by winner	Jim Gallagher Jr.	63	1993
Highest start by winner	Paul Azinger	70	1992
	Chad Campbell		2003
Lowest finish by winner	Phil Mickelson	66	2000
Highest finish by winner	Curtis Strange	74	1988
Best final-round comeback	Jim Gallagher Jr.	3 back	1993
Lowest 36-hole cut score	No cut		

MERCEDES CHAMPIONSHIPS

YEAR	WINNER	SCORE
	TOURNAMENT OF CHAMPIONS	
1953	Al Besselink	280
1954	Art Wall	278
1955	Gene Littler	280
1956	Gene Littler	281
1957	Gene Littler	285
1958	Stan Leonard	278
1959	Mike Souchak	281
1960	Jerry Barber	268
1961	Sam Snead	273
1962	Arnold Palmer	276
1963	Jack Nicklaus	273
1964	Jack Nicklaus	279
1965	Arnold Palmer	277
1966	*Arnold Palmer	283
1967	Frank Beard	278
1968	Don January	276
1969	Gary Player	284
1970	Frank Beard	278
1971	Jack Nicklaus	279
1972	*Bobby Mitchell	280
1973	Jack Nicklaus	276
1974	Johnny Miller	280
	MONY TOURNAMENT OF CHAMPIONS	
1975	*Al Geiberger	277
1976	Don January	277
1977	*Jack Nicklaus	281
1978	Gary Player	281
1979	Tom Watson	275
1980	Tom Watson	276
1981	Lee Trevino	273
1982	Lanny Wadkins	280
1983	Lanny Wadkins	280
1984	Tom Watson	274
1985	Tom Kite	275
1986	Calvin Peete	267
1987	Mac O'Grady	278
1988	Steve Pate	202
1989	Steve Jones	279
	INFINITI TOURNAMENT OF CHAMPIONS	
1990	Paul Azinger	272
1991	Tom Kite	272
1992	*Steve Elkington	279
1993	Davis Love III	272
	MERCEDES CHAMPIONSHIPS	
1994	*Phil Mickelson	276
1995	*Steve Elkington	278
1996	Mark O'Meara	271
1997	#Tiger Woods	202
1998	Phil Mickelson	271
1999	David Duval	266
2000	*Tiger Woods	276
2001	Jim Furyk	274
2002	*Sergio Garcia	274
2003	Ernie Els	261
2004	Stuart Appleby	270

* Playoff
# Rain-shortened

SONY OPEN IN HAWAII

YEAR	WINNER	SCORE
	HAWAIIAN OPEN	
1965	Gay Brewer	281
1966	Ted Makalena	271
1967	*Dudley Wysong	284
1968	Lee Trevino	272
1969	Bruce Crampton	272
1970	No tournament	
1971	Tom Shaw	273
1972	*Grier Jones	274
1973	John Schlee	273
1974	Jack Nicklaus	271
1975	Gary Groh	274
1976	Ben Crenshaw	270
1977	Bruce Lietzke	273
1978	*Hubert Green	274
1979	Hubert Green	267
1980	Andy Bean	266
1981	Hale Irwin	265
1982	Wayne Levi	277
1983	Isao Aoki	268
1984	*Jack Renner	271
1985	Mark O'Meara	267
1986	Corey Pavin	272
1987	*Corey Pavin	270
1988	Lanny Wadkins	271
1989	#Gene Sauers	197
1990	David Ishii	279
	UNITED AIRLINES HAWAIIAN OPEN	
1991	Lanny Wadkins	270
1992	John Cook	265
1993	Howard Twitty	269
1994	Brett Ogle	269
1995	John Morse	269
1996	*Jim Furyk	277
1997	*Paul Stankowski	271
1998	John Huston	260
	SONY OPEN IN HAWAII	
1999	Jeff Sluman	271
2000	Paul Azinger	261
2001	Brad Faxon	260
2002	Jerry Kelly	266
2003	*Ernie Els	264
2004	*Ernie Els	262

* Playoff
# Rain-shortened

BOB HOPE CHRYSLER CLASSIC

YEAR	WINNER	SCORE
	PALM SPRINGS GOLF CLASSIC	
1960	Arnold Palmer	338
1961	Billy Maxwell	345
1962	Arnold Palmer	342
1963	*Jack Nicklaus	345
1964	Tommy Jacobs	348
	BOB HOPE DESERT CLASSIC	
1965	Billy Casper	348
1966	*Doug Sanders	349
1967	Tom Nieporte	349
1968	*Arnold Palmer	348
1969	Billy Casper	345
1970	Bruce Devlin	339
1971	*Arnold Palmer	342
1972	Bob Rosburg	344
1973	Arnold Palmer	343
1974	Hubert Green	341
1975	Johnny Miller	339
1976	Johnny Miller	344
1977	Rik Massengale	337
1978	Bill Rogers	339
1979	John Mahaffey	343
1980	Craig Stadler	343
1981	Bruce Lietzke	335
1982	*Ed Fiori	335
1983	*Keith Fergus	335
	BOB HOPE CLASSIC	
1984	*John Mahaffey	340
1985	*Lanny Wadkins	333
	BOB HOPE CHRYSLER CLASSIC	
1986	Donnie Hammond	335
1987	Corey Pavin	341
1988	Jay Haas	338
1989	*Steve Jones	343
1990	Peter Jacobsen	339
1991	*Corey Pavin	331
1992	*John Cook	336
1993	Tom Kite	325
1994	Scott Hoch	334
1995	Kenny Perry	335
1996	Mark Brooks	337
1997	John Cook	327
1998	*Fred Couples	332
1999	David Duval	334
2000	Jesper Parnevik	331
2001	Joe Durant	324
2002	*Phil Mickelson	330
2003	Mike Weir	330
2004	*Phil Mickelson	330

* Playoff

FBR OPEN

YEAR	WINNER	SCORE
	PHOENIX OPEN	
1932	Ralph Guldahl	285
1933	Harry Cooper	281
1934	No tournament	
1935	Ky Laffoon	281
1936–		
1938	No tournaments	
1939	Byron Nelson	198
1940	Porky Oliver	205
1941	Porky Oliver	275
1942	Herman Barron	276
1943	No tournament	
1944	*Jug McSpaden	273
1945	Byron Nelson	274
1946	*Ben Hogan	273
1947	Ben Hogan	270
1948	Bobby Locke	268
1949	*Jimmy Demaret	278
1950	Jimmy Demaret	269

1951	Lew Worsham	272
1952	Lloyd Mangrum	274
1953	Lloyd Mangrum	272
1954	*Ed Furgol	272
1955	Gene Littler	275
1956	Cary Middlecoff	276
1957	Billy Casper	271
1958	Ken Venturi	274
1959	Gene Littler	268
1960	*Jack Fleck	273
1961	*Arnold Palmer	270
1962	Arnold Palmer	269
1963	Arnold Palmer	273
1964	Jack Nicklaus	271
1965	Rod Funseth	274
1966	Dudley Wysong	278
1967	Julius Boros	272
1968	George Knudson	272
1969	Gene Littler	263
1970	Dale Douglass	271
1971	Miller Barber	261
1972	*Homero Blancas	273
1973	Bruce Crampton	268
1974	Johnny Miller	271
1975	Johnny Miller	260
1976	Bob Gilder	268
1977	*Jerry Pate	277
1978	Miller Barber	272
1979	#Ben Crenshaw	199
1980	Jeff Mitchell	272
1981	David Graham	268
1982	Lanny Wadkins	263
1983	*Bob Gilder	271
1984	Tom Purtzer	268
1985	Calvin Peete	270
1986	Hal Sutton	267
1987	Paul Azinger	268
1988	*Sandy Lyle	269
1989	Mark Calcavecchia	263
1990	Tommy Armour III	267
1991	Nolan Henke	268
1992	Mark Calcavecchia	264
1993	Lee Janzen	273
1994	Bill Glasson	268
1995	*Vijay Singh	269
1996	*Phil Mickelson	269
1997	Steve Jones	258
1998	Jesper Parnevik	269
1999	Rocco Mediate	273
2000	Tom Lehman	270
2001	Mark Calcavecchia	256
2002	Chris DiMarco	267
2003	Vijay Singh	261
FBR OPEN		
2004	Jonathan Kaye	266

* Playoff
\# Rain-shortened

AT&T PEBBLE BEACH NATIONAL PRO-AM

YEAR	WINNER	SCORE
BING CROSBY PRO-AM		
1937	Sam Snead	68
1938	Sam Snead	139
1939	Dutch Harrison	138
1940	Ed Oliver	135
1941	Sam Snead	136
1942	Tie–Lloyd Mangrum/	133

	Leland Gibson	
1943–1946	No tournaments	
1947	Tie–Ed Furgol/	213
	George Fazio	
1948	Lloyd Mangrum	205
1949	Ben Hogan	208
1950	Tie–Sam Snead/Jack Burke, Jr./214	
	Smiley Quick/Dave Douglas	
1951	Byron Nelson	209
1952	Jimmy Demaret	145
BING CROSBY PRO-AM INVITATIONAL		
1953	Lloyd Mangrum	204
1954	Dutch Harrison	210
1955	Cary Middlecoff	209
BING CROSBY PRO-AM GOLF CHAMPIONSHIP		
1956	Cary Middlecoff	202
1957	Jay Hebert	213
1958	Billy Casper	277
BING CROSBY NATIONAL		
1959	Art Wall	279
1960	Ken Venturi	286
1961	Bob Rosburg	282
1962	*Doug Ford	286
1963	Billy Casper	285
BING CROSBY NATIONAL PRO-AM		
1964	Tony Lema	284
1965	Bruce Crampton	284
1966	Don Massengale	283
1967	Jack Nicklaus	284
1968	*Johnny Pott	285
1969	George Archer	283
1970	Bert Yancey	278
1971	Tom Shaw	278
1972	*Jack Nicklaus	284
1973	*Jack Nicklaus	282
1974	#Johnny Miller	208
1975	Gene Littler	280
1976	Ben Crenshaw	281
1977	Tom Watson	273
1978	*Tom Watson	280
1979	Lon Hinkle	284
1980	George Burns	280
1981	#*John Cook	209
1982	Jim Simons	274
1983	Tom Kite	276
1984	*Hale Irwin	278
1985	Mark O'Meara	283
AT&T PEBBLE BEACH NATIONAL PRO-AM		
1986	#Fuzzy Zoeller	205
1987	Johnny Miller	278
1988	*Steve Jones	280
1989	Mark O'Meara	277
1990	Mark O'Meara	281
1991	Paul Azinger	274
1992	Mark O'Meara	275
1993	Brett Ogle	276
1994	Johnny Miller	281
1995	Peter Jacobsen	271
1996	Cancelled due to rain	
1997	Mark O'Meara	268
1998	#Phil Mickelson	202
1999	#Payne Stewart	206
2000	Tiger Woods	273
2001	Davis Love III	272
2002	Matt Gogel	274
2003	Davis Love III	274
2004	Vijay Singh	272

* Playoff
\# Rain-shortened

BUICK INVITATIONAL

YEAR	WINNER	SCORE
SAN DIEGO OPEN		
1952	Ted Kroll	276
1953	Tommy Bolt	274
1954	a-Gene Littler	274
CONVAIR SAN DIEGO OPEN		
1955	Tommy Bolt	274
1956	Bob Rosburg	270
SAN DIEGO OPEN INVITATIONAL		
1957	Arnold Palmer	271
1958	No tournament	
1959	Marty Furgol	274
1960	Mike Souchak	269
1961	*Arnold Palmer	271
1962	*Tommy Jacobs	277
1963	Gary Player	270
1964	Art Wall	274
1965	*Wes Ellis	267
1966	Billy Casper	268
1967	Bob Goalby	269
ANDY WILLIAMS SAN DIEGO OPEN INVITATIONAL		
1968	Tom Weiskopf	273
1969	Jack Nicklaus	284
1970	Pete Brown	275
1971	George Archer	272
1972	Paul Harney	275
1973	Bob Dickson	278
1974	Bobby Nichols	275
1975	*J.C. Snead	279
1976	J.C. Snead	272
1977	Tom Watson	269
1978	Jay Haas	278
1979	Fuzzy Zoeller	279
1980	*Tom Watson	275
WICKES/ANDY WILLIAMS SAN DIEGO OPEN		
1981	*Bruce Lietzke	278
1982	Johnny Miller	270
ISUZU ANDY WILLIAMS SAN DIEGO OPEN		
1983	Gary Hallberg	271
1984	*Gary Koch	272
1985	*Woody Blackburn	269
SHEARSON LEHMAN BROTHERS ANDY WILLIAMS OPEN		
1986	*#Bob Tway	204
1987	George Burns	266
SHEARSON LEHMAN HUTTON ANDY WILLIAMS OPEN		
1988	Steve Pate	269
SHEARSON LEHMAN HUTTON OPEN		
1989	Greg Twiggs	271
1990	Dan Forsman	275
SHEARSON LEHMAN BROTHERS OPEN		
1991	Jay Don Blake	268
BUICK INVITATIONAL OF CALIFORNIA		
1992	#Steve Pate	200
1993	Phil Mickelson	278
1994	Craig Stadler	268
1995	Peter Jacobsen	269
BUICK INVITATIONAL		
1996	Davis Love III	269
1997	Mark O'Meara	275
1998	#Scott Simpson	204
1999	Tiger Woods	266
2000	Phil Mickelson	270
2001	*Phil Mickelson	269
2002	Jose Maria Olazabal	275
2003	Tiger Woods	272
2004	*John Daly	278

* Playoff
a- Amateur
\# Rain-shortened

NISSAN OPEN

YEAR	WINNER	SCORE
	LOS ANGELES OPEN	
1926	Harry Cooper	279
1927	Bobby Cruickshank	282
1928	Mac Smith	284
1929	Mac Smith	285
1930	Densmore Shute	296
1931	Ed Dudley	285
1932	Mac Smith	281
1933	Craig Wood	281
1934	Mac Smith	280
1935	*Vic Ghezzi	285
1936	Jimmy Hines	280
1937	Harry Cooper	274
1938	Jimmy Thomson	273
1939	Jimmy Demaret	274
1940	Lawson Little	282
1941	Johnny Bulla	281
1942	*Ben Hogan	282
1943	No tournament	
1944	Harold McSpaden	278
1945	Sam Snead	283
1946	Byron Nelson	284
1947	Ben Hogan	280
1948	Ben Hogan	275
1949	Lloyd Mangrum	284
1950	*Sam Snead	280
1951	Lloyd Mangrum	280
1952	Tommy Bolt	289
1953	Lloyd Mangrum	280
1954	Fred Wampler	281
1955	Gene Littler	276
1956	Lloyd Mangrum	272
1957	Doug Ford	280
1958	Frank Stranahan	275
1959	Ken Venturi	278
1960	Dow Finsterwald	280
1961	Bob Goalby	275
1962	Phil Rodgers	268
1963	Arnold Palmer	274
1964	Paul Harney	280
1965	Paul Harney	276
1966	Arnold Palmer	273
1967	Arnold Palmer	269
1968	Billy Casper	274
1969	*Charles Sifford	276
1970	*Billy Casper	276
	GLEN CAMPBELL LOS ANGELES OPEN	
1971	*Bob Lunn	274
1972	*George Archer	270
1973	Rod Funseth	276
1974	Dave Stockton	276
1975	Pat Fitzsimons	275
1976	Hale Irwin	272
1977	Tom Purtzer	273
1978	Gil Morgan	278
1979	Lanny Wadkins	276
1980	Tom Watson	276
1981	Johnny Miller	270
1982	*Tom Watson	271
1983	Gil Morgan	270
	LOS ANGELES OPEN	
1984	David Edwards	279
1985	Lanny Wadkins	264
1986	Doug Tewell	270
	LOS ANGELES OPEN PRESENTED BY NISSAN	
1987	*Tze-Chung Chen	275
1988	Chip Beck	267
	NISSAN LOS ANGELES OPEN	
1989	Mark Calcavecchia	272
1990	Fred Couples	266
1991	Ted Schulz	272
1992	*Fred Couples	269
1993	#Tom Kite	206
1994	Corey Pavin	271
	NISSAN OPEN	
1995	Corey Pavin	268
1996	Craig Stadler	278
1997	Nick Faldo	272
1998	*Billy Mayfair	272
1999	Ernie Els	270
2000	Kirk Triplett	272
2001	Robert Allenby	276
2002	Len Mattiace	269
2003	*Mike Weir	275
2004	Mike Weir	267

* Playoff
\# Rain-shortened

WGC-ACCENTURE MATCH PLAY CHAMPIONSHIP

YEAR	WINNER	SCORE
1999	Jeff Maggert	38 holes
2000	Darren Clarke	4 and 3
2001	Steve Stricker	2 and 1
2002	Kevin Sutherland	1 up
2003	Tiger Woods	2 and 1
2004	Tiger Woods	3 and 2

CHRYSLER CLASSIC OF TUCSON

YEAR	WINNER	SCORE
	TUCSON OPEN	
1945	Ray Mangrum	268
1946	Jimmy Demaret	268
1947	Jimmy Demaret	264
1948	Skip Alexander	264
1949	Lloyd Mangrum	263
1950	Chandler Harper	267
1951	Lloyd Mangrum	269
1952	Henry Williams	274
1953	Tommy Bolt	265
1954	No tournament	
1955	Tommy Bolt	265
1956	Ted Kroll	264
1957	Dow Finsterwald	269
1958	Lionel Hebert	265
1959	Gene Littler	266
1960	Don January	271
	HOME OF THE SUN OPEN INVITATIONAL	
1961	*Dave Hill	269
	TUCSON OPEN	
1962	Phil Rodgers	263
1963	Don January	266
1964	Jacky Cupit	274
1965	Bob Charles	271
1966	*Joe Campbell	278
1967	Arnold Palmer	273
1968	George Knudson	273
1969	Lee Trevino	271
1970	*Lee Trevino	275
1971	J.C. Snead	273
1972	Miller Barber	273
	DEAN MARTIN TUCSON OPEN	
1973	Bruce Crampton	277
1974	Johnny Miller	272
1975	Johnny Miller	263
	NBC TUCSON OPEN	
1976	Johnny Miller	274
	JOE GARAGIOLA TUCSON OPEN	
1977	*Bruce Lietzke	275
1978	Tom Watson	276
1979	Bruce Lietzke	265
1980	Jim Colbert	270
1981	Johnny Miller	265
1982	Craig Stadler	266
1983	*Gil Morgan	271
	SEIKO-TUCSON MATCH PLAY CHAMPIONSHIP	
1984	Tom Watson	2 and 1
1985	Jim Thorpe	4 and 3
1986	Jim Thorpe	67
	SEIKO TUCSON OPEN	
1987	Mike Reid	268
	NORTHERN TELECOM TUCSON OPEN	
1988	David Frost	266
1989	No tournament	
1990	Robert Gamez	270
	NORTHERN TELECOM OPEN	
1991	a-Phil Mickelson	272
1992	Lee Janzen	270
1993	Larry Mize	271
1994	Andrew Magee	270
1995	Phil Mickelson	269
	NORTEL OPEN	
1996	Phil Mickelson	273
	TUCSON CHRYSLER CLASSIC	
1997	Jeff Sluman	275
1998	David Duval	269
	TOUCHSTONE ENERGY TUCSON OPEN	
1999	*Gabriel Hjertstedt	276
2000	Jim Carter	269
2001	Garrett Willis	273
2002	Ian Leggatt	268
	CHRYSLER CLASSIC OF TUCSON	
2003	Frank Lickliter II	269
2004	Heath Slocum	266

* Playoff
a- Amateur

FORD CHAMPIONSHIP AT DORAL

YEAR	WINNER	SCORE
	DORAL CC OPEN INVITATIONAL	
1962	Billy Casper	283
1963	Dan Sikes	283
1964	Billy Casper	277
1965	Doug Sanders	274
1966	Phil Rodgers	278
1967	Doug Sanders	275
1968	Gardner Dickinson	275
1969	Tom Shaw	276
	DORAL-EASTERN OPEN INVITATIONAL	
1970	Mike Hill	279
1971	J.C. Snead	275
1972	Jack Nicklaus	276
1973	Lee Trevino	276
1974	Brian Allin	274
1975	Jack Nicklaus	275
1976	Hubert Green	270
1977	Andy Bean	277

1978	Tom Weiskopf	272
1979	Mark McCumber	279
1980	*Raymond Floyd	279
1981	Raymond Floyd	273
1982	Andy Bean	278
1983	Gary Koch	271
1984	Tom Kite	272
1985	Mark McCumber	284
1986	*Andy Bean	276

DORAL-RYDER OPEN

1987	Lanny Wadkins	277
1988	Ben Crenshaw	274
1989	Bill Glasson	275
1990	*Greg Norman	273
1991	*Rocco Mediate	276
1992	Raymond Floyd	271
1993	Greg Norman	265
1994	John Huston	274
1995	Nick Faldo	273
1996	Greg Norman	269
1997	Steve Elkington	275
1998	Michael Bradley	278
1999	Steve Elkington	275
2000	Jim Furyk	265

GENUITY CHAMPIONSHIP

2001	Joe Durant	270
2002	Ernie Els	271

FORD CHAMPIONSHIP AT DORAL

2003	*Scott Hoch	271
2004	*Craig Parry	271

*Playoff

THE HONDA CLASSIC

YEAR	WINNER	SCORE
	JACKIE GLEASON INVERRARY CLASSIC	
1972	Tom Weiskopf	276
	JACKIE GLEASON INVERRARY NATIONAL AIRLINES CLASSIC	
1973	Lee Trevino	279
	JACKIE GLEASON INVERRARY CLASSIC	
1974	Leonard Thompson	278
1975	Bob Murphy	273
1976	Hosted Players Championship	
1977	Jack Nicklaus	275
1978	Jack Nicklaus	276
1979	Larry Nelson	274
1980	Johnny Miller	274
	AMERICAN MOTORS INVERRARY CLASSIC	
1981	Tom Kite	274
	HONDA INVERRARY CLASSIC	
1982	Hale Irwin	269
1983	Johnny Miller	278
	THE HONDA CLASSIC	
1984	*Bruce Lietzke	280
1985	*Curtis Strange	275
1986	Kenny Knox	287
1987	Mark Calcavecchia	279
1988	Joey Sindelar	276
1989	Blaine McCallister	266
1990	John Huston	282
1991	Steve Pate	279
1992	*Corey Pavin	273
1993	#Fred Couples	207
1994	Nick Price	276
1995	Mark O'Meara	275
1996	Tim Herron	271
1997	Stuart Appleby	274
1998	Mark Calcavecchia	278

1999	Vijay Singh	277
2000	Dudley Hart	269
2001	Jesper Parnevik	270
2002	Matt Kuchar	269
2003	Justin Leonard	264
2004	Todd Hamilton	276

* Playoff
# Rain-shortened

BAY HILL INVITATIONAL PRESENTED BY MASTERCARD

YEAR	WINNER	SCORE
	FLORIDA CITRUS OPEN INVITATIONAL	
1966	Lionel Hebert	279
1967	Julius Boros	274
1968	Dan Sikes	274
1969	Ken Still	278
1970	Bob Lunn	271
1971	Arnold Palmer	270
1972	Jerry Heard	276
1973	Brian Allin	265
1974	Jerry Heard	273
1975	Lee Trevino	276
1976	*Hale Irwin	270
1977	Gary Koch	274
1978	Mac McLendon	271
	BAY HILL CITRUS CLASSIC	
1979	*Bob Byman	278
	BAY HILL CLASSIC	
1980	Dave Eichelberger	279
1981	Andy Bean	266
1982	*Tom Kite	278
1983	*Mike Nicolette	283
1984	*Gary Koch	272
	HERTZ BAY HILL CLASSIC	
1985	Fuzzy Zoeller	275
1986	#Dan Forsman	202
1987	Payne Stewart	264
1988	Paul Azinger	271
	THE NESTLÉ INVITATIONAL	
1989	*Tom Kite	278
1990	Robert Gamez	274
1991	#Andrew Magee	203
1992	Fred Couples	269
1993	Ben Crenshaw	280
1994	Loren Roberts	275
1995	Loren Roberts	272
	BAY HILL INVITATIONAL PRESENTED BY OFFICE DEPOT	
1996	Paul Goydos	275
1997	Phil Mickelson	272
	BAY HILL INVITATIONAL PRESENTED BY COOPER TIRES	
1998	Ernie Els	274
1999	*Tim Herron	274
2000	Tiger Woods	270
2001	Tiger Woods	273
2002	Tiger Woods	275
2003	Tiger Woods	269
	BAY HILL INVITATIONAL PRESENTED BY MASTERCARD	
2004	Chad Campbell	270

* Playoff
# Rain-shortened

THE PLAYERS CHAMPIONSHIP

YEAR	WINNER	SCORE
	TOURNAMENT PLAYERS CHAMPIONSHIP	
1974	Jack Nicklaus	272
1975	Al Geiberger	270
1976	Jack Nicklaus	269
1977	Mark Hayes	289
1978	Jack Nicklaus	289
1979	Lanny Wadkins	283
1980	Lee Trevino	278
1981	*Raymond Floyd	285
1982	Jerry Pate	280
1983	Hal Sutton	283
1984	Fred Couples	277
1985	Calvin Peete	274
1986	John Mahaffey	275
1987	*Sandy Lyle	274
	THE PLAYERS CHAMPIONSHIP	
1988	Mark McCumber	273
1989	Tom Kite	279
1990	Jodie Mudd	278
1991	Steve Elkington	276
1992	Davis Love III	273
1993	Nick Price	270
1994	Greg Norman	264
1995	Lee Janzen	283
1996	Fred Couples	270
1997	Steve Elkington	272
1998	Justin Leonard	278
1999	David Duval	285
2000	Hal Sutton	278
2001	Tiger Woods	274
2002	Craig Perks	280
2003	Davis Love III	271
2004	Adam Scott	276

* Playoff

BELLSOUTH CLASSIC

YEAR	WINNER	SCORE
	ATLANTA CLASSIC	
1967	Bob Charles	284
1968	Bob Lunn	280
1969	*Bert Yancey	277
1970	Tommy Aaron	275
1971	*Gardner Dickinson	275
1972	Bob Lunn	275
1973	Jack Nicklaus	272
1974	Hosted Players Championship	
1975	Hale Irwin	271
1976	No tournament	
1977	Hale Irwin	273
1978	Jerry Heard	269
1979	Andy Bean	265
1980	Larry Nelson	270
1981	*Tom Watson	277
	GEORGIA-PACIFIC ATLANTA GOLF CLASSIC	
1982	*Keith Fergus	273
1983	#Calvin Peete	206
1984	Tom Kite	269
1985	*Wayne Levi	273
1986	Bob Tway	269
1987	Dave Barr	265
1988	Larry Nelson	268
	BELLSOUTH ATLANTA GOLF CLASSIC	
1989	*Scott Simpson	278
1990	Wayne Levi	275
1991	*Corey Pavin	272

BELLSOUTH CLASSIC

1992	Tom Kite	272
1993	Nolan Henke	271
1994	John Daly	274
1995	Mark Calcavechia	271
1996	*Paul Stankowski	280
1997	Scott McCarron	274
1998	Tiger Woods	271
1999	David Duval	270
2000	*#Phil Mickelson	205
2001	Scott McCarron	280
2002	Retief Goosen	272
2003	Ben Crane	272
2004	Zach Johnson	275

* Playoff
# Rain-shortened

THE MASTERS

YEAR	WINNER	SCORE
1934	Horton Smith	284
1935	*Gene Sarazen	282
1936	Horton Smith	285
1937	Byron Nelson	283
1938	Henry Picard	285
1939	Ralph Guldahl	279
1940	Jimmy Demaret	280
1941	Craig Wood	280
1942	*Byron Nelson	280
1943–		
1945	No tournaments	
1946	Herman Keiser	282
1947	Jimmy Demaret	281
1948	Claude Harmon	279
1949	Sam Snead	282
1950	Jimmy Demaret	283
1951	Ben Hogan	280
1952	Sam Snead	286
1953	Ben Hogan	274
1954	*Sam Snead	289
1955	Cary Middlecoff	279
1956	Jack Burke, Jr.	289
1957	Doug Ford	282
1958	Arnold Palmer	284
1959	Art Wall, Jr.	284
1960	Arnold Palmer	282
1961	Gary Player	280
1962	*Arnold Palmer	280
1963	Jack Nicklaus	286
1964	Arnold Palmer	276
1965	Jack Nicklaus	271
1966	*Jack Nicklaus	288
1967	Gay Brewer	280
1968	Bob Goalby	277
1969	George Archer	281
1970	*Billy Casper	279
1971	Charles Coody	279
1972	Jack Nicklaus	286
1973	Tommy Aaron	283
1974	Gary Player	278
1975	Jack Nicklaus	276
1976	Raymond Floyd	271
1977	Tom Watson	276
1978	Gary Player	277
1979	*Fuzzy Zoeller	280
1980	Seve Ballesteros	275
1981	Tom Watson	280
1982	*Craig Stadler	284
1983	Seve Ballesteros	280
1984	Ben Crenshaw	277
1985	Bernhard Langer	282
1986	Jack Nicklaus	279
1987	*Larry Mize	285
1988	Sandy Lyle	281
1989	*Nick Faldo	283
1990	*Nick Faldo	278
1991	Ian Woosnam	277
1992	Fred Couples	275
1993	Bernhard Langer	277
1994	Jose Maria Olazabal	279
1995	Ben Crenshaw	274
1996	Nick Faldo	276
1997	Tiger Woods	270
1998	Mark O'Meara	279
1999	Jose Maria Olazabal	280
2000	Vijay Singh	278
2001	Tiger Woods	272
2002	Tiger Woods	276
2003	*Mike Weir	281
2004	Phil Mickelson	279

* Playoff

MCI HERITAGE

YEAR	WINNER	SCORE
	HERITAGE CLASSIC	
1969	Arnold Palmer	283
1970	Bob Goalby	280
	SEA PINES HERITAGE CLASSIC	
1971	Hale Irwin	279
1972	Johnny Miller	281
1973	Hale Irwin	272
1974	Johnny Miller	276
1975	Jack Nicklaus	271
1976	Hubert Green	274
1977	Graham Marsh	273
1978	Hubert Green	277
1979	Tom Watson	270
1980	*Doug Tewell	280
1981	Bill Rogers	278
1982	*Tom Watson	280
1983	Fuzzy Zoeller	275
1984	Nick Faldo	270
1985	*Bernhard Langer	273
1986	Fuzzy Zoeller	276
	MCI HERITAGE CLASSIC	
1987	Davis Love III	271
1988	Greg Norman	271
1989	Payne Stewart	268
1990	*Payne Stewart	276
1991	Davis Love III	271
1992	Davis Love III	269
1993	David Edwards	273
1994	Hale Irwin	266
1995	*Bob Tway	275
1996	Loren Roberts	265
1997	Nick Price	269
1998	Davis Love III	266
1999	*Glen Day	274
2000	Stewart Cink	270
	WORLDCOM CLASSIC	
2001	*Jose Coceres	273
2002	Justin Leonard	270
	MCI HERITAGE	
2003	*Davis Love III	271
2004	*Stewart Cink	274

* Playoff

SHELL HOUSTON OPEN

YEAR	WINNER	SCORE
	TOURNAMENT OF CHAMPIONS	
1946	Byron Nelson	274
1947	Bobby Locke	277
1948	No tournament	
1949	John Palmer	272
	HOUSTON OPEN	
1950	Cary Middlecoff	277
1951	Marty Furgol	277
1952	Jack Burke, Jr.	277
1953	*Cary Middlecoff	283
1954	Dave Douglas	277
1955	Mike Souchak	273
1956	Ted Kroll	277
1957	Arnold Palmer	279
1958	Ed Oliver	278
	HOUSTON CLASSIC	
1959	*Jack Burke, Jr.	277
1960	*Bill Collins	280
1961	*Jay Hebert	276
1962	*Bobby Nichols	278
1963	Bob Charles	268
1964	Mike Souchak	278
1965	Bobby Nichols	273
	HOUSTON CHAMPIONS INTERNATIONAL	
1966	Arnold Palmer	275
1967	Frank Beard	274
1968	Roberto De Vicenzo	274
1969	No tournament	
1970	*Gibby Gilbert	282
1971	*Hubert Green	280
	HOUSTON OPEN	
1972	Bruce Devlin	278
1973	Bruce Crampton	277
1974	Dave Hill	276
1975	Bruce Crampton	277
1976	Lee Elder	276
1977	Gene Littler	276
1978	Gary Player	270
1979	Wayne Levi	268
	MICHELOB HOUSTON OPEN	
1980	*Curtis Strange	266
1981	#Ron Streck	198
1982	*Ed Sneed	275
	HOUSTON COCA-COLA OPEN	
1983	David Graham	275
1984	Corey Pavin	274
	HOUSTON OPEN	
1985	Raymond Floyd	277
1986	*Curtis Strange	274
	BIG I HOUSTON OPEN	
1987	*Jay Haas	276
	INDEPENDENT INSURANCE OPEN	
1988	*Curtis Strange	270
1989	Mike Sullivan	280
1990	#Tony Sills	204
1991	Fulton Allem	273
	SHELL HOUSTON OPEN	
1992	Fred Funk	272
1993	#Jim McGovern	199
1994	Mike Heinen	272
1995	*Payne Stewart	276
1996	*Mark Brooks	274
1997	*Phil Blackmar	276
1998	David Duval	276
1999	Stuart Appleby	279
2000	*Robert Allenby	275
2001	Hal Sutton	278
2002	Vijay Singh	266

2003	Fred Couples	267
2004	Vijay Singh	277

* Playoff
# Rain-shortened

HP CLASSIC OF NEW ORLEANS

YEAR	WINNER	SCORE
GREATER NEW ORLEANS OPEN INVITATIONAL		
1938	Harry Cooper	285
1939	Henry Picard	284
1940	Jimmy Demaret	286
1941	Henry Picard	276
1942	Lloyd Mangrum	281
1943	No tournament	
1944	Sam Byrd	285
1945	*Byron Nelson	284
1946	Byron Nelson	277
1947	No tournament	
1948	Bob Hamilton	280
1949–		
1957	No tournament	
1958	*Billy Casper	278
1959	Bill Collins	280
1960	Dow Finsterwald	270
1961	Doug Sanders	272
1962	Bo Wininger	281
1963	Bo Wininger	279
1964	Mason Rudolph	283
1965	Dick Mayer	273
1966	Frank Beard	276
1967	George Knudson	277
1968	George Archer	271
1969	*Larry Hinson	275
1970	*Miller Barber	278
1971	Frank Beard	276
1972	Gary Player	279
1973	*Jack Nicklaus	280
1974	Lee Trevino	267
FIRST NBC NEW ORLEANS OPEN		
1975	Billy Casper	271
1976	Larry Ziegler	274
1977	Jim Simons	273
1978	Lon Hinkle	271
1979	Hubert Green	273
GREATER NEW ORLEANS OPEN		
1980	Tom Watson	273
USF&G NEW ORLEANS OPEN		
1981	Tom Watson	270
USF&G CLASSIC		
1982	#Scott Hoch	206
1983	Bill Rogers	274
1984	Bob Eastwood	272
1985	#Seve Ballesteros	205
1986	Calvin Peete	269
1987	Ben Crenshaw	268
1988	Chip Beck	262
1989	Tim Simpson	274
1990	David Frost	276
1991	*Ian Woosnam	275
FREEPORT MCMORAN CLASSIC		
1992	Chip Beck	276
1993	Mike Standly	281
1994	Ben Crenshaw	273
1995	*Davis Love III	274
FREEPORT MCDERMOTT CLASSIC		
1996	Scott McCarron	275
1997	Brad Faxon	272
1998	Lee Westwood	273

COMPAQ CLASSIC OF NEW ORLEANS		
1999	Carlos Franco	269
2000	*Carlos Franco	270
2001	David Toms	266
2002	K.J. Choi	271
2003	*Steve Flesch	267
HP CLASSIC OF NEW ORLEANS		
2004	Vijay Singh	266

*Playoff
#Rain-shortened

WACHOVIA CHAMPIONSHIP

YEAR	WINNER	SCORE
2003	David Toms	278
2004	*Joey Sindelar	277

* Playoff

EDS BYRON NELSON CHAMPIONSHIP

YEAR	WINNER	SCORE
TEXAS VICTORY OPEN		
1944	Byron Nelson	276
DALLAS OPEN		
1945	Sam Snead	276
1946	Ben Hogan	284
1947–		
1955	No tournament	
1956	Don January	268
1956A	*Peter Thomson	267
1957	Sam Snead	264
1958	*Sam Snead	272
1959	Julius Boros	274
1960	*Johnny Pott	275
1961	Earl Stewart, Jr.	278
1962	Billy Maxwell	277
1963	No tournament	
1964	Charles Coody	271
1965	No tournament	
1966	Roberto De Vicenzo	276
1967	Bert Yancey	274
BYRON NELSON GOLF CLASSIC		
1968	Miller Barber	270
1969	Bruce Devlin	277
1970	*Jack Nicklaus	274
1971	Jack Nicklaus	274
1972	*Chi Chi Rodriguez	273
1973	*Lanny Wadkins	277
1974	Brian Allin	269
1975	Tom Watson	269
1976	Mark Hayes	273
1977	Raymond Floyd	276
1978	Tom Watson	272
1979	*Tom Watson	275
1980	Tom Watson	274
1981	*Bruce Lietzke	281
1982	Bob Gilder	266
1983	Ben Crenshaw	273
1984	Craig Stadler	276
1985	*Bob Eastwood	272
1986	Andy Bean	269
1987	*Fred Couples	266
GTE BYRON NELSON GOLF CLASSIC		
1988	*Bruce Lietzke	271
1989	Jodie Mudd	265
1990	#Payne Stewart	202
1991	Nick Price	270

1992	#Billy Ray Brown	199
1993	Scott Simpson	270
1994	#*Neal Lancaster	132
1995	Ernie Els	263
1996	Phil Mickelson	265
1997	Tiger Woods	263
1998	John Cook	265
1999	*Loren Roberts	262
2000	*Jesper Parnevik	269
VERIZON BYRON NELSON CLASSIC		
2001	*Robert Damron	263
2002	Shigeki Maruyama	266
EDS BYRON NELSON CHAMPIONSHIP		
2003	Vijay Singh	265
2004	*Sergio Garcia	270

* Playoff
# Rain-shortened

BANK OF AMERICA COLONIAL

YEAR	WINNER	SCORE
COLONIAL NATIONAL INVITATION TOURNAMENT		
1946	Ben Hogan	279
1947	Ben Hogan	279
1948	Clayton Heafner	272
1949	No tournament	
1950	Sam Snead	277
1951	Cary Middlecoff	282
1952	Ben Hogan	279
1953	Ben Hogan	282
1954	Johnny Palmer	280
1955	Chandler Harper	276
1956	Mike Souchak	280
1957	Roberto De Vicenzo	284
1958	Tommy Bolt	282
1959	*Ben Hogan	285
1960	Julius Boros	280
1961	Doug Sanders	281
1962	*Arnold Palmer	281
1963	Julius Boros	279
1964	Billy Casper	279
1965	Bruce Crampton	276
1966	Bruce Devlin	280
1967	Dave Stockton	278
1968	Billy Casper	275
1969	Gardner Dickinson	278
1970	Homero Blancas	273
1971	Gene Littler	283
1972	Jerry Heard	275
1973	Tom Weiskopf	276
1974	Rod Curl	276
1975	*Al Geiberger	270
1976	Lee Trevino	273
1977	Ben Crenshaw	272
1978	Lee Trevino	268
1979	Al Geiberger	274
1980	Bruce Lietzke	271
1981	Fuzzy Zoeller	274
1982	Jack Nicklaus	273
1983	*Jim Colbert	278
1984	*Peter Jacobsen	270
1985	Corey Pavin	266
1986	#*Dan Pohl	205
1987	Keith Clearwater	266
1988	Lanny Wadkins	270
SOUTHWESTERN BELL COLONIAL		
1989	Ian Baker-Finch	270
1990	Ben Crenshaw	272
1991	Tom Purtzer	267

1992	*Bruce Lietzke	267
1993	Fulton Allem	264
1994	*Nick Price	266
COLONIAL NATIONAL INVITATION		
1995	Tom Lehman	271
MASTERCARD COLONIAL		
1996	Corey Pavin	272
1997	David Frost	265
1998	Tom Watson	265
1999	Olin Browne	272
2000	Phil Mickelson	268
2001	Sergio Garcia	267
2002	Nick Price	267
BANK OF AMERICA COLONIAL		
2003	Kenny Perry	261
2004	Steve Flesch	269

* Playoff
# Rain-shortened

FEDEX ST. JUDE CLASSIC

YEAR	WINNER	SCORE
MEMPHIS INVITATIONAL OPEN		
1958	Billy Maxwell	267
1959	*Don Whitt	272
1960	*Tommy Bolt	273
1961	Cary Middlecoff	266
1962	*Lionel Hebert	267
1963	*Tony Lema	270
1964	Mike Souchak	270
1965	*Jack Nicklaus	271
1966	Bert Yancey	265
1967	Dave Hill	272
1968	Bob Lunn	268
1969	Dave Hill	265
DANNY THOMAS MEMPHIS CLASSIC		
1970	Dave Hill	267
1971	Lee Trevino	268
1972	Lee Trevino	281
1973	Dave Hill	283
1974	Gary Player	273
1975	Gene Littler	270
1976	Gibby Gilbert	273
1977	Al Geiberger	273
1978	*Andy Bean	277
1979	*Gil Morgan	278
1980	Lee Trevino	272
1981	Jerry Pate	274
1982	Raymond Floyd	271
1983	Larry Mize	274
1984	Bob Eastwood	280
ST. JUDE MEMPHIS CLASSIC		
1985	*Hal Sutton	279
FEDERAL EXPRESS ST. JUDE CLASSIC		
1986	Mike Hulbert	280
1987	Curtis Strange	275
1988	Jodie Mudd	273
1989	John Mahaffey	272
1990	*Tom Kite	269
1991	Fred Couples	269
1992	Jay Haas	263
1993	Nick Price	266
1994	*Dicky Pride	267
FEDEX ST. JUDE CLASSIC		
1995	Jim Gallagher, Jr.	267
1996	John Cook	258
1997	Greg Norman	268
1998	*Nick Price	268
1999	Ted Tryba	265

2000	Notah Begay III	271
2001	Bob Estes	267
2002	Len Mattiace	266
2003	David Toms	264
2004	David Toms	268

* Playoff

THE MEMORIAL TOURNAMENT

YEAR	WINNER	SCORE
1976	*Roger Maltbie	288
1977	Jack Nicklaus	281
1978	Jim Simons	284
1979	Tom Watson	285
1980	David Graham	280
1981	Keith Fergus	284
1982	Raymond Floyd	281
1983	Hale Irwin	281
1984	*Jack Nicklaus	280
1985	Hale Irwin	281
1986	Hal Sutton	271
1987	Don Pooley	272
1988	Curtis Strange	274
1989	Bob Tway	277
1990	#Greg Norman	216
1991	*Kenny Perry	273
1992	*David Edwards	273
1993	Paul Azinger	274
1994	Tom Lehman	268
1995	Greg Norman	269
1996	Tom Watson	274
1997	#Vijay Singh	202
1998	Fred Couples	271
1999	Tiger Woods	273
2000	Tiger Woods	269
2001	Tiger Woods	271
2002	Jim Furyk	274
2003	Kenny Perry	275
2004	Ernie Els	270

* Playoff
# Rain-shortened

BUICK CLASSIC

YEAR	WINNER	SCORE
WESTCHESTER CLASSIC		
1967	Jack Nicklaus	272
1968	Julius Boros	272
1969	Frank Beard	275
1970	Bruce Crampton	273
1971	Arnold Palmer	270
1972	Jack Nicklaus	270
1973	*Bobby Nichols	272
1974	Johnny Miller	269
1975	*Gene Littler	271
AMERICAN EXPRESS WESTCHESTER CLASSIC		
1976	David Graham	272
1977	Andy North	272
1978	Lee Elder	274
MANUFACTURERS HANOVER WESTCHESTER CLASSIC		
1979	Jack Renner	277
1980	Curtis Strange	273
1981	Raymond Floyd	275
1982	Bob Gilder	261
1983	Seve Ballesteros	276

1984	Scott Simpson	269
1985	*Roger Maltbie	275
1986	Bob Tway	272
1987	*J.C. Snead	276
1988	*Seve Ballesteros	276
1989	*Wayne Grady	277
BUICK CLASSIC		
1990	Hale Irwin	269
1991	Billy Andrade	273
1992	David Frost	268
1993	*Vijay Singh	280
1994	Lee Janzen	268
1995	*Vijay Singh	268
1996	Ernie Els	271
1997	Ernie Els	268
1998	#*J.P. Hayes	201
1999	*Duffy Waldorf	276
2000	*Dennis Paulson	276
2001	Sergio Garcia	268
2002	Chris Smith	272
2003	Jonathan Kaye	271

* Playoff
# Rain-shortened

BOOZ ALLEN CLASSIC

YEAR	WINNER	SCORE
KEMPER OPEN		
1968	Arnold Palmer	276
1969	Dale Douglass	274
1970	Dick Lotz	278
1971	*Tom Weiskopf	277
1972	Doug Sanders	275
1973	Tom Weiskopf	271
1974	*Bob Menne	270
1975	Raymond Floyd	278
1976	Joe Inman	277
1977	Tom Weiskopf	277
1978	Andy Bean	273
1979	Jerry McGee	272
1980	John Mahaffey	275
1981	Craig Stadler	270
1982	Craig Stadler	275
1983	*Fred Couples	287
1984	Greg Norman	280
1985	Bill Glasson	278
1986	*Greg Norman	277
1987	Tom Kite	270
1988	*Morris Hatalsky	274
1989	Tom Byrum	268
1990	Gil Morgan	274
1991	*Billy Andrade	263
1992	Bill Glasson	276
1993	Grant Waite	275
1994	Mark Brooks	271
1995	*Lee Janzen	272
1996	Steve Stricker	270
1997	Justin Leonard	274
1998	Stuart Appleby	274
1999	Rich Beem	274
KEMPER INSURANCE OPEN		
2000	Tom Scherrer	271
2001	Frank Lickliter II	268
2002	Bob Estes	273
FBR CAPITAL OPEN		
2003	Rory Sabbatini	270

* Playoff

CIALIS WESTERN OPEN

YEAR	WINNER	SCORE
	WESTERN OPEN	
1899	*Willie Smith	156
1900	No tournament	
1901	Laurie Auchterlonie	160
1902	Willie Anderson	299
1903	Alex Smith	318
1904	Willie Anderson	304
1905	Arthur Smith	278
1906	Alex Smith	306
1907	Robert Simpson	307
1908	Willie Anderson	299
1909	Willie Anderson	288
1910	a-Chick Evans, Jr.	6&5
1911	Robert Simpson	2&1
1912	Mac Smith	299
1913	John McDermott	295
1914	Jim Barnes	293
1915	Tom McNamara	304
1916	Walter Hagen	286
1917	Jim Barnes	283
1918	No tournament	
1919	Jim Barnes	283
1920	Jock Hutchinson	296
1921	Walter Hagen	287
1922	Mike Brady	291
1923	Jock Hutchinson	281
1924	Bill Mehlhorn	293
1925	Mac Smith	281
1926	Walter Hagen	279
1927	Walter Hagen	281
1928	Abe Espinosa	291
1929	Tommy Armour	273
1930	Gene Sarazen	278
1931	Ed Dudley	280
1932	Walter Hagen	287
1933	Mac Smith	282
1934	*Harry Cooper	274
1935	Johnny Revolta	290
1936	Ralph Guldahl	274
1937	*Ralph Guldahl	288
1938	Ralph Guldahl	279
1939	Byron Nelson	281
1940	*Jimmy Demaret	293
1941	Ed Oliver	275
1942	Herman Barron	276
1943–		
1945	No tournament	
1946	Ben Hogan	271
1947	Johnny Palmer	270
1948	*Ben Hogan	281
1949	Sam Snead	268
1950	Sam Snead	282
1951	Marty Furgol	270
1952	Lloyd Mangrum	274
1953	Dutch Harrison	278
1954	*Lloyd Mangrum	277
1955	Cary Middlecoff	272
1956	*Mike Fetchick	284
1957	*Doug Ford	279
1958	Doug Sanders	275
1959	Mike Souchak	272
1960	*Stan Leonard	278
1961	Arnold Palmer	271
1962	Jacky Cupit	281
1963	*Arnold Palmer	280
1964	Chi Chi Rodriguez	268
1965	Billy Casper	270
1966	Bill Casper	283

1967	Jack Nicklaus	274
1968	Jack Nicklaus	273
1969	Billy Casper	276
1970	Hugh Royer	273
1971	Bruce Crampton	279
1972	Jim Jamieson	271
1973	Billy Casper	272
1974	Tom Watson	287
1975	Hale Irwin	283
1976	Al Geiberger	288
1977	Tom Watson	283
1978	*Andy Bean	282
1979	*Larry Nelson	286
1980	Scott Simpson	281
1981	Ed Fiori	277
1982	Tom Weiskopf	276
1983	Mark McCumber	284
1984	*Tom Watson	280
1985	a-Scott Verplank	279
1986	*Tom Kite	286
	BEATRICE WESTERN OPEN	
1987	#D.A. Weibring	207
1988	Jim Benepe	278
1989	*Mark McCumber	275
	CENTEL WESTERN OPEN	
1990	Wayne Levi	275
1991	Russ Cochran	275
1992	Ben Crenshaw	276
	SPRINT WESTERN OPEN	
1993	Nick Price	269
	MOTOROLA WESTERN OPEN	
1994	Nick Price	277
1995	Billy Mayfair	279
1996	Steve Stricker	270
1997	Tiger Woods	275
1998	Joe Durant	271
1999	Tiger Woods	273
	ADVIL WESTERN OPEN	
2000	*Robert Allenby	274
2001	Scott Hoch	267
2002	Jerry Kelly	269
	WESTERN OPEN	
2003	Tiger Woods	267

* Playoff
a- Amateur
Rain-shortened

JOHN DEERE CLASSIC

YEAR	WINNER	SCORE
	QUAD CITIES OPEN	
1972	Deane Beman	279
1973	Sam Adams	268
1974	Dave Stockton	271
	ED MCMAHON–JAYCEES QUAD CITY OPEN	
1975	Roger Maltbie	275
1976	John Lister	268
1977	Mike Morley	267
1978	Victor Regalado	269
1979	D.A. Weibring	266
	QUAD CITIES OPEN	
1980	Scott Hoch	266
1981	*Dave Barr	270
	MILLER HIGH-LIFE QUAD CITIES OPEN	
1982	Payne Stewart	268
1983	*Danny Edwards	266
1984	Scott Hoch	266
	LITE QUAD CITIES OPEN	
1985	Dan Forsman	267

	HARDEE'S GOLF CLASSIC	
1986	Mark Wiebe	268
1987	Kenny Knox	265
1988	Blaine McCallister	261
1989	Curt Byrum	268
1990	*Joey Sindelar	268
1991	D.A. Weibring	267
1992	David Frost	266
1993	David Frost	259
1994	Mark McCumber	265
	QUAD CITY CLASSIC	
1995	#D.A. Weibring	197
1996	Ed Fiori	268
1997	David Toms	265
1998	Steve Jones	263
	JOHN DEERE CLASSIC	
1999	*J.L. Lewis	261
2000	*Michael Clark II	265
2001	David Gossett	265
2002	J.P. Hayes	262
2003	Vijay Singh	268

* Playoff
# Rain-shortened

B.C. OPEN

YEAR	WINNER	SCORE
	BROOME COUNTY OPEN	
1971	^*Claude Harmon, Jr.	69
	B.C. OPEN	
1972	^Bob Payne	136
1973	Hubert Green	266
1974	*Richie Karl	273
1975	Don Iverson	274
1976	Bob Wynn	271
1977	Gil Morgan	270
1978	Tom Kite	267
1979	Howard Twitty	270
1980	Don Pooley	271
1981	Jay Haas	270
1982	Calvin Peete	265
1983	Pat Lindsey	268
1984	Wayne Levi	275
1985	Joey Sindelar	274
1986	Rick Fehr	267
1987	Joey Sindelar	266
1988	Bill Glasson	268
1989	*Mike Hulbert	268
1990	Nolan Henke	268
1991	Fred Couples	269
1992	John Daly	266
1993	Blaine McCallister	271
1994	Mike Sullivan	266
1995	Hal Sutton	269
1996	#*Fred Funk	202
1997	Gabriel Hjertstedt	275
1998	Chris Perry	273
1999	*Brad Faxon	273
2000	Brad Faxon	270
2001	*Jeff Sluman	276
2002	Spike McRoy	269
2003	Craig Stadler	267

* Playoff
# Rain-shortened
^ Second Tour event

U.S. BANK CHAMPIONSHIP IN MILWAUKEE

YEAR	WINNER	SCORE
	GREATER MILWAUKEE OPEN	
1968	Dave Stockton	275
1969	Ken Still	277
1970	Deane Beman	276
1971	Dave Eichelberger	270
1972	Jim Colbert	271
1973	Dave Stockton	276
1974	Ed Sneed	276
1975	Art Wall	271
1976	Dave Hill	270
1977	Dave Eichelberger	278
1978	*Lee Elder	275
1979	Calvin Peete	269
1980	Bill Kratzert	266
1981	Jay Haas	274
1982	Calvin Peete	274
1983	*Morris Hatalsky	275
1984	Mark O'Meara	272
1985	Jim Thorpe	274
1986	*Corey Pavin	272
1987	Gary Hallberg	269
1988	Ken Green	268
1989	Greg Norman	269
1990	*Jim Gallagher, Jr.	271
1991	Mark Brooks	270
1992	Richard Zokol	269
1993	*Billy Mayfair	270
1994	Mike Springer	268
1995	Scott Hoch	269
1996	*Loren Roberts	265
1997	Scott Hoch	268
1998	Jeff Sluman	265
1999	Carlos Franco	264
2000	Loren Roberts	260
2001	*Shigeki Maruyama	266
2002	Jeff Sluman	261
2003	Kenny Perry	268

* Playoff

BUICK OPEN

YEAR	WINNER	SCORE
	BUICK OPEN INVITATIONAL	
1958	Billy Casper	285
1959	Art Wall	282
1960	Mike Souchak	282
1961	Jack Burke, Jr.	284
1962	Bill Collins	284
1963	*Julius Boros	274
1964	Tony Lema	277
1965	Tony Lema	280
1966	Phil Rodgers	284
1967	Julius Boros	283
1968	Tom Weiskopf	280
1969	Dave Hill	277
1970–		
1971	No tournament	
	VERN PARSELL BUICK OPEN	
1972	^Gary Groh	273
	LAKE MICHIGAN CLASSIC	
1973	^Wilf Homenuik	215
	FLINT ELKS OPEN	
1974	^Bryan Abbott	135
1975	^Spike Kelley	208
1976	^Ed Sabo	279
1977	Bobby Cole	271

YEAR	WINNER	SCORE
	BUICK GOODWRENCH OPEN	
1978	*Jack Newton	280
1979	*John Fought	280
1980	Peter Jacobsen	276
	BUICK OPEN	
1981	*Hale Irwin	277
1982	Lanny Wadkins	273
1983	Wayne Levi	272
1984	Denis Watson	271
1985	Ken Green	268
1986	Ben Crenshaw	270
1987	Robert Wrenn	262
1988	Scott Verplank	268
1989	Leonard Thompson	273
1990	Chip Beck	272
1991	*Brad Faxon	271
1992	*Dan Forsman	276
1993	Larry Mize	272
1994	Fred Couples	270
1995	*Woody Austin	270
1996	Justin Leonard	266
1997	Vijay Singh	273
1998	Billy Mayfair	271
1999	Tom Pernice, Jr.	270
2000	Rocco Mediate	268
2001	Kenny Perry	263
2002	Tiger Woods	271
2003	Jim Furyk	267

* Playoff
^ Second-tour event

THE INTERNATIONAL

YEAR	WINNER	SCORE
	THE INTERNATIONAL	
1986	Ken Green	Plus 12
1987	John Cook	Plus 11
1988	Joey Sindelar	Plus 17
1989	Greg Norman	Plus 13
1990	Davis Love III	Plus 14
1991	Jose Maria Olazabal	Plus 10
1992	Brad Faxon	Plus 14
1993	Phil Mickelson	Plus 45**
	SPRINT INTERNATIONAL	
1994	*Steve Lowery	Plus 35
1995	Lee Janzen	Plus 34
1996	*Clarence Rose	Plus 31
1997	Phil Mickelson	Plus 48
1998	Vijay Singh	Plus 47
1999	David Toms	Plus 47
	INTERNATIONAL PRESENTED BY QWEST	
2000	Ernie Els	Plus 48
2001	Tom Pernice, Jr.	Plus 34
2002	Rich Beem	Plus 44
2003	Davis Love III	Plus 46

Scoring is by points in modified Stableford System.
* Playoff
**Scoring cumulative for four rounds beginning in 1993. In prior years, winning score is final-round score.

NEC WORLD SERIES OF GOLF

YEAR	WINNER	SCORE
	WORLD SERIES OF GOLF	
1962	Jack Nicklaus	135
1963	Jack Nicklaus	140
1964	Tony Lema	138

1965	Gary Player	139
1966	Gene Littler	143
1967	Jack Nicklaus	144
1968	Gary Player	143
1969	Orville Moody	141
1970	Jack Nicklaus	136
1971	Charles Coody	141
1972	Gary Player	142
1973	Tom Weiskopf	137
1974	*Lee Trevino	139
1975	Tom Watson	140
1976	Jack Nicklaus	275**
1977	Lanny Wadkins	267
1978	*Gil Morgan	278
1979	Lon Hinkle	272
1980	Tom Watson	270
1981	Bill Rogers	275
1982	Craig Stadler	278
1983	Nick Price	270
	NEC WORLD SERIES OF GOLF	
1984	Denis Watson	271
1985	Roger Maltbie	268
1986	Dan Pohl	277
1987	Curtis Strange	275
1988	*Mike Reid	275
1989	*David Frost	276
1990	Jose Maria Olazabal	262
1991	Tom Purtzer	279
1992	Craig Stadler	273
1993	Fulton Allem	270
1994	Jose Maria Olazabal	269
1995	*Greg Norman	278
1996	Phil Mickelson	274
1997	Greg Norman	273
1998	David Duval	269
	WGC-NEC INVITATIONAL	
1999	Tiger Woods	270
2000	Tiger Woods	259
2001	*Tiger Woods	268
2002	Craig Parry	268
2003	Darren Clarke	268

* Playoff
** 72-hole event beginning in 1976 (in prior years, a 36-hole exhibition)

RENO-TAHOE OPEN

YEAR	WINNER	SCORE
1999	Notah Begay III	274
2000	*Scott Verplank	275
2001	John Cook	271
2002	*Chris Riley	271
2003	Kirk Triplett	271

* Playoff

BUICK CHAMPIONSHIP

YEAR	WINNER	SCORE
	INSURANCE CITY OPEN	
1952	Ted Kroll	273
1953	Bob Toski	269
1954	*Tommy Bolt	271
1955	Sam Snead	269
1956	*Arnold Palmer	274
1957	Gardner Dickinson	272
1958	Jack Burke, Jr.	268
1959	Gene Littler	272
1960	*Arnold Palmer	270

Year	Winner	Score
1961	*Billy Maxwell	271
1962	*Bob Goalby	271
1963	Billy Casper	271
1964	Ken Venturi	273
1965	*Billy Casper	274
1966	Art Wall	266

GREATER HARTFORD OPEN INVITATIONAL

Year	Winner	Score
1967	Charlie Sifford	272
1968	Billy Casper	266
1969	*Bob Lunn	268
1970	Bob Murphy	267
1971	*George Archer	268
1972	*Lee Trevino	269

SAMMY DAVIS JR.
GREATER HARTFORD OPEN

Year	Winner	Score
1973	Billy Casper	264
1974	Dave Stockton	268
1975	*Don Bies	267
1976	Rik Massengale	266
1977	Bill Kratzert	265
1978	Rod Funseth	264
1979	Jerry McGee	267
1980	*Howard Twitty	266
1981	Hubert Green	264
1982	Tim Norris	259
1983	Curtis Strange	268
1984	Peter Jacobsen	269

CANON SAMMY DAVIS JR.
GREATER HARTFORD OPEN

Year	Winner	Score
1985	*Phil Blackmar	271
1986	*Mac O'Grady	269
1987	Paul Azinger	269
1988	*Mark Brooks	269
1989	Paul Azinger	267

CANON GREATER HARTFORD OPEN

Year	Winner	Score
1990	Wayne Levi	267
1991	*Billy Ray Brown	271
1992	Lanny Wadkins	274
1993	Nick Price	271
1994	David Frost	268
1995	Greg Norman	267
1996	D.A. Weibring	270
1997	Stewart Cink	267
1998	*Olin Browne	266
1999	Brent Geiberger	262
2000	Notah Begay III	260
2001	Phil Mickelson	264
2002	Phil Mickelson	266

GREATER HARTFORD OPEN

Year	Winner	Score
2003	Peter Jacobsen	266

* Playoff

DEUTSCHE BANK CHAMPIONSHIP

YEAR	WINNER	SCORE
2003	Adam Scott	264

BELL CANADIAN OPEN

YEAR	WINNER	SCORE
	CANADIAN OPEN	
1904	J.H. Oke	156
1905	George Cumming	148
1906	Charles Murray	170
1907	Percy Barrett	306
1908	Albert Murray	300
1909	Karl Keffer	309
1910	Daniel Kenny	303
1911	Charles Murray	314
1912	George Sargent	299
1913	Albert Murray	295
1914	Karl Keffer	300
1915–		
1918	No tournament	
1919	J. Douglas Edgar	278
1920	*J. Douglas Edgar	298
1921	W.H. Trovinger	293
1922	Al Watrous	303
1923	C.W. Hackney	295
1924	Leo Diegel	285
1925	Leo Diegel	295
1926	Mac Smith	283
1927	Tommy Armour	288
1928	Leo Diegel	282
1929	Leo Diegel	274
1930	*Tommy Armour	273
1931	*Walter Hagen	292
1932	Harry Cooper	290
1933	Joe Kirkwood	282
1934	Tommy Armour	287
1935	Gene Kunes	280
1936	Lawson Little	271
1937	Harry Cooper	285
1938	*Sam Snead	277
1939	Harold McSpaden	282
1940	*Sam Snead	281
1941	Sam Snead	274
1942	Craig Wood	275
1943–		
1944	No tournament	
1945	Byron Nelson	280
1946	*George Fazio	278
1947	Bobby Locke	268
1948	C.W. Congdon	280
1949	Dutch Harrison	271
1950	Jim Ferrier	271
1951	Jim Ferrier	273
1952	John Palmer	263
1953	Dave Douglas	273
1954	Pat Fletcher	280
1955	Arnold Palmer	265
1956	a-Doug Sanders	273
1957	George Bayer	271
1958	Wes Ellis	267
1959	Doug Ford	276
1960	Art Wall, Jr.	269
1961	Jacky Cupit	270
1962	Ted Kroll	278
1963	Doug Ford	280
1964	Kel Nagle	277
1965	Gene Littler	273
1966	Don Massengale	280
1967	*Billy Casper	279
1968	Bob Charles	274
1969	*Tommy Aaron	275
1970	Kermit Zarley	279
1971	*Lee Trevino	275
1972	Gay Brewer	275
1973	Tom Weiskopf	278
1974	Bobby Nichols	270
1975	*Tom Weiskopf	274
1976	Jerry Pate	267
1977	Lee Trevino	280
1978	Bruce Lietzke	283
1979	Lee Trevino	281
1980	Bob Gilder	274
1981	Peter Oosterhuis	280
1982	Bruce Lietzke	277
1983	*John Cook	277
1984	Greg Norman	278
1985	Curtis Strange	279
1986	Bob Murphy	280
1987	Curtis Strange	276
1988	Ken Green	275
1989	Steve Jones	271
1990	Wayne Levi	278
1991	Nick Price	273
1992	*Greg Norman	280
1993	David Frost	279

BELL CANADIAN OPEN

Year	Winner	Score
1994	Nick Price	275
1995	*Mark O'Meara	274
1996	#Dudley Hart	202
1997	Steve Jones	275
1998	*Billy Andrade	275
1999	Hal Sutton	275
2000	Tiger Woods	266
2001	Scott Verplank	266
2002	*John Rollins	272
2003	*Bob Tway	272

* Playoff
# Rain-shortened
a- Amateur

VALERO TEXAS OPEN

YEAR	WINNER	SCORE
	TEXAS OPEN	
1922	Bob MacDonald	281
1923	Walter Hagen	279
1924	Joe Kirkwood	279
1925	Joe Turnesa	284
1926	Mac Smith	288
1927	Bobby Cruickshank	272
1928	Bill Mehlhorn	297
1929	Bill Mehlhorn	277
1930	Denny Shute	277
1931	Abe Espinosa	281
1932	Clarence Clark	287
1933	No tournament	
1934	Wiffy Cox	283
1935–		
1938	No tournament	
1939	Dutch Harrison	271
1940	Byron Nelson	271
1941	Lawson Little	273
1942	*Chick Harbert	272
1943	No tournament	
1944	Johnny Revolta	273
1945	Sam Byrd	268
1946	Ben Hogan	264
1947	Ed Oliver	265
1948	Sam Snead	264
1949	Dave Douglas	268
1950	Sam Snead	265
1951	*Dutch Harrison	265
1952	Jack Burke, Jr.	260
1953	Tony Holguin	264
1954	Chandler Harper	259
1955	Mike Souchak	257
1956	Gene Littler	276
1957	Jay Hebert	271
1958	Bill Johnston	274
1959	Wes Ellis	276
1960	Arnold Palmer	276
1961	Arnold Palmer	270
1962	Arnold Palmer	273
1963	Phil Rodgers	268
1964	Bruce Crampton	273
1965	Frank Beard	270

1966	Harold Henning	272
1967	Chi Chi Rodriguez	277
1968	No tournament	
1969	*Deane Beman	274

SAN ANTONIO TEXAS OPEN

1970	Ron Cerrudo	273
1971	No tournament	
1972	Mike Hill	273
1973	Ben Crenshaw	270
1974	Terry Diehl	269
1975	*Don January	275
1976	*Butch Baird	273
1977	Hale Irwin	266
1978	Ron Streck	265
1979	Lou Graham	268
1980	Lee Trevino	265

TEXAS OPEN

1981	*Bill Rogers	266
1982	Jay Haas	262
1983	Jim Colbert	261
1984	Calvin Peete	266
1985	*John Mahaffey	268

VANTAGE CHAMPIONSHIP

1986	#Ben Crenshaw	196

TEXAS OPEN PRESENTED BY NABISCO

1987	Hosted Tour Championship	
1988	Corey Pavin	259
1989	Donnie Hammond	258

H.E.B. TEXAS OPEN

1990	Mark O'Meara	261
1991	*Blaine McCallister	269
1992	*Nick Price	283
1993	*Jay Haas	263

TEXAS OPEN

1994	Bob Estes	265

LACANTERA TEXAS OPEN

1995	Duffy Waldorf	268
1996	David Ogrin	275
1997	Tim Herron	271

WESTIN TEXAS OPEN

1998	Hal Sutton	270
1999	*Duffy Waldorf	270
2000	Justin Leonard	261

TEXAS OPEN AT LACANTERA

2001	Justin Leonard	266

VALERO TEXAS OPEN

2002	Loren Roberts	261
2003	Tommy Armour III	254

* Playoff
# Rain-shortened

84 LUMBER CLASSIC

YEAR	WINNER	SCORE
	SEI PENNSYLVANIA CLASSIC	
2000	Chris DiMarco	270
	MARCONI PENNSYLVANIA CLASSIC	
2001	Robert Allenby	269
	SEI PENNSYLVANIA CLASSIC	
2002	Dan Forsman	270
	84 LUMBER CLASSIC	
2003	J.L. Lewis	266

WGC-AMERICAN EXPRESS CLASSIC

YEAR	WINNER	SCORE
1999	*Tiger Woods	278
2000	Mike Weir	277

2001	No tournament	
2002	Tiger Woods	263
2003	Tiger Woods	274

* Playoff

SOUTHERN FARM BUREAU CLASSIC

YEAR	WINNER	SCORE
	MAGNOLIA STATE CLASSIC	
1968	*Mac McLendon	269
1969	Larry Mowry	272
1970	Chris Blocker	271
1971	Roy Pace	270
1972	Mike Morley	269
1973	Dwight Nevil	268
1974	#Dwight Nevil	133
1975	Bob Wynn	270
1976	Dennis Meyer	271
1977	Mike McCullough	269
1978	Craig Stadler	268
1979	Bobby Walzel	272
1980	#*Roger Maltbie	65
1981	*Tom Jones	268
1982	Payne Stewart	270
1983	^#Russ Cochran	203
1984	^#*Lance Ten Broeck	201
1985	^#*Jim Gallagher, Jr.	131
	DEPOSIT GUARANTY GOLF CLASSIC	
1986	Dan Halldorson	263
1987	David Ogrin	267
1988	Frank Conner	267
1989	#*Jim Booros	199
1990	Gene Sauers	268
1991	*Larry Silveira	266
1992	Richard Zokol	267
1993	Greg Kraft	267
1994	#*Brian Henninger	135
1995	Ed Dougherty	272
1996	Willie Wood	268
1997	Billy Ray Brown	271
1998	Fred Funk	270
	SOUTHERN FARM BUREAU CLASSIC	
1999	#Brian Henninger	202
2000	*Steve Lowery	266
2001	Cameron Beckman	269
2002	#Luke Donald	201
2003	John Huston	268

* Playoff
# Rain-shortened
^ Second Tour event
Event became official in 1994

LAS VEGAS INVITATIONAL

YEAR	WINNER	SCORE
	PANASONIC LAS VEGAS PRO-CELEBRITY CLASSIC	
1983	Fuzzy Zoeller	340
	PANASONIC LAS VEGAS INVITATIONAL	
1984	Denis Watson	341
1985	Curtis Strange	338
1986	Greg Norman	333
1987	#Paul Azinger	271
1988	#Gary Koch	274
	LAS VEGAS INVITATIONAL	
1989	*Scott Hoch	336
1990	*Bob Tway	334
1991	*Andrew Magee	329

1992	John Cook	334
1993	Davis Love III	331
1994	Bruce Lietzke	332
1995	Jim Furyk	331
1996	*Tiger Woods	332
1997	Bill Glasson	340
1998	Jim Furyk	335
1999	Jim Furyk	331

INVENSYS CLASSIC AT LAS VEGAS

2000	Billy Andrade	332
2001	Bob Estes	329
2002	Phil Tataurangi	330

LAS VEGAS INVITATIONAL

2003	*Stuart Appleby	328

* Playoff
# Rain shortened

CHRYSLER CLASSIC OF GREENSBORO

YEAR	WINNER	SCORE
	GREATER GREENSBORO OPEN	
1938	Sam Snead	272
1939	Ralph Guldahl	280
1940	Ben Hogan	270
1941	Byron Nelson	276
1942	Sam Byrd	279
1943–		
1944	No tournament	
1945	Byron Nelson	271
1946	Sam Snead	270
1947	Vic Ghezzi	286
1948	Lloyd Mangrum	278
1949	*Sam Snead	276
1950	Sam Snead	269
1951	Art Doering	279
1952	Dave Douglas	277
1953	*Earl Stewart	275
1954	*Doug Ford	283
1955	Sam Snead	273
1956	*Sam Snead	279
1957	Stan Leonard	276
1958	Bob Goalby	273
1959	Dow Finsterwald	278
1960	Sam Snead	270
1961	Mike Souchak	276
1962	Billy Casper	275
1963	Doug Sanders	270
1964	*Julius Boros	277
1965	Sam Snead	273
1966	*Doug Sanders	276
1967	George Archer	267
1968	Billy Casper	267
1969	*Gene Littler	274
1970	Gary Player	271
1971	*Brian Allin	275
1972	*George Archer	267
1973	Chi Chi Rodriguez	267
1974	Bob Charles	270
1975	Tom Weiskopf	275
1976	Al Geiberger	268
1977	Danny Edwards	276
1978	Seve Ballesteros	282
1979	Raymond Floyd	282
1980	Craig Stadler	273
1981	*Larry Nelson	281
1982	Danny Edwards	285
1983	Lanny Wadkins	275
1984	Andy Bean	280
1985	Joey Sindelar	285

1986	Sandy Lyle	275
1987	Scott Simpson	282

KMART GREATER GREENSBORO OPEN
1988	Sandy Lyle	271
1989	Ken Green	277
1990	Steve Elkington	282
1991	*Mark Brooks	275
1992	Davis Love III	272
1993	Rocco Mediate	281
1994	Mike Springer	275
1995	Jim Gallagher, Jr.	274

GREATER GREENSBORO CHRYSLER CLASSIC
1996	Mark O'Meara	274
1997	*Frank Nobilo	274
1998	*Trevor Dodds	276
1999	Jesper Parnevik	265
2000	Hal Sutton	274
2001	Scott Hoch	272
2002	Rocco Mediate	272
2003	Shigeki Maruyama	266

* Playoff

FUNAI CLASSIC AT THE WALT DISNEY WORLD RESORT

YEAR	WINNER	SCORE

WALT DISNEY WORLD OPEN INVITATIONAL
1971	Jack Nicklaus	273
1972	Jack Nicklaus	267
1973	Jack Nicklaus	275

WALT DISNEY WORLD NATIONAL TEAM CHAMPIONSHIP
1974	Hubert Green/ Mac McLendon	255
1975	Jim Colbert/ Dean Refram	252
1976	*Woody Blackburn/ Bill Kratzert	260
1977	Gibby Gilbert/ Grier Jones	253
1978	Wayne Levi/ Bob Mann	254
1979	George Burns/ Ben Crenshaw	255
1980	Danny Edwards/ David Edwards	253
1981	Vance Heafner/ Mike Holland	275

WALT DISNEY WORLD GOLF CLASSIC
1982	*Hal Sutton	269
1983	Payne Stewart	269
1984	Larry Nelson	266

WALT DISNEY WORLD/ OLDSMOBILE CLASSIC
1985	Lanny Wadkins	267
1986	*Ray Floyd	275
1987	Larry Nelson	268
1988	*Bob Lohr	263
1989	Tim Simpson	272
1990	Tim Simpson	264
1991	Mark O'Meara	267
1992	John Huston	262
1993	Jeff Maggert	265
1994	Rick Fehr	265
1995	#Brad Bryant	198
1996	Tiger Woods	267

1997	*David Duval	270

NATIONAL CAR RENTAL GOLF CLASSIC
1998	John Huston	272
1999	Tiger Woods	271
2000	Duffy Waldorf	262
2001	Jose Coceres	265

DISNEY GOLF CLASSIC
2002	Bob Burns	263

FUNAI CLASSIC AT THE WALT DISNEY WORLD RESORT
2003	Vijay Singh	265

* Playoff
# Rain-shortened

CHRYSLER CHAMPIONSHIP

YEAR	WINNER	SCORE

TAMPA BAY CLASSIC
2000	John Huston	271
2001	No tournament	
2002	K.J. Choi	267

CHRYSLER CHAMPIONSHIP
2003	Retief Goosen	272

THE TOUR CHAMPIONSHIP

YEAR	WINNER	SCORE

NABISCO CHAMPIONSHIPS OF GOLF
1987	Tom Watson	268

NABISCO GOLF CHAMPIONSHIPS
1988	*Curtis Strange	279

NABISCO CHAMPIONSHIPS
1989	*Tom Kite	276
1990	*Jodie Mudd	273

THE TOUR CHAMPIONSHIP
1991	*Craig Stadler	279
1992	Paul Azinger	276
1993	Jim Gallagher, Jr.	277
1994	*Mark McCumber	274
1995	Billy Mayfair	280
1996	Tom Lehman	268
1997	David Duval	273
1998	*Hal Sutton	274
1999	Tiger Woods	269
2000	Phil Mickelson	267
2001	*Mike Weir	270
2002	Vijay Singh	268
2003	Chad Campbell	268

* Playoff

RECORDS AND STATISTICS | *All-Time PGA Tour Records*

SCORING RECORDS

72 HOLES:
254—Tommy Armour III (64-62-63-65), The Resort at LaCantera, 2003 Texas Open (26 under par).
256—Mark Calcavecchia (65-60-64-67), TPC of Scottsdale, 2001 Phoenix Open (28 under par).
257—Mike Souchak (60-68-64-65), Brackenridge Park GC, 1955 Texas Open (27 under par).
258—Donnie Hammond (65-64-65-64), Oak Hills CC, 1989 Texas Open (22 under par).
258—John Cook (64-62-63-69), TPC at Southwind, 1996 FedEx St. Jude Classic (26 under par).
258—Steve Jones (62-64-65-67), TPC of Scottsdale, 1997 Phoenix Open (26 under par).
259—Byron Nelson (62-68-63-66), Broadmoor GC, 1945 Seattle Open (21 under par).
259—Chandler Harper (70-63-63-63), Brackenridge Park GC, 1954 Texas Open (25 under par).
259—Tim Norris (63-64-66-66), Wethersfield CC, 1982 Sammy Davis Jr. Greater Hartford Open (25 under par).
259—Corey Pavin (64-63-66-66), Oak Hills CC, 1988 Texas Open (21 under par).
259—David Frost (68-63-64-64), Oakwood CC, 1993 Hardee's Golf Classic (21 under par).
259—Tiger Woods (64-61-67-67), Firestone CC, 2000 WGC-NEC Invitational (21 under par).
259—Joe Durant (65-61-67-66), four courses, 2001 Bob Hope Chrysler Classic (29 under par).*
259—Tim Herron (69-64-61-65), four courses, 2003 Bob Hope Chrysler Classic (29 under par).*
259—Stuart Appleby (62-68-63-66), three courses, 2003 Las Vegas Invitational (28 under par).*
*Through four rounds of 90-hole tournament.

90 HOLES:
324—Joe Durant (65-61-67-66-65), four courses, 2001 Bob Hope Chrysler Classic.
325—Tom Kite (67-67-64-65-62), four courses, 1993 Bob Hope Chrysler Classic.
327—John Cook (66-69-67-62-63), four courses, 1997 Bob Hope Chrysler Classic.

MOST SHOTS UNDER PAR:
72 holes:
31—Ernie Els, 2003 Mercedes Championships, 261.
29—Joe Durant, 2001 Bob Hope Chrysler Classic, 259.*
29—Tim Herron, 2003 Bob Hope Chrysler Classic, 259.*
28—John Huston, 1998 United Airlines Hawaiian Open, 260.
28—Mark Calcavecchia, 2001 Phoenix Open, 256.
28—Stuart Appleby, 2003 Las Vegas Invitational, 259.*
27—Ben Hogan, 1945 Portland Invitational, 261.
27—Mike Souchak, 1955 Texas Open, 257.
27—Mark Calcavecchia, 1997 Bob Hope Chrysler Classic, 261.*
27—Jonathan Byrd, 2002 Buick Challenge, 261.
27—Steve Flesch, 2003 Las Vegas Invitational, 260.*
*Through first four rounds of 90-hole tournament.

90 holes:
36—Joe Durant, 2001 Bob Hope Chrysler Classic, 324.
35—Tom Kite, 1993 Bob Hope Chrysler Classic, 325.
33—John Cook, 1997 Bob Hope Chrysler Classic, 327.

54 HOLES:
Opening rounds:
189—John Cook (64-62-63), TPC at Southwind, 1996 FedEx St. Jude Classic

(24 under par).
189—Mark Calcavecchia (65-60-64), TPC of Scottsdale, 2001 Phoenix Open (24 under par).
189—Tommy Armour III (64-62-63), The Resort at LaCantera, 2003 Valero Texas Open (21 under par).
191—Johnny Palmer (65-62-64), Brackenridge Park GC, 1954 Texas Open (22 under par).
191—Gay Brewer (66-64-61), Pensacola CC, 1967 Pensacola Open (25 under par).
191—Steve Jones (62-64-65), TPC of Scottsdale, 1997 Phoenix Open (22 under par).
Consecutive rounds:
189—Chandler Harper (63-63-63), Brackenridge Park GC, rounds 2-4, 1954 Texas Open (24 under par).
189—John Cook (64-62-63), TPC at Southwind, rounds 1-3, 1996 FedEx St. Jude Classic (24 under par).
189—Mark Calcavecchia (65-60-64), TPC of Scottsdale, rounds 1-3, 2001 Phoenix Open (24 under par).
189—Tommy Armour III (64-62-63), The Resort at LaCantera, rounds 1-3, 2003 Valero Texas Open.

36 HOLES:
Opening rounds:
125—Tiger Woods (64-61), Firestone CC, 2000 WGC-NEC Invitational (15 under par).
125—Mark Calcavecchia (65-60), TPC of Scottsdale, 2001 Phoenix Open (17 under par).
125—Tom Lehman (63-62), two courses, 2001 Invensys Classic at Las Vegas (19 under par).
126—Tommy Bolt (64-62), Cavalier Yacht & CC, 1954 Virginia Beach Open (12 under par).
126—Paul Azinger (64-62), Oak Hills CC, 1989 Texas Open (14 under par).
126—John Cook (64-62), TPC at Southwind, 1996 FedEx St. Jude Classic (16 under par).
126—Rick Fehr (64-62), two courses, 1996 Las Vegas Invitational (17 under par).
126—Steve Jones (62-64), TPC of Scottsdale, 1997 Phoenix Open (16 under par).
126—David Frost (63-63), TPC at Southwind, 1999 FedEx St. Jude Classic (16 under par).
126—Joe Durant (65-61), two courses, 2001 Bob Hope Chrysler Classic (18 under par).
126—Tommy Armour III (64-62), The Resort at LaCantera, 2003 Valero Texas Open (14 under par).
126—Steve Flesch (62-64), two courses, 2003 Las Vegas Invitational (17 under par).
126—Scott Verplank (64-62), two courses, 2003 Las Vegas Invitational (17 under par).
Consecutive rounds:
124—Mark Calcavecchia (60-64), TPC of Scottsdale, rounds 2-3, 2001 Phoenix Open (18 under par).
125—Gay Brewer (64-61), Pensacola CC, rounds 2-3, 1967 Pensacola Open (19 under par).
125—Ron Streck (63-62), Oak Hills CC, rounds 3-4, 1978 Texas Open (15 under par).
125—Blaine McCallister (62-63), Oakwood CC, rounds 2-3, 1988 Hardee's Golf Classic (15 under par).
125—John Cook (62-63), TPC at Southwind, rounds 2-3, 1996 FedEx St. Jude Classic (17 under par).
125—Tiger Woods (64-61), Firestone CC, rounds 1-2, 2000 WGC-NEC Invitational (15 under par).
125—Mark Calcavecchia (65-60), TPC of Scottsdale, rounds 1-2, 2001 Phoenix Open (17 under par).
125—Tom Lehman (63-62), two courses, rounds 1-2, 2001 Invensys Classic at Las Vegas (19 under par).
125—Tim Herron (62-63), two courses, rounds 2-3, 2003 Bob Hope Chrysler Classic (19 under par).

125—Kenny Perry (64-61), Colonial CC, rounds 2-3, 2003 Bank of America Colonial (15 under par).
125—Tommy Armour III (62-63), The Resort at LaCantera, rounds 2-3, 2003 Valero Texas Open (15 under par).

18 HOLES:
59—Al Geiberger, Colonial CC, second round, 1977 Memphis Classic (13 under par).
59—Chip Beck, Sunrise GC, third round, 1991 Las Vegas Invitational (13 under par).
59—David Duval, PGA West (Palmer Course), fifth round, 1999 Bob Hope Chrysler Classic (13 under par).
60—Al Brosch, Brackenridge Park GC, third round, 1951 Texas Open (11 under par).
60—Bill Nary, Brackenridge Park GC, third round, 1952 Texas Open (11 under par).
60—Ted Kroll, Brackenridge Park GC, third round, 1954 Texas Open (11 under par).
60—Wally Ulrich, Cavalier Yacht & CC, second round, 1954 Virginia Beach Open (9 under par).
60—Tommy Bolt, Wethersfield CC, second round, 1954 Insurance City Open (11 under par).
60—Mike Souchak, Brackenridge Park GC, first round, 1955 Texas Open (11 under par).
60—Sam Snead, Glen Lakes CC, second round, 1957 Dallas Open (11 under par).
60—David Frost, Randolph Park GC, second round, 1990 Northern Telecom Tucson Open (12 under par).
60—Davis Love III, Waialae CC, second round, 1994 United Airlines Hawaiian Open (12 under par).
60—Grant Waite, TPC of Scottsdale, final round, 1996 Phoenix Open (11 under par).
60—Steve Lowery, Callaway Gardens (Mountain View Course), first round, 1997 Buick Challenge (12 under par).
60—Tommy Armour III, Las Vegas CC, second round, 1999 Las Vegas Invitational (12 under par).
60—Mark Calcavecchia, TPC of Scottsdale, second round, 2001 Phoenix Open (11 under par).
60—Robert Gamez, Indian Wells CC, third round, 2004 Bob Hope Chrysler Classic (12 under par).

BEST VARDON TROPHY SCORING AVERAGE:
Non-adjusted:
68.17—Tiger Woods, 2000
68.87—Tiger Woods, 2001
69.00—Tiger Woods, 2002
69.11—Vijay Singh, 2003
69.16—Phil Mickelson, 2001
69.23—Sam Snead, 1950
69.28—Jim Furyk, 2003
69.30—Ben Hogan, 1948
Adjusted (since 1988):
67.69—Tiger Woods, 2000
68.41—Tiger Woods, 2003
68.43—Tiger Woods, 1999
68.56—Tiger Woods, 2002
68.54—Vijay Singh, 2003
Note: Byron Nelson's scoring average in 1945 was 68.34, but the Vardon Trophy was not awarded in 1942-46.

MOST BIRDIES IN A ROW:
8—Bob Goalby, Pasadena GC, final round, 1961 St. Petersburg Open.
8—Fuzzy Zoeller, Oakwood CC, first round, 1976 Quad Cities Open.
8—Dewey Arnette, Warwick Hills G&CC, first round, 1987 Buick Open.
8—Edward Fryatt, Doral Golf Resort (Blue Course), second round, 2000 Doral-Ryder Open.
8—J.P. Hayes, PGA West (Palmer Course), first round, 2002 Bob Hope Chrysler Classic.
8—Jerry Kelly, TPC at Summerlin, third round, 2003 Las Vegas Invitational.

BEST BIRDIE-EAGLE STREAK:
8—Billy Mayfair, 7 birdies, 1 eagle, Warwick Hills G&CC, final round, 2001 Buick Open
8—Briny Baird, 7 birdies, 1 eagle, Disney Palm Course, second round, 2003

Funai Classic at Walt Disney World Resort.
7—Al Geiberger, 6 birdies, 1 eagle, Colonial CC, second round, 1977 Danny Thomas Memphis Classic.
7—Webb Heintzelman, 6 birdies, 1 eagle, Spanish Trail G&CC, third round, 1989 Las Vegas Invitational.
7—Davis Love III, 6 birdies, 1 eagle, Pebble Beach GL, final round, 2001 AT&T Pebble Beach National Pro-Am.

MOST BIRDIES IN A ROW TO WIN:
6—Mike Souchak, 1956 St. Paul Open (last six holes).
5—Jack Nicklaus, 1978 Jackie Gleason Inverrary Classic (last five holes).
5—Tom Weiskopf, 1971 Kemper Open (last four holes plus first playoff hole).

MOST BIRDIES, 72 HOLES:
32—Mark Calcavecchia, 2001 Phoenix Open.
32—Paul Gow, 2001 B.C. Open.
31—John Huston, 1998 United Airlines Hawaiian Open.

MOST BIRDIES, 90 HOLES:
37—Joe Durant, 2001 Bob Hope Chrysler Classic.

MOST CONSECUTIVE ROUNDS PAR OR BETTER:
52—Tiger Woods, third round, 2000 GTE Byron Nelson Classic, through first round, 2001 Phoenix Open.

VICTORY RECORDS

MOST VICTORIES DURING CAREER (PGA TOUR COSPONSORED AND/OR APPROVED TOURNAMENTS ONLY):
82—Sam Snead
73—Jack Nicklaus
64—Ben Hogan
62—Arnold Palmer
52—Byron Nelson
51—Billy Casper

MOST CONSECUTIVE YEARS WINNING AT LEAST ONE TOURNAMENT:
17—Jack Nicklaus (1962-78)
17—Arnold Palmer (1955-71)
16—Billy Casper (1956-71)

MOST CONSECUTIVE VICTORIES:
11—Byron Nelson, March 8-11 to August 2-4, 1945 (Miami Four-Ball, Charlotte Open, Greensboro Open, Durham Open, Atlanta Open, Montreal Open, Philadelphia Inquirer Invitational, Chicago Victory National Open, PGA Championship, Tam O'Shanter Open, Canadian Open).
6—Ben Hogan, June 9-12 to August 19-22, 1948 (U.S. Open, Inverness Round-Robin, Motor City Open, Reading Open, Western Open, Denver Open).
6—Tiger Woods, August 26-29, 1999 to February 3-6, 2000 (WGC-NEC Invitational, National Car Rental Golf Classic, Tour Championship, WGC-American Express Championship, Mercedes Championships, AT&T Pebble Beach National Pro-Am).
4—Byron Nelson, October 11-14, 1945 to January 10-13, 1946 (Seattle Open, Glen Garden Invitational, Los Angeles Open, San Francisco Open).
4—Jack Burke, Jr., February 14-17 to March 6-9, 1952 (Texas Open, Houston Open, Baton Rouge Open, St. Petersburg Open).
4—Ben Hogan, April 9-12 to June 10-13, 1953 (Masters, Pan American, Colonial, U.S. Open).

MOST VICTORIES IN A SINGLE EVENT:
8—Sam Snead, Greater Greensboro Open (1938, 1946, 1949, 1950, 1955, 1956, 1960, 1965).
6—Harry Vardon, British Open (1896, 1898, 1899, 1903, 1911, 1914).
6—Alex Ross, North & South Open (1902, 1904, 1907, 1908, 1910, 1915).
6—Sam Snead, Miami Open (1937, 1939, 1946, 1950, 1951, 1955).
6—Jack Nicklaus, Masters (1963, 1965, 1966, 1972, 1975, 1986).

MOST CONSECUTIVE VICTORIES IN A SINGLE EVENT:
4—Tom Morris Jr., British Open, 1868-70 (no event in 1871), 1872.
4—Walter Hagen, PGA Championship, 1924-27.
4—Gene Sarazen, Miami Open, 1926 (schedule change), 1928-1930.
4—Tiger Woods, Bay Hill Invitational, 2000-2003.

MOST VICTORIES IN CALENDAR YEAR:
18—Byron Nelson, 1945
13—Ben Hogan, 1946
11—Sam Snead, 1950
10—Ben Hogan, 1948
9—Paul Runyan, 1933
9—Tiger Woods, 2000
8—Horton Smith, 1929
8—Gene Sarazen, 1930
8—Sam Snead, 1938
8—Byron Nelson, 1944
8—Arnold Palmer, 1960
8—Johnny Miller, 1974
8—Tiger Woods, 1999

MAJOR CHAMPIONSHIP WINS (AMATEUR AND PROFESSIONAL):
20—Jack Nicklaus, 1959-86 (6 Masters, 4 U.S. Opens, 3 British Opens,
5 PGAs, 2 U.S. Amateurs).
13—Bobby Jones, 1923-30 (4 U.S. Opens, 3 British Opens, 5 U.S. Amateurs, 1
British Amateur).
11—Walter Hagen, 1914-29 (2 U.S. Opens, 4 British Opens, 5 PGAs).
11—Tiger Woods, 1994-2002 (3 Masters, 2 U.S. Opens, 1 British Open, 2
PGAs, 3 U.S. Amateurs).
9—John Ball, 1888-1912 (1 British Open, 8 British Amateurs).
9—Ben Hogan, 1946-53 (2 Masters, 4 U.S. Opens, 1 British Open, 2 PGAs).
9—Gary Player, 1959-78 (3 Masters, 1 U.S. Open, 3 British Opens, 2 PGAs).
8—Arnold Palmer, 1954-64 (4 Masters, 1 U.S. Open, 2 British Opens, 1 U.S.
Amateur).
8—Tom Watson, 1975-83 (2 Masters, 1 U.S. Open, 5 British Opens).

MAJOR CHAMPIONSHIP WINS (PROFESSIONAL ONLY):
18—Jack Nicklaus
11—Walter Hagen
9—Ben Hogan
9—Gary Player
8—Tom Watson
8—Tiger Woods
7—Harry Vardon
7—Bobby Jones
7—Gene Sarazen
7—Sam Snead
7—Arnold Palmer
6—Lee Trevino
6—Nick Faldo

MOST YEARS BETWEEN VICTORIES:
15—Butch Baird (1961-76)
14—Ed Fiori (1982-96)
14—Joey Sindelar (1990-2004)

MOST YEARS FROM FIRST VICTORY TO LAST:
29—Raymond Floyd (1963-92)
28—Sam Snead (1937-65)
24—Tom Watson (1974-98)
24—Macdonald Smith (1912-36)
24—Jack Nicklaus (1962-86)

MOST WINS BY PLAYERS IN THEIR 20s:
40—Tiger Woods
30—Jack Nicklaus

MOST WINS BY PLAYERS IN THEIR 30s:
42—Arnold Palmer
40—Ben Hogan

MOST WINS BY PLAYERS AFTER 40:
17—Sam Snead

YOUNGEST WINNERS:
19 years, 10 months—Johnny McDermott, 1911 U.S. Open
20 years, 0 months—Gene Sarazen, 1922 Southern Open
20 years, 1 month—Chick Evans, 1910 Western Open
20 years, 4 months—Francis Ouimet, 1913 U.S. Open
20 years, 4 months—Gene Sarazen, 1922 U.S. Open

20 years, 5 months—Horton Smith, 1928 Oklahoma City Open
20 years, 5 months—Gene Sarazen, 1922 PGA Championship
20 years, 6 months—Raymond Floyd, 1963 St. Petersburg Open
20 years, 6 months—Phil Mickelson, 1991 Northern Telecom Open

OLDEST WINNERS:
52 years, 10 months—Sam Snead, 1965 Greater Greensboro Open
51 years, 7 months—Art Wall, Jr., 1975 Greater Milwaukee Open
51 years, 3 months—Jim Barnes, 1937 Long Island Open
51 years, 1 month—John Barnum, 1962 Cajun Classic
50 years, 1 month—Craig Stadler, 2003 B.C. Open

LARGEST WINNING MARGIN:
16—J.D. Edgar, 1919 Canadian Open
16—Joe Kirkwood Sr., 1924 Corpus Christi Open
16—Bobby Locke, 1948 Chicago Victory National Championship
15—Tiger Woods, 2000 U.S. Open
14—Ben Hogan, 1945 Portland Invitational
14—Johnny Miller, 1975 Phoenix Open

BIGGEST FINAL-ROUND COMEBACK:
10—Paul Lawrie, 1999 British Open
9—Stewart Cink, 2004 MCI Heritage
8—Jack Burke, Jr., 1956 Masters
8—Ken Venturi, 1959 Los Angeles Open
8—Mark Lye, 1983 Bank of Boston Classic
8—Hal Sutton, 1985 St. Jude Memphis Classic
8—Chip Beck, 1990 Buick Open
8—Scott Simpson, 1998 Buick Invitational
8—Craig Stadler, 2003 B.C. Open

MISCELLANEOUS RECORDS

MOST CONSECUTIVE EVENTS WITHOUT MISSING CUT:
124—Tiger Woods, Buick Invitational, February 5-8, 1998, through the
Memorial Tournament, June 3-6, 2004.
113—Byron Nelson, Bing Crosby National Pro-Am, January 26, 1941, through
Colonial National Invitation, May 27-30, 1948.
105—Jack Nicklaus, Sahara Open, October 29-November 1, 1970, through
World Series of Golf, September 2-5, 1976.

YOUNGEST PRO SHOOTING AGE:
67—Sam Snead, 66, fourth round, 1979 Quad Cities Open
67—Sam Snead, 67, third rounds, 1979 Quad Cities Open

LONGEST SUDDEN-DEATH PLAYOFF:
11 holes—Cary Middlecoff and Lloyd Mangrum declared co-winners, 1949
Motor City Open.
8 holes—Dick Hart defeated Phil Rodgers, 1965 Azalea Open.
8 holes—Lee Elder defeated Lee Trevino, 1978 Greater Milwaukee Open.
8 holes—Dave Barr defeated Woody Blackburn, Dan Halldorson, Frank
Conner, and Victor Regalado, 1981 Quad Cities Open.
8 holes—Bob Gilder defeated Rex Caldwell, Johnny Miller, and Mark
O'Meara, 1983 Phoenix Open.

MONEY-WINNING RECORDS

MOST MONEY WON IN A SINGLE SEASON:
$9,188,321—Tiger Woods, 2000
$7,573,907—Vijay Singh, 2003
$6,912,625—Tiger Woods, 2002
$6,673,413—Tiger Woods, 2003
$6,616,585—Tiger Woods, 1999

MOST MONEY WON BY A ROOKIE:
$1,864,584—Carlos Franco, 1999
$1,520,632—Charles Howell III, 2001
$1,502,888—Jose Coceres, 2001

ALL-TIME TOUR WINNERS

1.	Sam Snead	82
2.	Jack Nicklaus	73
3.	Ben Hogan	64
4.	Arnold Palmer	62
5.	Byron Nelson	52
6.	Billy Casper	51
7.	Walter Hagen	44
T8.	Cary Middlecoff	40
T8.	Tiger Woods	40
T10.	Gene Sarazen	39
T10.	Tom Watson	39
12.	Lloyd Mangrum	38
13.	Horton Smith	32
T14.	Harry Cooper	31
T14.	Jimmy Demaret	31
16.	Leo Diegel	30
T17.	Gene Littler	29
T17.	Paul Runyan	29
T17.	Lee Trevino	29
20.	Henry Picard	26
T21.	Tommy Armour	25
T21.	Johnny Miller	25
T23.	Gary Player	24
T23.	Macdonald Smith	24
25.	Phil Mickelson	23
T26.	Johnny Farrell	22
T26.	Raymond Floyd	22
T28.	Willie Macfarlane	21
T28.	Lanny Wadkins	21
T28.	Craig Wood	21
T31.	James Barnes	20
T31.	Hale Irwin	20
T31	Bill Mehlhorn	20
T31.	Greg Norman	20
T31.	Doug Sanders	20
T36.	Ben Crenshaw	19
T36.	Doug Ford	19
T36.	Hubert Green	19
T36.	Tom Kite	19
T40.	Nick Price	18
T40.	Julius Boros	18
T40.	Jim Ferrier	18
T40.	E.J. Harrison	18
T40.	Davis Love III	18
T40.	Johnny Revolta	18
T40.	Vijay Singh	18
T47.	Jack Burke, Jr.	17
T47.	Bobby Cruickshank	17
T47.	Harold McSpaden	17
T47.	Curtis Strange	17
T51	Ralph Guldahl	16
T51	Mark O'Meara	16
T51.	Tom Weiskopf	16

PGA TOUR COURSES RANKED BY LENGTH

COURSE	LENGTH	PAR
Torrey Pines GC (South)	7568	72
Castle Pines GC	7559	72
Redstone GC (Rees Jones)	7550	72
TPC of Louisiana	7519	72
Montreux G&CC	7472	72
Quail Hollow CC	7438	72
CC at Mirasol (Sunrise)	7416	72
TPC of Boston	7415	71
Cog Hill G&CC	7320	72
Westin Innisbrook (Copperhead)	7315	71
Forest Oaks CC	7311	72
TPC at Sugarloaf	7293	72
Augusta National GC	7290	72
Firestone CC (South)	7283	70
Nemacolin Woodlands Resort	7276	72
Doral Resort & Spa	7266	72
Muirfield Village GC	7265	72
Plantation Course at Kapalua	7263	73
Riviera CC	7260	71
La Costa Resort & Spa	7247	72
TPC at Summerlin	7243	72
Bay Hill Club & Lodge	7239	72
TPC of Scottsdale	7216	71
Magnolia GC	7200	72
Annandale GC	7199	72
TPC at Deere Run	7183	72
Harding Park GC	7141	70
East Lake GC	7132	70
Omni Tucson National Resort	7109	72
TPC at Southwind	7103	71
TPC at Sawgrass	7093	72
Colonial CC	7080	70
TPC at the Canyons	7063	71
La Quinta CC	7060	72
Waialae CC	7060	70
TPC Four Seasons Las Colinas	7016	70
TPC at Avenel	7005	71
Shaughnessy G&CC	6996	70
En-Joie GC	6974	72
Harbour Town GL	6973	71
Palm GC	6957	72
Bermuda Dunes CC	6927	72
PGA West (Palmer)	6921	72
Resort at LaCantera	6881	71
Tamarisk CC	6881	72
Torrey Pines GC (North)	6874	72
Spyglass Hill GC	6858	72
Cottonwood Valley GC	6846	70
Poppy Hills GC	6833	72
TPC at River Highlands	6820	70
Pebble Beach GL	6816	72
Westchester CC	6783	71
Brown Deer Park GC	6759	70

RANK	COURSE	PAR	YDG	SCORE	O/U PAR	EGL	BIRD	PARS	BOG	DBL BOG	TPL BG+	TOURNAMENT NAME
1	Augusta National GC	72	7290	74.640	2.640	13	712	3079	1124	144	22	The Masters
2	Spyglass Hill GC	72	6862	74.592	2.592	4	460	1980	656	98	24	AT&T Pebble Beach
3	Capital City Club	70	7189	72.417	2.417	13	774	3064	1182	140	11	WGC-American Express
4	Poppy Hills GC	72	6833	74.023	2.023	30	540	1830	644	113	29	AT&T Pebble Beach
5	Hamilton G&CC	70	6983	71.630	1.630	34	1291	5247	1774	150	18	Bell Canadian Open
6	Riviera CC	71	7222	72.507	1.507	26	1224	4807	1593	149	13	Nissan Open
7	Westin Innisbrook (Copperhead)	71	7315	72.351	1.351	15	1145	4565	1395	131	21	Chrysler Championship
8	Torrey Pines (South)	72	7568	73.277	1.277	7	862	3430	1055	92	8	Buick Invitational
9	Muirfield Village GC	72	7265	73.253	1.253	27	1091	3725	1155	166	28	The Memorial Tournament
10	Firestone CC (South)	70	7283	71.253	1.253	27	1015	3759	1174	124	21	WGC-NEC Invitational
11	TPC at Avenel	71	6987	72.215	1.215	24	1427	5110	1488	210	39	FBR Capital Open
12	Bay Hill Club	72	7239	72.955	0.955	24	1174	4588	1168	156	36	Bay Hill Invitational
13	Quail Hollow Club	72	7396	72.902	0.902	26	1361	5090	1448	158	17	Wachovia Championshop
14	Pebble Beach GL	72	6798	72.794	0.794	35	803	2614	799	104	19	AT&T Pebble Beach
15	TPC at Four Seasons	70	7017	70.763	0.763	19	974	3592	967	124	12	EDS Byron Nelson Champ.
16	Brown Deer Park GC	70	6759	70.748	0.748	12	1327	5525	1431	120	9	Greater Milwaukee Open
17	Westchester CC	71	6783	71.556	0.556	23	1452	5137	1422	141	15	Buick Classic
18	TPC at Sawgrass	72	7093	72.541	0.541	42	1433	4625	1312	176	26	The Players Championship
19	TPC at Sugarloaf	72	7293	72.505	0.505	39	1487	4673	1269	200	36	BellSouth Classic
20	TPC at River Highlands	70	6820	70.489	0.489	17	1452	5388	1259	163	37	Greater Hartford Open
21	TPC at Deere Run	71	7183	71.452	0.452	29	1431	4906	1299	164	19	John Deere Classic
22	TPC at Boston	71	7415	71.438	0.438	39	1521	4991	1395	169	21	Deutsche Bank Champ.
23	Montreux G&CC	72	7472	72.308	0.308	28	1424	4528	1187	169	26	Reno-Tahoe Open
24	Colonial CC	70	7080	69.941	-0.059	12	1233	4436	960	110	17	Bank of America Colonial
25	Cog Hill G&CC	72	7320	71.938	-0.062	52	1620	4920	1312	153	25	Western Open
26	Waialae CC	70	7060	69.880	-0.120	53	1487	4988	1296	100	14	Sony Open in Hawaii
27	Harbour Town GL	71	6973	70.621	-0.379	28	1415	4898	1032	119	14	MCI Heritage
28	TPC at Southwind	71	7069	70.474	-0.526	66	1725	5090	1154	180	29	FedEx St. Jude Classic
29	Cottonwood Valley GC	70	6846	69.419	-0.581	15	563	1749	426	34	3	EDS Byron Nelson Champ.
30	Champions GC	71	7301	70.290	-0.710	14	445	1425	316	28	4	The Tour Championship
31	Omni Tucson National	72	7109	71.273	-0.727	41	1703	5331	1068	152	21	Chrysler Classic of Tucson
32	Redstone GC (Fall Creek)	72	7508	71.264	-0.736	42	1640	5194	1104	128	10	Shell Houston Open
33	Doral Resort & Spa (Blue)	72	7125	71.153	-0.847	52	1734	5064	1133	138	15	Ford Championship at Doral
34	Forest Oaks CC	72	7311	71.105	-0.895	19	1703	4927	1138	81	16	Chrysler Classic of Greensboro
35	Annandale GC	72	7199	70.912	-1.088	57	1532	4517	963	94	19	Southern Farm Bureau Classic
36	PGA West (Palmer)	72	6930	70.601	-1.399	38	904	2018	522	69	14	Bob Hope Chrysler Classic
37	Warwick Hills G&CC	72	7127	70.555	-1.445	36	1830	5096	1001	105	14	Buick Open
38	Resort Course at LaCantera	70	6881	68.554	-1.446	35	1779	5168	916	108	22	Valero Texas Open
39	En-Joie GC	72	6974	70.538	-1.462	28	1826	5081	967	116	10	B.C. Open
40	Magnolia Course	72	7200	70.365	-1.635	12	1173	3530	629	35	3	FUNAI Classic - Disney
41	English Turn G&CC	72	7116	70.242	-1.758	60	2042	5000	1090	114	10	HP Classic of New Orleans
42	Nemacolin Woodlands (Mystic Rock)	72	7276	70.201	-1.799	37	1678	4541	830	87	9	84 Lumber Classic of Penn.
43	TPC of Scottsdale	71	7089	69.132	-1.868	50	1717	4634	836	102	5	Phoenix Open
44	La Quinta CC	72	7060	70.071	-1.929	11	559	1415	269	29	3	Bob Hope Chrysler Classic
45	Southern Highlands GC	72	7465	70.000	-2.000	20	687	1519	304	53	9	Las Vegas Invitational
46	Torrey Pines (North)	72	6874	69.941	-2.059	15	622	1799	300	17	1	Buick Invitational
47	Palm Course	72	6957	69.465	-2.535	20	653	1593	257	26	7	FUNAI Classic - Disney
48	TPC at The Canyons	71	7063	68.385	-2.615	19	632	1671	214	33	5	Las Vegas Invitational
49	TPC at Summerlin	72	7243	69.248	-2.752	72	1500	3205	572	85	20	Las Vegas Invitational
50	CC at Mirasol (Sunset)	72	7157	69.075	-2.925	54	2082	4980	656	88	24	The Honda Classic
51	Plantation Course at Kapalua	73	7263	69.160	-3.840	22	776	1570	185	36	3	Mercedes Championships
52	Bermuda Dunes CC	73	6927	67.929	-4.071	23	646	1449	161	7		Bob Hope Chrysler Classic
53	Indian Wells CC	72	6478	67.619	-4.381	34	694	1357	164	13	6	Bob Hope Chrysler Classic

RANK	COURSE	HOLE	PAR	YDG	AVG SCORE	O/U PAR	EGL	BIRD	PARS	BOG	DBL BOG	TPL BOG+	TOURNAMENT NAME
1	Spyglass Hill GC	16	4	462	4.486	.486		8	92	66	10	3	AT&T Pebble Beach
2	Quail Hollow Club	18	4	478	4.478	.478	1	29	214	170	33	3	Wachovia Championship
3	Torrey Pines (South)	12	4	477	4.419	.419		12	163	118	9	1	Buick Invitational
4	Poppy Hills GC	5	4	426	4.418	.418		20	90	45	17	5	AT&T Pebble Beach
5	Augusta National GC	11	4	490	4.410	.410		17	152	96	17	1	The Masters
5	Augusta National GC	18	4	465	4.410	.410		13	158	97	13	2	The Masters
7	Capital City Club	16	4	486	4.403	.403		21	149	101	15	2	WGC-American Express
8	Poppy Hills GC	6	3	181	3.401	.401		7	104	56	8	2	AT&T Pebble Beach
9	Torrey Pines (South)	4	4	471	4.399	.399		14	162	119	8		Buick Invitational
10	Cog Hill G&CC	18	4	480	4.396	.396		34	244	132	37	2	Western Open
10	Capital City Club	9	4	475	4.396	.396		19	146	113	10		WGC-American Express
12	Firestone CC (South)	16	5	667	5.388	.388		37	184	86	21	12	WGC-NEC Invitational
13	TPC at Avenel	12	4	472	4.377	.377		25	276	127	28	5	FBR Capital Open
14	Spyglass Hill GC	8	4	399	4.374	.374		11	101	58	7	2	AT&T Pebble Beach
15	TPC at Sugarloaf	9	4	465	4.369	.369		38	244	106	31	9	BellSouth Classic
16	Waialae CC	1	4	488	4.361	.361		25	255	145	9	7	Sony Open in Hawaii
17	Westchester CC	12	4	485	4.360	.360		20	267	154	12	2	Buick Classic
18	English Turn G&CC	18	4	471	4.357	.357		19	285	136	19	3	HP Classic of New Orleans
19	Poppy Hills GC	16	4	439	4.356	.356		14	102	50	6	5	AT&T Pebble Beach
19	Cog Hill G&CC	13	4	482	4.356	.356		34	249	142	21	3	Western Open
21	Pebble Beach GL	8	4	418	4.354	.354		20	130	81	11	1	AT&T Pebble Beach
21	TPC at Four Seasons	3	4	490	4.354	.354		23	177	98	17	1	EDS Byron Nelson Champ.
23	TPC at River Highlands	1	4	434	4.353	.353		42	270	113	26	11	Greater Hartford Open
23	Hamilton G&CC	18	4	446	4.353	.353		33	262	159	17	2	Bell Canadian Open
25	Hamilton G&CC	6	3	224	3.345	.345	1	23	278	158	9	4	Bell Canadian Open
26	Brown Deer Park GC	4	4	485	4.342	.342		28	266	160	14		Greater Milwaukee Open
27	Riviera CC	2	4	463	4.341	.341		27	255	131	19	2	Nissan Open
28	Capital City Club	18	4	466	4.340	.340		24	159	89	15	1	WGC-American Express
29	PGA West (Palmer)	5	3	233	3.333	.333		16	114	57	8	3	Bob Hope Chrysler Classic
30	TPC at Sugarloaf	8	3	248	3.332	.332		20	264	129	12	3	BellSouth Classic
30	Westin Innisbrook (Copperhead)	6	4	465	4.332	.332		28	237	120	15	4	Chrysler Championship
32	Hamilton G&CC	11	4	481	4.328	.328		31	272	157	10	3	Bell Canadian Open
33	Westin Innisbrook (Copperhead)	16	4	475	4.327	.327		37	224	122	16	5	Chrysler Championship
34	Poppy Hills	11	3	203	3.322	.322	1	13	98	58	7		AT&T Pebble Beach
35	TPC at Southwind	14	3	231	3.321	.321		33	281	113	28	3	FedEx St. Jude Classic
36	Omni Tucson National	18	4	465	4.320	.320		39	267	126	29	1	Chrysler Classic Tucson
36	TPC at Sugarloaf	7	4	458	4.320	.320		38	236	135	17	2	BellSouth Classic
36	Quail Hollow Club	17	3	217	3.320	.320		38	268	116	21	7	Wachovia Championship
39	Poppy Hills GC	8	4	390	4.316	.316		11	105	55	6		AT&T Pebble Beach
39	Riviera CC	15	4	487	4.316	.316		22	261	143	8		Nissan Open
41	Augusta National GC	10	4	495	4.314	.314		22	165	85	8	3	The Masters
42	TPC at Sugarloaf	5	4	418	4.313	.313	1	48	242	98	31	8	BellSouth Classic
43	Bay Hill Club	17	3	219	3.312	.312		20	255	103	16	3	Bay Hill Invitational
43	Firestone CC (South)	4	4	471	4.312	.312		26	190	116	8		WGC-NEC Invitational
45	Pebble Beach GL	5	3	188	3.309	.309		20	139	75	7	2	AT&T Pebble Beach
46	Spyglass Hill GC	5	3	183	3.307	.307		8	118	48	2	3	AT&T Pebble Beach
47	Riviera CC	4	3	236	3.306	.306		21	271	130	12		Nissan Open
48	Capital City Club	14	4	480	4.302	.302		24	166	85	13		WGC-American Express
49	Augusta National GC	12	3	155	3.300	.300		22	182	61	13	5	The Masters
50	TPC at Sawgrass	18	4	447	4.298	.298		52	228	112	27	4	The Players Championship
51	Augusta National GC	1	4	435	4.297	.297		14	178	84	7		The Masters
52	Capital City Club	10	4	459	4.295	.295		23	170	82	13		WGC-American Express
53	Doral Resort & Spa	13	3	245	3.294	.294		23	284	135	9	1	Ford Championship at Doral
53	TPC at Deere Run	18	4	463	4.294	.294		40	253	119	23	1	John Deere Classic
55	Riviera CC	9	4	458	4.288	.288		31	259	132	12		Nissan Open
55	Riviera CC	12	4	460	4.288	.288	1	40	241	137	15		Nissan Open
55	Muirfield Village GC	17	4	478	4.288	.288		28	211	89	10	6	The Memorial Tournament
58	Quail Hollow Club	6	3	250	3.287	.287		29	273	138	10		Wachovia Championship
58	TPC at Deere Run	9	4	485	4.287	.287		31	266	123	15	1	John Deere Classic
60	Spyglass Hill GC	13	4	445	4.285	.285		17	105	48	7	2	AT&T Pebble Beach
61	Poppy Hills GC	2	3	174	3.277	.277		13	116	37	8	3	AT&T Pebble Beach

RANK	COURSE	AVG HOLE	PAR	O/U YDG	SCORE	PAR	EGL	BIRD	PARS	DBL BOG	BOG	TPL BOG	TOURNAMENT NAME
62	Redstone GC (Fall Creek)	7	4	498	4.275	.275		40	271	116	24		Shell Houston Open
63	Firestone CC (South)	18	4	464	4.274	.274		28	207	89	16		WGC-NEC Invitational
64	Cottonwood Valley GC	15	4	441	4.271	.271		10	95	48	2		EDS Byron Nelson Champ.
65	Quail Hollow Club	16	4	478	4.269	.269		25	288	130	5	2	Wachovia Championship
66	TPC at Four Seasons	15	4	475	4.266	.266		28	186	94	7	1	EDS Byron Nelson Champ.
66	Westchester CC	15	4	462	4.266	.266		33	285	122	13	2	Buick Classic
68	Cog Hill G&CC	4	4	434	4.265	.265		58	237	134	17	3	Western Open
69	Waialae CC	5	4	466	4.263	.263		25	289	113	14		Sony Open in Hawaii
69	Pebble Beach GL	12	3	202	3.263	.263		13	154	75	1		AT&T Pebble Beach
71	Riviera CC	8	4	433	4.260	.260		35	270	112	15	2	Nissan Open
71	Capital City Club	15	3	220	3.260	.260		20	181	80	6	1	WGC-American Express
73	Westchester CC	11	4	442	4.257	.257		27	294	125	8	1	Buick Classic
74	Muirfield Village GC	2	4	455	4.256	.256		23	228	77	15	1	The Memorial Tournament
74	Muirfield Village GC	12	3	166	3.256	.256		44	201	74	19	6	The Memorial Tournament
76	TPC at Avenel	18	4	444	4.254	.254		55	254	134	16	2	FBR Capital Open
76	TPC of Boston	14	4	495	4.254	.254		32	285	124	10	1	Deutsche Bank Champ.
78	Hamilton G&CC	13	3	236	3.254	.254	1	30	300	132	10		Bell Canadian Open
79	Champions GC	11	4	460	4.250	.250		6	82	35	1		The Tour Championship
80	Poppy Hills GC	1	4	413	4.249	.249		8	124	39	5	1	AT&T Pebble Beach
80	Bay Hill Club	18	4	441	4.249	.249		53	242	68	23	11	Bay Hill Invitational
82	Doral Resort & Spa	4	3	236	3.246	.246		42	288	95	24	3	Ford Championship at Doral
83	TPC at Avenel	7	4	461	4.245	.245		43	285	113	17	3	FBR Capital Open
83	TPC at Southwind	11	3	185	3.245	.245	1	59	297	53	35	13	FedEx St. Jude Classic
85	Poppy Hills	3	4	406	4.243	.243		17	109	42	9		AT&T Pebble Beach
85	TPC at Avenel	15	4	467	4.243	.243		55	258	129	19		FBR Capital Open
87	Torrey Pines (North)	11	4	467	4.242	.242		16	87	47	3		Buick Invitational
88	Spyglass Hill GC	9	4	431	4.240	.240		10	121	43	5		AT&T Pebble Beach
89	Quail Hollow Club	4	4	458	4.238	.238		48	263	124	14	1	Wachovia Championship
90	PGA West (Palmer)	13	4	447	4.237	.237		26	119	37	12	4	Bob Hope Chrysler Classic
91	TPC at Sawgrass	7	4	442	4.234	.234		44	253	110	15	1	The Players Championship
92	TPC at Avenel	3	3	239	3.232	.232		31	303	116	11		FBR Capital Open
93	TPC at Summerlin	17	3	196	3.231	.231		34	184	67	17	1	Las Vegas Invitational
94	Riviera CC	18	4	451	4.230	.230		37	274	112	8	3	Nissan Open
94	Augusta National GC	5	4	455	4.230	.230	1	20	183	72	6	1	The Masters
96	Torrey Pines (South)	7	4	462	4.228	.228		29	183	84	7		Buick Invitational
96	Annandale GC	14	4	473	4.228	.228		23	274	93	7	2	Southern Farm Bureau Classic
98	TPC at Deere Run	15	4	465	4.227	.227		55	243	123	14	1	John Deere Classic
99	Firestone CC (South)	13	4	471	4.226	.226		33	211	84	10	2	WGC-NEC Invitational
99	Champions GC	12	3	232	3.226	.226		12	80	25	6	1	The Tour Championship

INDEX

ACKNOWLEDGMENTS

My thanks go to Duke Butler, Ward Clayton, Bob Combs, Dave Lancer, Chris Smith, and John Snow at PGA Tour headquarters for their assistance with the many moving parts of this book, to Laurie Platt Winfrey and Cristian Pena at Carousel for their indefatigable photo research, and to David Barrett, my longtime friend and colleague, for catching my errors and adding numerous facts and insights to the text. At Harry N. Abrams, the publisher of all three editions of this book, I'm indebted to Managing Editor Harriet Whelchel and her assistant Jon Cipriaso for bringing the production together so smoothly, to Art Director Bob McKee for yet another brilliant design, and to Executive Editor Margaret Kaplan for two decades of support and friendship.

George Peper
St. Andrews, Scotland
June 2004

PHOTO CREDITS

Annandale Golf Club/Michelle Corley: 250 bottom, 252 top

AP/Wide World: 11, 31 top, 42 (all), 59 bottom left & right, 74 left, 81 top & bottom, 119 right, 175 right, 190 bottom, 194 bottom left, 207, 213, 238 center, 274 bottom

Phil Arnold/Golfscape: 113, 114, 156, 156–157, 158

Stan Badz/PGA Tour Images: 12–13, 16 right, 48 center, 73 bottom, 87 bottom, 89, 90–91, 132, 135 bottom, 147 top, 150 (all), 154 bottom, 163 bottom, 226 top, 228, 235

David Bean: 68 top & bottom

Aidan Bradley: 2, 54 top & bottom, 56 top, 57 bottom, 138 top, 141 top, 202, 203 bottom, 204, 105

Chris Condon/PGA Tour Images: 16 left, 31 bottom, 46, 49, 51 (2), 52, 56 top, 62 top, 65 (all), 94 bottom, 101 center, 161 top, 165 top, 169 top & bottom, 203 top, 243

Tom Craig/Opulence Studio/PGA Tour Images: 254–257 (all)

Culver Pictures: 263 bottom

Courtesy Deere & Company: 182–187

Joann Dost Golf Editions: 37, 244, 245, 246 (all)

Dick Durrance II/PGA Tour: 29 top & center, 90 (all), 96–97, 98, 150–151, 152–153, 153 top, 154, 170, 172 bottom, 173 (2), 220, 221, 222 top, 224–225, 225, 226 bottom, 227 (2)

Getty Images: 25 left & center, 30, 53, 74 right, 87, 175 left, 194 right, 281 bottom

Golf Images, Inc.: 93, 132–133, 134, 135 top, 136, 145 top, 146, 164, 165 bottom, 166 (all), 166–167, 171, 192, 193 top, 209 top, 210 (all), 210–211, 218–219, 240, 240–241, 242 top & center, 250 top, 250–251, 277, 278–279, 279 top & center, 283 top

Harbour Town Golf Links/Sea Pines Resort/Chip Henderson: Cover, 116 center & bottom

Harbour Town Golf Links/Sea Pines Resort/David Soliday: 115 top

Chip Henderson: 70, 71, 72–73

Henebry Photography: 8 top & center, 8–9, 18, 18–19, 20, 20–21, 22 (2), 46–47, 177 top left, 177 top right, 179 top, 188 center & bottom, 214 bottom, 215

Historic Golf Photos: 68 right, 111 center & bottom, 142 bottom, 169 center, 181, 201 top, 222 bottom, 248 left & right, 252 bottom, 259 right

Bob Huxtable/Hux.net: 231, 232 (2), 234–235

Rusty Jarrett/PGA Tour Images: 68, 92, 94 top

John R. Johnson: 6, 7, 8 bottom, 14–15, 14 top, 41 bottom, 48 top & bottom, 50–51, 54–55, 56 bottom, 57 bottom, 83, 112–113, 153 center & bottom, 176, 178 top, 193, 196 bottom, 197, 198–199, 208–209, 211–212, 230–231, 233, 266 top

Mike Klemme/Golfoto: 1, 34–35, 40, 41 top, 106, 179 bottom, 21 (L.C. Lambrecht)

L.C. Lambrecht Photography: 32–33, 35, 38, 84, 104–105, 114 bottom, 115 bottom, 279 bottom

La Cantera/Gary Perkins: 236–237

La Costa Resort and Spa/Jay Jenks: 60–61, 61, 62 bottom, 63

Martin Miller: 246–247

Montreux Golf and Country Club/Talbot Photography: 24 top, 216 top & bottom

Gary Perkins: 237 top & bottom, 238 top & bottom

Michael Pugh: 96, 99 top, 99 bottom, 101 bottom

Dan Routh: 260–262 (all)

Phil Sheldon Golf Library: 36, 102–103, 105–106, 108, 109, 147 top (Dave Shopland)

Talbot Photography: 25 right, 39, 43 top & center

TPC of Louisiana/Jerry Ward: 127, 128

TPC of Scottsdale/Dick Durrance II: 26 top & bottom, 27, 28–29, 29 bottom

Westin Innisbrook Resort/Dick Durrance II: 270, 271 bottom, 272, 272–273

Westin Innisbrook Resort/Al Messerschmidt: 271 top, 274 top

Project Manager: Margaret L. Kaplan
Editor: David Barrett
Editorial Assistant: Jon Cipriaso
Designer: Robert McKee
Photo Research: Laurie Platt Winfrey, Cristian Pena, Carousel Research, Inc.
Production Managers: Stanley Redfern, Norman Watkins

Library of Congress Cataloging-in-Publication Data
Peper, George.
Golf courses of the PGA Tour / by George Peper.—3rd ed.
p. cm.
Includes index.
ISBN 0–8109–4950–4 (alk. paper)
1. Golf courses—United States. 2. PGA Tour.
I. Title.
GV981.P46 2004
796.'352'06'873—dc22   2004017097

10 9 8 7 6 5 4 3 2 1

Harry N. Abrams, Inc.
100 Fifth Avenue
New York, N.Y. 10011
www.abramsbooks.com

Abrams is a subsidiary of

LA MARTINIÈRE